2611X

Renaissance Drama
& the English Church Year

"Though their voice be taught to sound to present occasions, their sense or doth or should always lay hold on more removed mysteries."

Ben Jonson on court masques in *Hymenaei*

"The sight of such glorious earthly spectacles advantageth our Ladyes conceit by infinite multiplication thereof to consider of heaven."

Thomas Fuller on court masques in
The Holy State and the Profane State

"Though your Poets who enjoy by Patent a particular privilege to draw downe any of the Dieties from Twelfnight till Shrove-tuesday [for] a most familiar entercourse between the two Courts [of heaven and earth], have as yet never invited me to these Solemnities, yet . . . I . . . may most properly assist."

Momus speaking in *Coelum Britannicum*,
a Shrovetide masque

"The next day being Innocente day, it was expected, & partly determined by or selves, that the Tragedy of Philomela should have bene publikely acted, wch (as wee thought) would well have fitted the day by reason of the murder of Innocent Itis."

Griffin Higgs, *The Christmas Prince*

"King Charles cou'd not have thought of a better *entertainment*, for the *Sundays* after *Evening prayer*, than a diversion which tended to the confirmation of the Doctrine of the day."

The Stage, Acquitted

Renaissance Drama
& the English Church Year

R. Chris Hassel, Jr.

UNIVERSITY OF NEBRASKA PRESS

LINCOLN AND LONDON

The publication of this book was assisted by
a grant from The Andrew M. Mellon Foundation
and from Vanderbilt University.

Publishers on the Plains

UNP

Library of Congress Cataloging in Publication Data

Hassel, Rudolph Chris, 1939–
   Renaissance drama and the English church year.

   Bibliography: p. 205
   Includes index.
   1. English drama—Early modern and Elizabethan,
1500–1600—History and criticism. 2. English drama—
17th century—History and criticism. 3. Christianity in
literature. 4. Church year. 5. Church of England.
Book of common prayer. I. Title.
PR658.R43H3   822'.3'09   78-24233
ISBN 0-8032-2304-8

To my family,
for their faith and love

Contents

Acknowledgments

In preparing this book I have received a great deal of generous assistance. Scott Colley and Robert Hunter have been kind enough to read various stages of the manuscript and offer valuable suggestions for improving it. Leeds Barroll and Robert Knoll have offered encouragement and advice at the right moments. The staffs of the Folger Shakespeare Library and the Vanderbilt Library have both been extremely helpful. I also gratefully acknowledge a Folger Summer Research Fellowship; a sabbatical leave and several research and typing grants from Vanderbilt University; and the patience and competence of the departmental secretaries. I would finally like to thank the many colleagues, students, and friends who have taken an interest in my work.

Renaissance Drama
& the English Church Year

Renaissance Drama & the English Church Year

Evidence encouraging a new and productive approach to Renaissance drama has long been available in the records of Renaissance court performances compiled by E. K. Chambers and Gerald Eades Bentley.[1] Over fifty years ago Chambers noticed the persistent correlation between the dates of dramatic performance at Elizabeth's court and certain liturgical festivals of the English church year.

> Whether in Whitehall or elsewhere, the twelve days of Christmas from the Nativity to the Epiphany, were a season of high revels. . . . Twelfth Night [6 Jan.] itself, with St. Stephen's [26 Dec.], St. John's [27 Dec.], Innocents' [28 Dec.], and New Year's Day [circumcision], were regularly appointed for plays and masks, which often overflowed on to other nights during the period. . . . The revels were renewed for Candlemas [2 Feb.] and for Shrovetide [Sunday, Monday, and Tuesday before Ash Wednesday], either at the Christmas headquarters or at some other palace to which the court had meanwhile removed. . . . Easter, with the distribution of alms and washing of feet on Maunday Thursday, and Whitsuntide, were kept as ecclesiastical, rather than secular feasts. [1:19-20]

Gradually emerging during the sixteenth century, this calendar tradition seems to have peaked in the period 1570–85, continued strong until Elizabeth's death, diminished and changed somewhat during the Jacobean and Caroline periods, and then disappeared completely after 1640. In all, ninety-three extant masques and plays are recorded as performed at court during this period on ten traditional festival days of the English church year.

Surprisingly, there has never been a systematic study of possible thematic, narrative, or imagistic correlations between these works and their liturgical occasions.[2] Enid Welsford in *The Court Masque* observes of Thomas Middleton's *Inner Temple Masque:* "This piece of Middleton's is by no means the only masque in which the plot is nothing but a symbolical setting forth either of the particular holiday which was being celebrated, or else more generally of the flight of time, the succession of day and night, the round of seasons, months, and festivals" (p. 209). But Welsford chooses not to deal with these liturgical aspects of the masques; in fact, she seems almost impatient with them. Yet elsewhere Welsford suggests that the masque is the best example of art's "impulse to express the joy and value of existence" (p. 392). Since many in the Renaissance audience still understand that joy and value in basically Christian terms, it would hardly be surprising if their masques should sometimes parallel the liturgical celebrations they are designed to grace. The details of this whole tradition of festival masques and plays would seem to deserve more attention, for their implications could establish a new and major context for the understanding of Renaissance drama.

For the period before 1570 the record of these performances is uneven and defies a precise analysis. But it clearly indicates that a tradition of festival performances at court reaches at least all the way back to 1510. Epiphany and Shrovetide are the most popular festivals for such entertainments; they will remain so throughout most of the tradition. During Edward VI's brief kingship in the late 1540s and early fifties, these festival entertainments seem to have become especially frequent, with Christmas 1552 graced by ten masques. However, Mary's reign marks the abrupt if brief interruption of a thriving tradition. From the beginning of her rule until almost 1570 there is evidently little court drama and almost no correlation between what there is and the church year. Chambers assumes that poor records from 1560 to 1570 may disguise an earlier resurgence of the tradition at the beginning of Elizabeth's reign.³ But even if he is wrong, by 1552, within a decade of Shakespeare's birth, the English court traditionally hosted dramatic entertainments on seven selected holy days during Christmastide and Shrovetide.

In 1570, when extensive records resume, the tradition of dramatic performances on these seven liturgical occasions seems again in exceptional health. A summary of the statistics concerning court performance during Elizabeth's reign reveals the strength of this dramatic tradition. Of the 328 performances Chambers records at court from 1558 to 1603, 289, or 88 percent, fall again and again on the same seven festival days. Each year, with a regularity approaching and paralleling that of the liturgical year itself, performances fall on the two or three holy days immediately after Christmas Day, then on New Year's, Epiphany, and Shrove Sunday and Tuesday (I count Shrovetide as one of the seven "occasions" because of the liturgical homogeneity of the three days). Occasionally Shrove Monday and Candlemas are added. Elizabeth's court averages only one nonfestival performance a year for the thirty-nine years of her reign. And, of these 39 plays, 21 are also performed during the twelve days of Christmas, from 29 December through 5 January. During her reign, Elizabeth's court would have enjoyed, then, an average of seven holy-day performances each season, almost as many as the liturgical calendar could hold.

With this rich evidence of a tradition of festival performance at Elizabeth's court, however, come two disappointments. Almost all of the fifty-five to sixty titles scrupulously recorded on specific festival dates from 1570 to 1585 are lost.⁴ And around 1585, when we begin to have a higher number of extant plays, the recorder of these performances becomes hopelessly imprecise with titles and dates. Consequently, for the period from 1570 to 1584, when the chronological tradition seems to have been most vigorous, we have elaborate records of festival performance but no extant plays. For the next fifteen to twenty years we have many extant plays but few records of specific performances. When the records finally improve again, we are in the middle of the first decade of the seventeenth century. Ninety percent of the hundred recorded performances of extant plays and masques occur during the Jacobean and Caroline periods. Although they will evidence impressive correlations with their liturgical occasions, they cannot counterbalance those elusive three decades at the end of the sixteenth century.

Upon James's accession, an increase in the number of dramatic performances at court becomes immediately apparent. As Chambers suggests, the king and his court seem to have loved the theater not wisely but too well.[5] The inevitable corollary of the increased number of plays at court is relatively fewer festival performances. For while there are many more secular dates to host these performances, there are almost no more holy days. By 1610, seven years into James's reign, only forty-five plays have been specifically recorded on holy days; sixty-two have occurred at other times. By 1616, the date of Shakespeare's death and the last year of Chambers's study, James's court has witnessed 70 recorded festival performances, but 125 nonfestival dates. This is a meager 36 percent of all court performances, as against 88 percent for the holy days during Elizabeth's tenure. Even considering that the records are not as precise as before and that 40 additional dates of performance fall within the Advent to Shrovetide season, only 55 percent of these court performances occur within the Christmas season in its largest possible liturgical sense, as against 94 percent in Elizabeth's court. This statistical decline suggests that the festival performance begins to lose its importance during this first part of James's reign as the central and isolated highlight of the dramatic season.

With the appointment of Sir Henry Herbert as Master of Revels around 1622, records indicate something of a resurgence of the Elizabethan correspondence of holy day and dramatic performance. For the last five years of James's reign, 1621–25, twenty-two out of thirty-eight recorded court performances (58 percent) fall on the seven holy days, for an average of over five per year. Eighty percent fall sometime during the Christmas season. For the first time since Elizabeth's reign, then, the familiar liturgical dates of 26, 27, 28 December, 1 and 6 January, 2 February, and Shrovetide come back into prominence on the court's dramatic calendar. If anything the older tradition seems to have become reinvigorated after the initial exuberance of the Jacobean court for almost continuous dramatic fare. Even during its quantitative waning, there is some evidence that the tradition remains qualitatively strong. Starting around 1605 court masques begin to be commissioned for annual performance on Epiphany and Shrovetide. This new tradition seems to have continued right through 1635. In fact, Alfred Harbage and Samuel Schoenbaum record ten new Epiphany and Shrovetide masques performed at court from 1604 to 1626, and no new plays. In contrast to the avalanche of purely secular plays, these masques with their pronounced thematic and allegorical bias and their genesis within the festival context might be expected to grace their holy days with particular if subtle aptness. In fact, we shall discover that they often do.

Although the records of court performances during Charles's reign are just as poor as those for James's, it is clear that after 1625 nonfestival performances increase and holy day performances diminish, with two important exceptions. We have even more specially commissioned masques for Shrovetide. And Easter Monday and Tuesday begin to host plays with considerable regularity. As well as we can ascertain from these uneven records, fewer than 33 percent of the recorded court performances fall on holy days from 1626–1635, at which time most of the chronological correlations cease entirely. But many of these performances, especially the commissioned masques and the Easter plays, will prove unusually relevant to the holy day. The death knell of the tradition is perhaps most decisively sounded on 6 January 1640 and 1641. On those nights, for the first recorded times since early in the sixteenth century, Epiphany masques are performed not at court but in private residences, the earl of Chesterfield's and Lord Strange's, respectively. None would have imagined in the previous 130 years risking the wrath of even a tottering monarch by conflicting with his calendar of Christmas festivity. Obviously by now the court has stopped observing even the oldest and most frequent of the traditional festival performances.

A tradition that has gradually emerged during the reign of

Henry VIII flourishes for thirty years during Elizabeth's rule. Then it gradually diminishes during the Jacobean and Caroline period until its quiet extinction around 1640, a date near the closing of the theaters in 1642. During the whole period 70 percent (397 of 561) of the recorded dramatic performances at court occur on the same ten liturgical festivals.[6] Over 80 percent (450 of 561) occur sometime during Christmastide. Such a long and intense chronological correlation between dramatic performances and holy days certainly invites our investigation of the degree to which these plays and masques may share narrative, thematic, and imagistic patterns with the liturgical festivals on which they were performed.

But first we must ask if it is reasonable to assume that members of the Renaissance court audience might have perceived narrative, imagistic, and thematic parallels between what was obviously a basically secular entertainment and its liturgical context. Are there historical precedents, for example, for such a tradition? Would the court audience have been familiar enough with the specific liturgical character of each of the festivals involved to have perceived parallels to the plays and masques in question? Are the festivals themselves unique in ways that would encourage such perceptions? And finally, crucially, do we have any witnesses who actually testify to the operation of such a tradition in Renaissance drama? The answer to each of these questions is affirmative.

The most obvious precedents for drama with explicit liturgical overtones are the Catholic miracle and mystery plays performed in England until nearly the end of the sixteenth century. Many of the subjects they celebrate are identical with these same days in the English church year. The play of Herod's slaughter of the innocents, for example, is at the center of the Holy Innocents' celebration, as is the journey of the Magi central to the Epiphany. The interlude of Saint John the Evangelist likewise finds its obvious liturgical counterpart in the Saint John's festival. The purification plays celebrate the mysteries of Candlemas, and the Resurrection plays those of Easter. Most of the medieval Corpus Christi plays with New Testament subject matter, as well as the two earliest Quem quaeritis tropes, inevitably dramatize the events connected with the two focal points of the Christian year—Christmas and Easter. Shakespeare's contemporaries, growing up in the last four decades of the sixteenth century, would surely have looked forward to these mystery plays as a staple of English life and associated them with both the whole cyclical church year and its unique liturgical moments.[7] These many connections of style, structure, and narrative scheme make it reasonable for us to assume that an Elizabethan courtier might have been predisposed to perceive apposite liturgical echoes when they surfaced during these predominantly secular performances at court. In fact, it might not be entirely coincidental that this decade of the seventies marks not only the suppression of the popular and widespread mysteries but also the establishment of a new tradition of regular court performances on prominent Anglican liturgical festivals.

It is equally reasonable for us to assume that these liturgical festivals would have been well known in Renaissance England. For Elizabeth's subjects were forced not only to use the prescribed Anglican Prayer Book exclusively, but also to attend services weekly and on all holy days. Horton Davies summarizes these pressures and analyzes their implications through his admittedly ecumenical but still thoroughly reliable historical perspective.

The three Tudor Books of Common Prayer were a coerced formulary of worship intended for "soul control"—that is, to force the parson and people in a direction predetermined by their sovereign and Council. . . . Every minister declining to use the Prayer Book or using other forms of worship was subject to an ascending series of punishments, ending, for the third offense, in deprivation and life imprisonment. Any lay person depraving the book or obstructing the use of it was subject to heavy penalties. Absence from church on Sundays or holy days was punishable by a fine of 12 pence for each offense, the sum to be levied by the churchwardens for the use of the poor of the parish. The later Elizabethan Acts against Recusants and Puritans contained even stiffer penalties, including imprisonment and in extreme cases, death.[8]

Obviously most of Shakespeare's contemporaries, if not all of them, were exposed week after week, holy day after holy day, to the liturgical formulations of their universal prayer book. From 1559 through Shakespeare's lifetime its prescribed prayers, litanies, sacraments, and biblical readings were the required common inheritance of the English people. There were reluctant hearers, to be sure, and inattentive ones too.[9] But the very life of the Elizabethan, his sense of the calendar year as well as his doctrinal and liturgical orientation, was inevitably touched by this dominant cultural force. Only the very ignorant or the very obstinate could have escaped its influences.

One can still imagine the indoctrinary power of this constantly reiterated Anglican liturgy. Even the most inattentive would have been saturated with the basic tenets and liturgical rhythms of Anglican Christianity in England. What is harder to imagine is the equal effect of the Prayer Book on the Elizabethan's sense of the year itself. For many today the year is first fiscal, or academic, or just purely chronological, a calendar prescribed by the monthly sequence of bills, the passing of the seasons, scattered political or religious holidays, or the periodic renewal of subscriptions and professional memberships. But in the Renaissance the year was the church year, clearly organized around a predictable succession of major religious festivals and compulsory weekly church attendance. This way of thinking influences many of the activities of the Elizabethan and Jacobean courts, including their schedules of dramatic performances.

The *Book of Common Prayer* carefully organizes the church year. It begins, in fact, with elaborate calendars which prescribe biblical readings not only for each of the Sundays and festival days of the year, but for every single day. So important are these calendars that the two great pulpit Bibles of the day, the Bishops (1568) and the King James (1611), include them in red letters just before Genesis. As they are today, the two major focal points of the Renaissance church year are Christmas and Easter. The first festively celebrates the nativity of Christ; the second pensively celebrates his death and resurrection. The first considers the benefits accruing to man in this life, the lessons of Christ to the living; the second presents and considers those of the world beyond, the message of eternal life. Although there are other prominent festival days, the Anglican church year focuses on the anticipation, the celebration, the remembrance, and the understanding of the birth and the resurrection of Christ.[10]

Advent begins the church year with four Sundays preparatory to Christ's birth. Christmas itself, the highest festival day of this season, is followed by twelve days of further celebration and remembrance. The holy days of the season, Saint Stephen's (26 December), Saint John's (27 December), Holy Innocents' (28 December), and New Year's (the Feast of the Circumcision, 1 January), lead up to the culminating festival of Epiphany (6 January). The first through the fifth Sundays after Epiphany similarly celebrate this season of the discovery of Christ and his message for mankind and are obviously named for that relationship. One other holy day, Candlemas (2 February), is closely associated with the Christmas season. In all, then, eleven Sundays of the church year and six other holy days are devoted to the general celebration of Christmas. As we have seen, these are the same six holy days that with Shrovetide are exclusively and repeatedly graced by dramatic performances during Elizabeth's reign.

The Easter season is as richly attended by festival services. In addition to the six Sundays in Lent, culminating with Palm Sunday, there are also two to three pre-Lenten Sundays of preparation, concluding with the three final holy days of Shrovetide, Shrove Sunday, Monday, and Tuesday. The next day is Ash Wednesday, the official beginning of Lent. The overlapping during these three Shrovetide days of Christmas festivity and Lenten pensiveness and the psychological, sociological, and liturgical conflict occasioned by that overlapping are vividly embodied in Peter Brueghel the Elder's painting *The Battle of Carnival and Lent*. We shall see that the conflict also finds its way into the structure and thematic concerns of many of the Shrovetide masques and plays. During the days surrounding Easter Sunday occurs another cluster of seven holy days. Then five Sundays after Easter, leading to Ascension Sunday, Whitsunday, and Trinity Sunday, conclude this festival season. Only Shrovetide, Easter Monday, and Easter Tuesday share the celebratory spirit of the six holy days after Christmas, though they share as well touches of the penitential mood of Eastertide. Perhaps because of these affinities of spirit, these pre-Lenten and post-Easter holy days are also the other festivals most frequently graced by dramatic performances at court.

Although it is just as elaborately organized, the other half of the liturgical year is far less distinctive for its festival days. The twenty-five Sundays after Trinity are virtually indistinguishable by name or thematic focus. As a result, from "the First Sunday after Trinity" through "the Twenty-fifth Sunday after Trinity" the church year quietly awaits another Advent, another Lent, and the distinctive liturgical festivals of Christmas and Easter associated with them. A season of liturgical rest is thus carefully counterpoised against a season of liturgical activity, just as surely as the birth of Christ is followed by his death and resurrection, year after year in the liturgical calendar.

With equal ritualistic regularity the same Anglican preachers offer sermons in the same places on the same festivals year after year. Lancelot Andrewes preaches seventeen Christmas sermons from 1605 to 1624, all of them before King James at Whitehall. Several refer back to previous sermons, confident that the homogeneous audience will remember the last occasion. Just as regularly, John Donne always preaches at Whitehall on Shrovetide, and at Saint Paul's on Christmas and Easter Days. Such calendar traditions, not to mention such a permanent and homogeneous social and religious community, we can hardly imagine today. But court in the Renaissance constituted the theatrical audience as well as the liturgical congregation.

The almost symphonic order of the church year also reaches extensively into the Elizabethans' secular sense of time.[11] In fact, so extensive is this influence that to many of them distinctions between secular and religious calendars would have been unnecessary. Repeatedly the title pages of most individually published plays and masques give two facts of their performance equal billing: the performance at court and the festival day on which it occurs. "Played before the Queenes Maiestie at Greenewiche on Candlemas day at night," or "Played before the Kings Maiestie at Whitehall upon St. Stephen night" are characteristic inscriptions. Nonfestival performances at court record no date at all on their title pages. The separately published Shrovetide and Epiphany masques from 1605 to 1635, with only one exception, continue this tradition into the seventeenth century. Further, the characteristic references both on title pages and in the Revels Accounts call a holy day by its liturgical name, not its calendar date. That reminds us that the days, and probably their liturgical significance, were much more familiar in the Renaissance than they are today. The reader might have been invited to share the same festival context as the original court audience by this reminder.

Even in the "purely secular" realm, rents, accounts, hirings, elections, and contracts all traditionally came due at the start of Michaelmas term, one of the four "quarters" of the church year.[12] Until recently school semesters were governed by a similar liturgical calendar. The progress of the court to and from London seems also to have been defined in terms of the church year. One expected the court to be at Whitehall from All Saints' (or Michaelmas) through Easter, and to make its progress through the realm between. Even as James and Charles add secular days of court performance to Elizabeth's rigidly observed festival calendar, they do so within the framework of the church year. One of these expansions, into Lent, must have filled that penitential season, albeit briefly, with unaccustomed joy. Like most of the court calendar, these expansions of the dramatic tradition are always defined in terms of the church year, illustrating the potency of its influence in the Renaissance.

The uniqueness of the most prominent of these festival days in the English church year may also help to explain their unusual amenability to pertinent dramatic performances. First, most of them fall during the Christmas and Easter season, the festive focal points of the church year. At this time the court was usually in London, which is of course the focal point of theatrical activity as well. Thus the spirit of the seasons would have coincided with the availability of drama. Second, the Orders of Evening or Morning Prayer and Holy Communion, the basic services in the *Book of Common Prayer*, are usually celebrated on Sundays. In contrast, most of these festival days fall during the week, creating a special blend of secular and religious in the calendar context. Since attendance was required as on Sundays, there is still considerable assurance of a large common audience. Third, the great comfort and strength of the normal prayer or Communion service lies in its sonorous repetition of familiar forms of worship. Sunday after Sunday one Morning Prayer is virtually indistinguishable from another, one Communion from the next, in form as in content. The prescribed prayers for the days, the "Collects," like the prescribed biblical readings, articulate general doctrinal and moral truths with little distinctive thematic or narrative focus from one week to the next.

In complete contrast, these ten festival days, while they are celebrated within the general Order of Morning Prayer or Holy Communion, have a sharp narrative and thematic focus unique in the church year. That focus is announced and reinforced by the equally unique naming of a mysterious or miraculous event (e.g., Innocents', Epiphany, Resurrection, All Saints'), the unique imagery (e.g., lights, candles), or the particular spiritual discipline which is to be celebrated (e.g., circumcision, purification, shriving). The prescribed biblical readings are often either descriptive of this saint, event, image, or theme, or parallel to it. And the Collect names the day and persistently drives home its special meaning. This unusual thematic, imagistic, and narrative focus would produce in the congregation on these unique festival days a deep impression of their liturgical "point." It would also be more naturally amenable to the dramatic experience to follow, since character, action, image, and theme are common to both forms. As V. A. Kolve suggests concerning the Corpus Christi mystery tradition, only the most vivid narrative, dramatic, and figural patterns can be transmitted from the liturgy to the stage with immediate affective power.[13] All of these distinctive characteristics would have provided a liturgical context especially favorable to a tradition of pertinent dramatic performances.

The significance of many of these liturgical festivals would also have remained prominent in Renaissance England through social traditions rich in liturgical significance. Of Saint Stephen's

Day, for example, Dorothy Spicer observes that rough sports commemorate Saint Stephen's stoning. The Saint Stephen's mummers play, with its traditional enactment of the death and subsequent rebirth of either Saint George or his Saracen enemy, must have suggested similar patterns of martyrdom. Holy Innocents', celebrating Herod's slaughter of the innocent children of Israel and the deliverance of Christ, was known as a time of "special indulgence to children," but also as a day of muffled church bells. In fact, unusual severity rather than unusual indulgence could also characterize the day; into the seventeenth century in England children were whipped in bed on Innocents' morning to remind them of the mournfulness of the day.[14] Such traditions are difficult to forget.

Of court traditions, we learn from Spicer, Ethel Urlin, and Leslie Hotson that the English monarchs, including Elizabeth, traditionally delivered the Magi's offerings of gold, frankincense, and myrrh to the altar during the Epiphany service at the Chapel Royal in St. James Palace. This chapel was right next to the great hall where the subsequent play would be performed that same evening before virtually the same audience that attended the chapel service.[15] Thus were the social and the liturgical celebrations tightly interwoven in the Renaissance court. The Shrovetide Lord of Misrule was also an almost universal presence in noble houses in England and embodied before the assembled worthies not only good Saturnalian fun but also all of the sins of the flesh, all of the indulgences of carnival, which they would have to repent and give over by the end of Shrovetide and the beginning of Lent. The common emblems of such Christmas and Shrovetide Lords of Misrule, their lions, asses, goats, apes, and fools, would also have been parading around the court throughout the holiday season in the festival mummings.[16] When their dramatic analogues, if not the creatures themselves, then appeared in the culminating masques as well, their pertinency to the season could hardly have been missed. The traditional Shrovetide pancakes similarly suggest the fasting that is associated with the lenten season. In fact one Shrovetide lord is called "First Founder of the Fritters,"[17] because of this association. Easter too had its "Pace-Egging" tradition of boys going about in fantastic garb and performing the old mummers play of Saint George and the Dragon, with its explicit overtones of death and resurrection. And all of the egg-throwing, egg-rolling, and egg-hitting contests of Easter also signified the festive conclusion of the fast started with the Shrovetide pancakes; for the eggs were eaten after their shells were broken (Spicer, *Yearbook of English Festivals*, pp. 212–13). Parallels like these between social and liturgical traditions suggest again the visibility of the basic outlines of such liturgical occasions in the Renaissance.

It would seem reasonable, then, to assume that the Renaissance courtier would have perceived liturgical echoes when they occurred in court performances on festival days. Those occasions are themselves unusually amenable to pertinent dramatic performances. Such pertinency has in the Renaissance a strong historical precedent in the recently suppressed Catholic mysteries. Further, the virtually universal and compulsory indoctrination of the Prayer Book would have combined with the strength of complementary Renaissance calendar traditions to have created an especially strong affective context for these performances. But witnesses to such affective power would cap off the reliability of such a thesis much better than argumentation. Welsford notices one such piece of external evidence in a description of a Shrovetide masque for 1577: "a device of 7: speeches framed correspondant to the daie."[18] Its very matter-of-factness may suggest how expected such correspondence was. But more impressive testimony is offered by Griffin Higgs, Oxonian, in 1607, and seconded by the anonymous author of *The Stage Acquitted* later in the century.

The Christmas Prince contains Higgs's contemporary account of pertinent Christmastide performances in 1607 at Saint John's College, Oxford. After supper on Christmas day an interlude "contayninge the order of ye Saturnall's" also showed "the first cause of Christmas-candles, and in the ende there was an application made to the Day, and Nativitie of Christ."[19] As in many of the festival masques to come, Saturnalian and liturgical strands are joyously if incongruously joined. Their English observer does not miss them; he seems to take them rather for granted. In fact, Higgs and his friends subsequently engineer the appropriate performance of the "purely secular" *Tragedy of Philomela* for Holy Innocents' Night: "The next day being Innocente day, it was expected, & partly determined by or selves, that the Tragedy of Phylomela should have bene publikely acted, wch (as wee thought) would well have fitted the day by reason of the murder of Innocent Itis" (p. 56). That the play is secular and its subject classical is obviously no deterrent to their sense of its appropriateness to Holy Innocents'. Of course this is Oxford and not the court. Still, Higgs's account in 1607 is an important piece of firsthand, external evidence of the actual operation of a general tradition of apposite festival plays early in the seventeenth century. Higgs and his friends not only perceive such pertinency; they actually plan it.

Late in the century an anonymous defense of the theater against Puritan attacks, *The Stage Acquitted* (1699), [20] provides our best evidence of near-contemporary awareness of this tradition of pertinent festival performances. Many of the other defenses of the stage—one ironically attributed to William Pyrnn in 1649, Richard Baker's in 1662, and John Dennis's in 1737— follow Sir Philip Sidney's argument that plays could edify morally. They also suggest that if the king and queen, the Anglican clergy, and pious gentlemen had attended plays at the Elizabethan, Jacobean, and Caroline courts, those plays could hardly have been as morally offensive as the Puritans claimed. Christian plays, written by Christian playwrights for Christian audiences, could edify those audiences concerning both natural and revealed religion. [21] But at least one of the essays in defense should have cited the specific tradition of appropriate performances, since its existence through 1640 would have been a persuasive counterblow to the critics. *The Stage Acquitted* is that essay.

For the most part it follows the traditional arguments in defense of the stage, seriously and reasonably. The Anglican clergy and the crown supported performances at court because "drama is the best Lesson of Morality that can be invented by the Wit of man" (p. 22). But the author of *The Stage Acquitted* argues uniquely that the drama at court not only was supportive of general moral principles but was specifically pertinent to its liturgical occasions. How else could Queen Elizabeth and King Charles I, not to mention Bishop William Laud, have considered dramatic entertainments on holy days.

> King Charles cou'd not have thought of a better *entertainment,* for the *Sundays* after *Evening prayer,* than a diversion which tended to the confirmation of the Doctrine of the day; in purging our minds even in our Recreations from those faults which might have crept into our *morality,* that is, in our duty to God, our selves, and our Neighbours. . . . 'Tis no new observation, but confirm'd by the consent of all Mankind, that *Example* is of more force than *Precept,* and therefore the bringing such *Examples* that may move our Aversion to Vice, and our Love of Virtue, was a design worthy both the day and the King; for the *Masques* or *Plays* was but a continuing the instruction, and fixing it in the minds of the Auditory. [Pp. 56-57]

Perhaps this is a little too generous to Charles's court. But the connection assumed by this seventeenth-century writer between dramatic performance and liturgical occasion is every bit as extensive, and much more consciously edifying, than any suggested in the study which follows.

Given such a potentially edifying drama, why did the Puritans so oppose it? The answer is as persuasive as it is brutal.

> I am of opinion that if the *Plays* had not exposed the *darling* sins of the *Saints* [Puritans], the Saints had not been such violent Enemies to the Stage. . . . On the contrary, when they must know that the business of the *Stage* is to expose Vice and Folly, they ought not to declare themselves such utter Enemies to the Stage, which is a *Foe to Hypocrisie, and false pretender[s] to Virtue and Religion.* . . . 'Tis no wonder therefore that Mr. R—th should be an enemy to those Plays, which King *Charles* and the Church of *England* encouraged. [Pp. 61-62]

Having disposed of the Puritans, the author goes on to show how pertinent one of the Epiphany masques, *Britannia Triumphans,* was to its festival occasion and how uncomfortable it must have made a Puritan:

> But let us examine even from his [Collier's] own quotations, the subject of his Masque, which he attacks in his 2d Chapter, entituled *Britannia Triumphans,* and spight of Mr. R—th's zeal for *Imposture,*

see if the exposing Falshood be not a good prosecution of the business of the *day,* in which they were taught to value the Doctrine of *Truth,* to love our Neighbour as our selves, to love our Enemies, and to do as we would be done by. . . . Now the exposing *Imposture* [a character in the masque] was to take away a notorious enmity to all these admirable Doctrines. . . . So that this [sombre dress] is so far from a *reflection* on the *graver sort,* that 'tis a compliment to 'em, by shewing that to make the Devil appear like an Angel of Light, he was feign to borrow the best outside he cou'd find. . . . [Pp. 63-64]

Further, the portrayal of Imposture not only illustrates Epiphany's virtue of truth by exposing its opposite; it also portrays the ugly enmity of the chief opponent of episcopacy and the crown.

For when the Poet here brings in Imposture speaking against *Episcopacy,* he will needs have it mean the Fanaticks or Dissenters; they are oblig'd to our *Drawcansir,* who spares neither *Friend* nor *Foe.* But is it so unpardonable a Crime, for a Friend of Episcopacy to jerk its Enemies and that for what they were guilty of? he follows not his own Rule; he is very unmercifully dealing with King *Charles.* [P. 65]

Even more extensively than Griffin Higgs, the anonymous author of *The Stage Acquitted* has precisely described the whole general tradition of pertinent festival performances at court, has shown some of its specific operation, sociological and liturgical, in one of the court masques, and has given it a firm historical grounding in the Anglican tradition. In answering charges against King Charles and the Anglican clergy, this sophisticated seventeenth-century critic has helped us answer one of our most difficult questions as well. For he has shown us, with Griffin Higgs, how readily members of the seventeenth-century audience might perceive the fitness of these dramatic works to their liturgical occasions.

Having established the fact that Renaissance drama was traditionally performed at court on ten nights of religious festivity and the likelihood that some of the ninety-three extant masques and plays of festival performance, plus three festival namesakes, might have been perceived as appropriate to those festivals, it now remains for us to look at the most interesting of these dramatic works in the light of this tradition.

The methodology of the rest of the study will be as simple as
the material allows. Its organization follows the church year as
it is set forth in the Prayer Book, beginning with the post-
Christmas holy days. A reading of the Collect and biblical passages prescribed for each holy day of repeated dramatic performance establishes the basic liturgical context. These readings
are supplemented by pertinent marginal glosses from the Geneva Bible, dated sermons by John Donne, Lancelot Andrewes,
and others, and commentary by the Fathers of the English
Church to re-create the fullest possible sense of a festival's
unique thematic, imagistic, and narrative dimensions.[22] This
primary material is then supplemented by Robert Nelson's *A
Companion for the Festivals and Fasts of the Church of England,* the standard, conservative, eighteenth-century guide to
Anglican liturgical life.[23] It is also checked against such standard contemporary works as C. H. George and Katherine
George, *The Protestant Mind of the English Reformation*;
Horton Davies, *Worship and Theology in England*; and *The
Prayer-Book Dictionary*. Social customs, C. L. Barber's province,
are mentioned only when they pertain to both the dramatic
and the liturgical experience. This liturgical context, though
recoverable today only through such research, was emphatically
not book-learning in the Renaissance. It was a weekly or a
monthly indoctrination shared by most Englishmen from 1558
to 1642. Such knowledge permeates the mind through decades
of exposure; it is also refreshed every time a particular festival
is celebrated again. The Renaissance courtier would have known
his liturgical festivals well enough to have responded to their
echoes in festival plays.

Once the liturgical tradition for a given day has been established, all of the plays and masques performed on that day are
considered for their possible correlations to it. We might expect
two general kinds of correlation to exist between these plays
and their holy days. One can be called "genetic" and the other
"affective."[24] *Genetic* would describe each work which was
clearly *named for a festival or written for festival performance,*
works into whose *genesis* the significance of the day might
enter. The masques commissioned for Epiphany and Shrovetide

plus those few for New Year's and Candlemas are certainly in this category. So are *Twelfth Night* and *Michaelmas Terme,* with their obvious festival namesakes. Roughly a third of these works have such a festival genesis. In the second and much larger *affective* category would fall all of the other plays performed on the holy days. There is no reason to assume that any of them were written for the festival day of their eventual performance at court, though some, of course, could have been so composed. But there is a good chance, given the uniqueness of these ten festivals and the demonstrated strength of the calendar tradition, that the play's significance might have been affected for the court audience by its liturgical occasion. This affective thesis does not try to account for the correlation of these plays and their holy days, though it does not rule out the sometimes attractive possibility that particularly apposite plays—Thomas Dekker's *Olde Fortunatus* for Saint John's, Jonson's *Alchemist* for New Year's, Shakespeare's *Merchant of Venice* for Shrovetide, or his *Winter's Tale* for Easter Tuesday— might occasionally have been chosen (à la Griffin Higgs) by the Lord Chamberlain or the Master of Revels for their unusual fitness. It does not insist that every perceived parallel would have been noticed by every courtier, or even any courtier. What it does suggest is that a courtier who had just had such and such a biblical or liturgical or homiletic passage read to him in the Chapel Royal on one of these unique and familiar festival days might very well have made affective connections while watching the subsequent play that would never have occurred to him on Guy Fawkes's Day. Such associations can often enrich our understandings of these works.

Obviously the quality of such correlations will vary considerably from play to play and from festival to festival. Given the complexity of these plays and their liturgical context, the attempt to demonstrate their relationships or to measure affective power is not an exact science, and should not be. Several festivals share common thematic and imagistic motifs, especially those of the Christmas season; so do some of their plays. Obversely, one of the most interesting Candlemas masques celebrates the entire festival tradition rather than that single day. Several works—*King Lear* and *Twelfth Night* among them—grace more than one festival with almost equal pertinency. Some works are only slightly appropriate; others are extensively so. To deal tactfully with such variables throughout the study, and to make the concluding analysis of the quantity and quality of all the correlations a little more sophisticated, distinctions are drawn between slight, moderate, and extensive correlations. These distinctions are admittedly rough, but they are also useful.

That final analysis clarifies and interprets the weight and significance of all the available evidence for a tradition of apposite festival performances at court. For its figures to have any validity, the study considers all of the ninety-six works and tries to determine the nature and degree of their correlation to their liturgical occasion. But because so many of these performances evidence a slight to moderate correlation to their festival, the study considers in detail only the most interesting forty or so of these works, those which evidence an obvious or "extensive correlation." The curtailed discussion of the plays of moderate and slight correlation should imply, however, neither the lack of good evidence of correlation within the plays nor their unimportance among these works of festival performance.

Shakespeare, Jonson, and Beaumont and Fletcher, with fifty-six of the recorded ninety-six works and many of the most extensively pertinent performances, are especially prominent in this tradition. So, predictably, are many of the commissioned masques. More surprisingly, fifteen to twenty of the plays with a purely secular genesis also show extensive correlations. Though the discussion which follows must restrict itself to the ways in which these plays and masques parallel their festival occasions, that focus is not meant to imply that such consonance is the only way to understand these works, or even the most important way. Still, the presence of frequent and intense parallels between these works and their festival occasions will reveal a hitherto unimagined relationship between Renaissance drama and the English church year. It should also encourage revised assessments of the ways the Elizabethan, Jacobean, and Caroline audiences might have associated their basically secular drama with the religious insights that drama seems potentially to have contained and reflected.

CHAPTER 2

Performances on Saint Stephen's through New Year's

In Elizabeth's reign the scheduling of plays at court on the four festival days immediately following Christmas Day—Saint Stephen's, Saint John's, Innocents', and New Year's—is almost automatic, year after year. But though these days remain fairly prominent in the Jacobean and Caroline calendars of court performance, they attract few of the commissioned masques that will make the Epiphany, Candlemas, and Shrovetide performances so much more important in this dramatic tradition. The study therefore begins with some of its least impressive data. Countering this disadvantage is the opportunity to begin with the simplest of questions about the affective dimensions of the tradition we are about to consider. What associations might the liturgical experience earlier in the day have elicited in the courtier as he later watched these plays of purely secular genesis? The correlations that emerge between plays and festivals are surprisingly rich and frequent even in these least impressive cases.

It is also valuable to discuss these plays together because their holy days share the immediate liturgical context of Christmas and the general post-Christmas liturgical emphasis upon celebrated humility. The ass and the infant in the manger figure prominently in the Innocents' and New Year's feastings of folly. Most of these festivals celebrate together universal imperfection—man's folly and his worldliness—as they urge its mortification. The Christ child's humble birth reassures us of the normalcy of this imperfection and its forgiveness, by God and among men of good will, men unlike Malvolio. Robert Nelson's glosses on the Christmas liturgy conventionally stress these general motifs: charity, love of enemies, patience in adversity, but especially humility: "That we might learn *Humility*, this Prince of Glory condescended to the Poverty of a Stable; this Wisdom of the Father became dumb, and was reduced to the Simplicity of an Infant."[1] Such common liturgical strands help explain how a few of these plays might seem equally at home on several festival days. But since their genesis almost surely had nothing to do with the liturgical occasion they were later chosen to entertain, these first plays are most remarkable for the frequency of their unique suitability to their own festival.

The Saint Stephen's Collect provides the theme common to the first festival and most of its plays: "Graunt us, o Lorde, to learne to love our enemies, by thexample of thy Martir sainct

Table 1

26 December: Saint Stephen's Performances

Dates	Titles	Authorities
1604	*Measure for Measure*	Chambers, 4:119
1606	*King Lear*	Chambers, 4:121
1611	*A King and No King*	Chambers, 4:125
1621	*The Island Princess*	Bentley, 7:41
1622	*The Spanish Curate*	Bentley, 7:45
1623	*The Maid of the Mill*	Bentley, 7:50
1624	*Rule a Wife and Have a Wife*	Bentley, 7:56
1630	*The Duchess of Malfi*	Bentley, 7:76
1636	*Arviragus*, part 1	Bentley, 7:104

Source: E. K. Chambers, *The Elizabethan Stage,* and Gerald Eades Bentley, *The Jacobean and Caroline Stage.*

Stephen who praied for his persecutours." The prescribed
biblical readings continually stress the same values: patience in
adversity ("a time for all things" in Eccles. 3) the reward of the
righteous (in Isa. 56 and Prov. 28), and of course Saint Stephen's
Christ-like example of forgiving his persecutors as they stoned
him to death (Acts 7:55–end).[2] Eight of the nine plays performed on Saint Stephen's contain positive or negative exemplars of these peculiarly Christian virtues of loving one's enemies and praying for and forgiving one's persecutors. Such a
frequent correspondence to this uniquely Christian theme
certainly suggests that whoever attended these plays on Saint
Stephen's day at night could have caught these similarities and
enjoyed them.

The first of the recorded and extant plays, *Measure for
Measure,* is extensively relevant. In fact, its central value system,
ironically articulated in the title, is precisely that of the Saint
Stephen's festival: measure should not be meted out for measure in the new dispensation. As Christ advises during the
Sermon on the Mount, to which the Collect as well as the
play's title are verbally indebted, "Judge not, that ye be not
judged, For with what judgement ye judge, ye shall be judged,
and with what measure ye mette, it shall be measured to you
againe."[3] The Old Law of righteousness and justice is being
supplanted in the Christian tradition by the New Law of humility and mercy: "Ye have heard that it hathe bene said, Thou
shalt love thy neighbour, and hate thine enemie [or "an eye for
an eye, & a tooth for a tooth" (Matt. 5:38)], But I say unto
you, Love your enemies, blesse them that curse you: do good to
them that hate you, and praye for them which hurt you, and
persecute you" (Matt. 5:43–44).

In paraphrasing the same biblical passage in his Saint Stephen's commentary, Robert Nelson's *Companion* makes its
centricity to the festival quite clear. What does this festival
teach? "We must love our *Enemies,* blesse them that curse us,
pray for them that despitefully use us and persecute us, a Perfection of Charity peculiar to the Gospel Institution, in which
St. *Stephen* copied the Example of his blessed Master, which we
might have thought impossible to have imitated, if the *Saint*

of this Day had not convinced us of the contrary" (pp. 81–82).
Nelson adds with the familiar biblical rhetoric of the play's
title the almost impossible injunction that we should not even
think badly of our enemies: "It is also plainly contrary to our
Lord's Rule, who warneth us not to *judge, that we be not
judged,* because, *with what Measure we mete, it will be measured to us again"* (p. 83). Donne explains in a Saint Stephen's
sermon that Saint Stephen's martyrdom exemplifies for us both
a forgiving and a regenerating charity: "If *St. Stephen* had not
praid for *Saul,* the Church had had no *Paul.*"[4] Paul, of course,
was the cornerstone of organized Christianity.

Angelo is the enemy and the persecutor in *Measure for
Measure,* as well as the exemplar of the literalness and severity
of the Old Law. Through his charitable strategems, the duke-
priest Vincentio gradually leads Isabella to forgive her enemy
and her brother's persecutor. Mariana also gladly forgives
Angelo, but then she is betrothed to him and loves him. Isabella's love is thus pure charity, exemplary and disinterested
love; Mariana's is something less, though it is still impressive in
its forgiveness. Although the court is almost too generous in
its forgiveness of Angelo, it seems unusually harsh in its treat-
ment of Lucio. However, we might recall from the homilies
that edification through punishment was another established
function of charity.[5] The Saint Stephen's audience could probably have perceived and enjoyed many of these general but
central parallels to their festival night, especially in a play called
Measure for Measure. They might also have found it easier to
forgive Angelo and even Lucio than we do today, if only because of the unique liturgical setting of this performance.[6]

A Saint Stephen's play by Beaumont and Fletcher, *The
Island Princess,* is even more strikingly apposite to this festival
of martyrdom and the forgiveness of persecutors. The persistently vengeful and malicious governor of Ternata is confronted
first by the patience of the king of Tidore as he persecutes him.
Then his second victim, Armusia, confronts his villainy with a
saintlike willingness to be persecuted and die for his Christian
faith. Quisara, the lovely Mohammedan princess whom he loves,
asks Armusia to renounce his Christian faith for her hand in

marriage. In the explicitly doctrinal scene which follows, he refuses, rails against her faith and in favor of Christianity, and is overheard by the king (Quisara's brother) and the vengeful governor of Ternata. Armusia's outspoken opposition to the faith of his pagan hosts allows Ternata to insist on Armusia's persecution and eventual martyrdom. Quisara's pleading to her father suggests how appropriate this action could have appeared on Saint Stephen's:

> Thou hast persecuted goodness, innocence;
> And laid a hard and violent hand on virtue.[7]

Like Saint Stephen, Armusia is ready to die for his faith:

> Touch my life,
> 'Tis ready for ye, put it to what test
> It shall please ye, I am patient; but for the rest
> You may remove Rocks with your little fingers
> Or blow a mountain out o' th'way, with bellows,
> As soon as stir my faith; use no more arguments.
>
> [8:162]

Quisara is immediately converted to Christianity by Armusia's saintly example; she accepts his love, his persecution, and the glory of martyrdom for faith as her own (8:163).

Of course, in tragicomedy the promised martyrdom of Armusia and Quisara never occurs. The treacherous governor is exposed and imprisoned, and the Portugese Christians and the Mohammedans of Tidore end the play in the unity of love and the veiled promise of a new faith. The pagan king has the final words of the play, and they are the Christian words of forgiveness of enemies and persecutors alike. He pronounces benediction on Armusia's exemplary suffering and suggests its miraculous effects:

> Come, Friends and Lovers all, come noble Gentlemen,
> No more Guns now, nor hates, but joyes and triumphs,
> An universal gladness fly about us:
> And know however subtle men dare cast,
> And promise wrack, the gods give peace at last.
>
> [8:170]

The pertinency of this Saint Stephen's entertainment in 1621 rivals any that we will subsequently find in singly performed plays. It is close to the surface of the play for all who have just experienced the Saint Stephen's liturgy. The appropriateness of John Webster's *Duchess of Malfi* is just as impressive. For the duchess, as Webster's editor F. L. Lucas makes quite clear, is herself a clear example of cruelly persecuted goodness: "Hers is a sadder and more pensive, though not less undaunted, soul [than Webster's Vittoria]; and at the last, in her prison darkness gibbered around by madmen, she sits before us silently with the sad and terrible patience of a Mater Dolorosa."[8] The contrast to Vittoria is instructive, for *The Duchess* is the only play by Webster ever to grace one of these festival occasions and seems the only one suitable for them. As Lucas suggests, the duchess accepts her persecution with a religious dignity, in sharp contrast to the heroic, Roman defiance of Vittoria: "While Vittoria dies, like a Roman Emporer, standing, her gentler counterpart bows her head to the murderer's cord and kneels humbly before that cold star-lit heaven whence no hand stoops to save" (p. 19). Webster's characteristic brooding darkness surrounds them both; but the duchess, in accepting it with "the enduring courage of a martyr" (p. 20), could have moved court officials to perceive in her tragedy an extended analogy to the festival which celebrates Saint Stephen's own martyrdom.

Descriptions of her martyrdom in the play would have enhanced the chances of this association with Saint Stephen's. Her patience in adversity is so exemplary, it "gives a majestie to adversitie" (4.1.4-7). The duchess certainly dies like a Christian martyr; as she says,

> Who would be afraid on't [death]
> Knowing to meete such excellent company
> In th' other world.
>
> [4.2.217-19]

Even at the moment of her murder by strangulation she dies much like Saint Stephen, humbly kneeling, forgiving the executioners as her deliverers, and hoping for eternal life:

Pull, and pull strongly, for your able strength
Must pull downe heaven upon me:
Yet stay, heaven gates are not so highly arch'd
As Princes pallaces—they that enter there
Must go upon their knees.

[4.2.237–41]

We must agree with Bosola when he says of her body, "O sacred innocence, that sweetly sleepes" (4.2.382). Such moments in the portrayal of the duchess make it likely that her example on Saint Stephen's night could have evoked the memory of that martyred saint as well. A more appropriate secular drama could hardly be imagined.

Five other Saint Stephen's plays evidence at least a moderate correlation to their festival occasion. The first is Shakespeare's *King Lear*, a work dominated by extraordinarily cruel persecutors who could never be realistically forgiven by believable human agents. At the same time, the forgiveness of those who wrong others ignorantly and are themselves persecuted for their mistakes (Lear and Gloucester) is a prominent virtue in the play. So is the strenuously achieved patience of Lear in his persecution. Cordelia gladly forgives and prays for her enemy and persecutor Lear and briefly restores him to love and sanity. Kent and Edgar are equally forgiving. Like most of these plays, the tragic vision of *Lear* is vastly more complex and uncertain than the thematic thrust of Saint Stephen's. But the play has some interesting festival associations.

So do three other Saint Stephen's plays by Beaumont and Fletcher. *A King and No King* resolves in a contrived series of forgiven and loved persecutors. Tigranes needs Spaconia's forgiveness for breaking his vow of eternal love. She needs his forgiveness for her overly harsh upbraiding of him (1:200). This chain reaction of love and forgiveness allows the play to end in an amity strikingly consonant with the spirit of Saint Stephen's. In *The Maid of the Mill* Florimel and Otrante, members of feuding families, gradually come to love one another. The woman is persecuted by the man, but eventually fulfills the injunction of the Saint Stephen's Collect by loving, forgiving, and regenerating her "enemy." *The Spanish Curate* contains the cuckolded lawyer Bartolus and the dishonored Violante, both of whom plan an orgy of vengeance in the final act quite opposed to the ideal of forgiveness prescribed in the Collect for the Day. But their acts of vengeance are forestalled by the wise, wronged, but forgiving Don Jamie, whose ability to forgive those who have wronged him redeems the flawed plotters and the vengeful couple and resolves the plot in a muted concord. Enemies are again regenerated through an unusual act of forgiveness.

The last Saint Stephen's play, *Arviragus and Philicia,* is also at least moderately consonant with its festival occasion, but only if we take the two parts as a thematic whole with which the audience was fairly familiar. The threatened martyrdom of Arviragus in part 1 would suggest Saint Stephen's martyrdom. But the more impressive parallels occur in the second part, which was performed the next night in 1636 (with absolutely no correlation with Saint John's). In part 2, the magnanimity with which Arviragus and his brother Guiderius (Cymbeline's sons, of course) offer to die for one another is intensified by our knowledge that they have been bitter enemies—rivals for Philicia's love—and have now become reconciled through forgiveness.[9] Thus neatly do the motifs of forgiveness and martyrdom coalesce in the play's central action. Wholesale forgiveness transforms all but the most depraved of Arviragus's enemies at the end of the play, completing our sense of its moderate affective power.

Rule a Wife and Have a Wife seems to be the only recorded Saint Stephen's performance with no correlation at all to the liturgical festival. The other eight contain considerable enough correlation with the festival occasion for us to infer that the court audience could probably have perceived each of those similarities and enjoyed their enrichment of the theatrical experience. In three cases, *Measure for Measure, The Island Princess,* and *The Duchess of Malfi,* this affective power is almost a certainty.

Of the eight Saint John's plays only the earliest, *Olde Fortunatus,* and Jonson's *Volpone* seem persistently and extensively relevant to motifs characteristic of the holy day. Two others

Table 2

Correlations of Saint Stephen's Performances

None	Slight	Moderate	Extensive
Rule a Wife (1624)	*King Lear* (1606)	*Measure for Measure* (1604)	
	A King and No King (1611)	*The Island Princess* (1621)	
	The Spanish Curate (1622)	*The Duchess of Malfi* (1630)	
	The Maid of the Mill (1623)		
	Arviragus, part 1 (1636)		

Table 3

27 December: Saint John's Performances

Dates	Titles	Authorities
1599	*Olde Fortunatus* (?)	Chambers, 4:112
1611	*Greene's Tu Quoque*	Chambers, 4:125
1622	*Beggar's Bush*	Bentley, 7:45
1623	*The Bondman*	Bentley, 7:50
1624	*Volpone*	Bentley, 7:56
1630	*The Scornful Lady*	Bentley, 7:76
1636	*Arviragus,* part 2	Bentley, 7:104
1638	*The Passionate Lovers,* part 2	Bentley, 7:113

however, *Greene's Tu Quoque* and *Beggar's Bush,* share an interest in the traditional comic theme of the vanity of human wishes which is also the central lesson of this second post-Christmas festival. So does another, *The Scornful Lady,* but its hedonistic value system is uniquely opposed to the festival's message. The Collect, like the prescribed biblical readings, Ecclesiastes 5 and 6, Revelation 1 and 22, Isaiah 59, and 1 John 1, advises the worshipper to eschew the worldly in favor of "thy everlasting gyftes."[10] Eccles. 5:14, for example, contains the famous passages "As he came forthe of his mothers belly, he shal returne naked to go as he came, & shal beare away nothing of his labour, which he hathe caused to passe by his hand," and Eccles. 5:9, "He that loveth silver, shal not be satisfied with silver, & he that loveth riches, shalbe without the frute thereof: this also is vanitie." The other prescribed passages are insistently similar in theme and imagery.

So are comments by Bishops Nicholas Ridley and John Whitgift concerning the essential features of Saint John's. A letter by Ridley suggests that the theme of the vanity of the world was characteristically associated with Saint John. "And the saying of St. John is true: 'All that is in the world, as the lust of the flesh, the lust of the eyes and the pride of life, is not of the Father, but of the world; and the world passeth away and the lust thereof, but he that doth the will of God abideth forever.' "[11] In a sermon preached at Greenwich on Saint John, Whitgift stresses the same liturgical theme with proverbial eloquence.

First, worldly things are but momentary, they have no continuance. . . . : to-day as a beautiful flower, to-morrow as the withered grass. . . . Secondly, worldly things how pleasant soever they are and delectable, yet in the end they wax loathsome. . . , for there is in them deceitful pleasure, unprofitable labour, perpetual fear, dangerous dignity or promotion: the beginning is without wisdom, and the end with repentance. . . . "What will it profit a man to win the whole world, and to lose his own soul?"[12]

The four apposite plays complement several of the prescribed biblical readings by dividing up their final societies into the flawed and the pure, with a judgmental finality. As the Angel of the Lord said to Saint John in Rev. 22:10-15:

> The time is at hand. He that is unjust, let him be unjust stil: & he which is filthie, let him be filthie still: & he yt is righteous, let him be righteous still: & he yt is holie, let him be holie still. And beholde, I come shortly, & my rewarde is with me, to give everie man according as his worke shalbe. I am a and ω, the beginning & the end, the first and the last. Blessed are they, that do his commandements, that their right may be in the tre of life, & may entre in through the gates into the citie. For without shalbe dogges & enchanters, & whoremongers, & murtherers, & idolaters, & whosoever loveth or maketh lyes.

The marginal gloss to this passage is equally clear in its warning of the last judgment: "Let them be afraid of Gods horrible judgements, & assone as thei heare the Lambe call, let them come." Isaiah 59 catalogues the iniquities that will separate men from God when "the Redemer shal come unto Zion." *Volpone,* with its severely and explicitly judgmental ending in a court of law, and *Olde Fortunatus,* with its more literal rendition of the last judgment, could clearly refract this aspect of the Saint John's tradition.

In fact, *Volpone* is persistently about the vanity and iniquity of human wishes. As Alvin Kernan suggests, the play opens with Volpone's blasphemous celebration of his gold: "He first elevates—as the host is raised in the mass—a round gold coin. . . . Gold is the new Creator of the Volpone Universe, the unmoved mover, the still point, around which all existence now circles and from which it must draw its life."[13] Volpone also replaces old human relations of "wife, child, parent, ally, or servant," with "grotesque relationships based on gold" (p. 3): "From this golden center the infection spreads outward, re-creating the world beyond. In hopes of fortune Corbaccio disinherits his son, Corvino is willing to whore his wife, Lady Wouldbe offers her virtue, and Voltore, who for a few pennies would 'plead against his maker,' dishonors his profession" (p. 3). So extreme is this world's commitment to vanity that all values are finally traduced: "Not only are individuals, professions, and social institutions remade by the power of gold, but the yellow metal ultimately becomes the standard by which all things material and spiritual are measured" (p. 3). This is the iniquity of Isaiah and Revelation gone stark mad but appearing pure sanity, even religion, to those who pursue it. As Kernan suggests, Volpone and Mosca "transcend mere miserliness" in the intensity of their commitment (p. 6). Ultimately, of course, "the iteration of this theme reveals that a world and men given over entirely to materialism are unreal, mere pretenses" (p. 11). This is but the shadow world of Ecclesiastes and of the Saint John's liturgy, drawn in ironic but compelling splendor. And as that world dissolves, so this with its foxes, flies, vultures, and crows, virtually eats itself up. It feeds, cormorantlike, on itself until there is nothing left to eat. Left to inherit the earth are the two innocents Celia and Bonario. Gone to judgment are Volpone and his worldly confederates. Their judgment is fittingly literal in the play. They are tried and sentenced at the end, though their appetites have already degenerated to the point of self-destruction long before. As Kernan suggests in his conclusion, Jonson's moral vision would have allowed no other end.

> Volpone and the views he represents were, in Jonson's time, only the latest in a long series of challenges to society and established order. They were as contemporary and shining new as a fresh-minted coin, and yet they were as old as Satan himself. And the end was the same in both cases. With the predictable regularity of a machine, each step upward in defiance of nature becomes a step downward. [P. 25]

With judgmental finality, then, "the court locks these Proteans into the shapes they have wrought for themselves" (p. 26). Iniquity is its own brutal punishment, though the forces of society and religion assist in its final execution. *Volpone,* of course, has dimensions untouched by this discussion. But on Saint John's day, it would have been an impressively pertinent play.

Olde Fortunatus is even more closely related to the festival than *Volpone.* The play is obsessed with the theme of the vanity of human wishes. At least eight times there are extended discussions of this central thematic pattern, several of them two to three pages long.[14] In addition, the plot inevitably revolves around the unfortunate repercussions of Fortunatus's choice among Fortune's proffered gifts, "wisdom, strength, health, beautie, long life, and riches" (1.1.211). Like all of his predecessors, Fortunatus hardly has a chance, unless he chooses wisdom. But they never choose wisdom:

> Farewel, vaine covetous foole, thou wilt repent,
> That for the love of drosse thou hast despised
> Wisedomes divine embrace, she would have borne thee
> On the rich wings of immortalitie;
> But now goe dwell with cares and quickly die.

[1.2.308-12]

One feels especially sorry for Fortunatus, since both Ecclesiastes and later Paul consider earthly wisdom a thing of this world only. Like Paris, Fortunatus had little chance to choose aright. His name, of course, suggests his worldly dilemma.

Like Whitgift and Ridley, both the Lessons and the Collect for Saint John's Day persistently stress this theme of the vanity of human wishes. Isaiah 59, like Ecclesiastes 5 mentioned above, is frightening in its statements of the futility of human judgment or earthly riches. Ecclesiastes 6 even articulates a premise similar to the narrative strategy of *Volpone* and *Olde Fortunatus*:

> 2 A man to whome God hathe given riches and treasures and honour, and he wanteth nothing for his soule of all that it desireth: but God giveth him not power to eat thereof, but a strange man shal eat it up; this is vanitie, and this is an evil sicknes.
>
> 12 (or 7:2) For who knoweth what is good for man in the life & in the nomber of the dayes of the life of his vanitie, seing he maketh them as a shadow? For who can shewe unto man what shalbe after him under ye sun?

Olde Fortunatus persistently asks this same question. It also contains a character appropriately named *Shadow,* who is among the frequent articulators of this truth about ephemeral and lasting gifts. Just after the choice of wealth, for example, Shadow warns, angellike, against the whole spectrum of earthly vanity:

> I am out of my wits, to see fat gluttons feede all day long, whilst I that am leane, fast every day: I am out of my wits, to see our Famagosta

fooles, turne halfe a shop of wares into a suite of gay apparrell, onely
to make other Ideots laugh, and wise men to crie who's the foole now?
I am mad, to see Souldiours beg, and cowards brave: I am mad, to see
Schollers in the Brokers shop, and Dunces in the Mercers; I am mad, to
see men that have no more fashion in them then poore Shaddow, yet
must leape thrice a day into three orders of fashions: I am mad, to see
many things, but horne-mad, that my mouth feeles nothing. [1.2.111-
20]

As Andolucia comments, this fool has spoken the truth of the
play: "Why, now Shaddow, I see thou hast a substance: I am
glad to see thee thus mad" (11. 121-22). As in *Volpone,* what
has appeared the sanity of the world has been proven madness;
what has appeared substance has become accidence. Shadow's
unworldly folly has become the greatest wisdom.

The image of light naturally contrasts in the play with that
of the world as a shadowy place. Light is, of course, a common
poetic and Neoplatonic symbol for truth, vision, and even God.
But since John the Evangelist's imagery for his own festival day
is so similar, the Master of Revels or the court audience could
have made the connection. In the first chapter of Revelation,
Saint John is transported into heaven. There he perceives the
brilliance of God's truth, imaged by golden candlesticks and a
Christ-like figure amidst them "girde about the pappes with a
golden girdle. His head, and heeres were white as white woll, &
as snowe, and his eyes were as a flame of fyre, And his fete like
unto fine brasse burning as in a fornace. . . . He had in his right
hand seven starres . . . & his face *shone* as the sunne shineth in
his strength" (Rev. 1:12-16, passim). That fire, that gold and
brass, that whiteness of the stars and the sun and truth itself
enter *Olde Fortunatus* in both ironic and straightforward ways.
On the ironic side, Fortune appears to Fortunatus in a stunning
"bright Eminence" (1.1.146); her first speech is loaded with
imagery of gold. Yet in spite of these images we know, because
the play explicitly tells us (11. 80-138), that she is of the
shadow world. True eminence, properly imaged by brilliance,
lies in the true queen, Gloriana, who also can create "two eyes
strucke blinde with admiration." "Our eyes are dazled by Elizaes
beames," amidst the "starrie Candlestickes" of the night, so
that she deserves our "prayers and praises" (p. 113). Or is she

sacred wisdom, as bright as the beams of light Saint John himself saw:

> O sacred wisdome,
> Had Fortunatus been enamored
> Of thy celestiall beautie, his two sonnes
> Had shin'd like two bright Sunnes.

[5.2.162-65]

Instead, of course, the sons also die and are carted off to Hell
by Vice, leaving Shadow a servant without "substance." As in
Volpone, this horrifying judgmental ending is reminiscent not
only of the morality tradition from which it so obviously
derives, but also has its counterpart in the liturgical tradition of
Saint John's Day.

One other general connection between *Olde Fortunatus* and
the Christmas holiday season seems manifest in the pair of
closely parallel songs which mark the entrance of Fortune as
the reigning goddess at the beginning of the play (1.1.64–79),
and the presence of Vertue as the reigning goddess at the end
(5.2.347–58). By replacing the name *Fortune* with *Vertue* in
the second song, Dekker effectively illustrates that the shadowy, transient values of the world have been finally replaced
by the everlasting favor of Vertue herself. While "Vertue's
love is Heaven, her Hate is Hell." In this line we have moved a
major thematic distance from the identical comment about
Fortune. The first statement is merely a manner of speaking;
the last is strikingly close to the Christian doctrine of Revelation. When we hear hymns to Vertue's deity, we are likewise
far removed from the purer secularity of the parallel statement
about Fortune. For in this second case, Vertue's deity is God
himself, who should be hymned and honored on holy days. The
refrain "Cry holyday" is another reminder of this same parallel
to religious festivity, as is the second statement of that phrase,
which has neatly become "Crie holly day." Unless this is a
typesetter's error, this second holy day is reminiscent of the
specific liturgical season in which Saint John's occurs, Christmas. Reminded that we should "tremble when her eyes doe
lowre" and cry holly day "where she smiles," we are not far

Table 4

Correlations of Saint John's Performances

None	Slight	Moderate	Extensive
The Bondman (1623)	*Tu Quoque* (1611)		*Olde Fortunatus* (1599)
The Scornful Lady (1630)	*Beggar's Bush* (1622)		*Volpone* (1624)
Arviragus (1636)			
The Passionate Lovers (1638)			

at all from the joyous but threatening lesson of the liturgical celebration or its saint, John the Evangelist.

Although three of the eight recorded Saint John's plays have no relationship to the liturgical festival, one runs diametrically against its thematic center, and two others show only a slight thematic relationship; *Olde Fortunatus* is impressively parallel in plot, theme, and images. *Volpone* also evidences a persistent thematic affinity. Of all the plays recorded performed at one time on a festival, *Olde Fortunatus* seems most likely to have been written with the festival in mind. But that relationship will almost certainly remain Dekker's secret, for we cannot presently penetrate it any more than Fortunatus could penetrate the riddles of Fortune.

For Holy Innocents' Day, 28 December, though there was evidently a strong tradition of annual court performances in Elizabeth's and James's reigns, we have only three recorded titles. Actually, *The Comedy of Errors* twice entertained the festival, once at court, once at Gray's Inn. *Cupid's Revenge* and *The Northern Lass* are recorded much later in the tradition. Because *The Comedy of Errors* is the only play twice performed on one of these first four holy days, because it is performed

Table 5

Holy Innocents' Performances

Dates	Titles	Authorities
1594	*The Comedy of Errors* (Grey's)	*Gesta Greyorum,* pp. 14–23
1604	*The Comedy of Errors*	Chambers, 4:119
1624	*Cupid's Revenge*	Bentley, 7:56
1638	*The Northern Lass*	Bentley, 7:113

early in the tradition, and because it is unusually resonant with festival associations, we will look at its affinities with some care. One is tempted to attribute their intensity to a festival genesis, and contemporary reports indicate that at the very least some of its festival relevancies were not missed by the revellers at Gray's Inn.

The account of the Gray's Inn Christmas revels for 1594 includes almost unmistakable references to the performance of *The Comedy of Errors* as part of the festivity "upon Innocents-Day at night."[15] We learn that after great confusion and revelry upon the stage of mock ceremony and misrule, and in the face of

> Throngs and Tumults . . . able to disorder and confound any good Inventions whatsoever, it was thought good not to offer any thing of Account, saving Dancing and Revelling with Gentlewomen; and after such Sports, a Comedy of Errors (like to *Plautus* his *Menechmus*) was played by the Players. So that Night was begun, and continued to the end, in nothing but Confusion and Errors; whereupon, it was ever afterwards called, *The Night of Errors.* [Pp. 20, 22]

This unusual piece of contemporary commentary indicates that the play fit easily into the night's context of wild, drunken revelry. Several critics have suggested that *The Comedy of Errors* was written precisely for the traditional misrule and confusion of Innocents' night, either this particular one or one earlier.[16] But the secular festival's traditions of misrule and universal confusion are combined in the play and the *Gesta Greyorum* with a more profound celebration of universal human absurdity, a celebration with liturgical overtones. That combination gives us an unusually complete understanding of the general and specific context of the play's festival performance.

Error seems to have been the traditional hallmark of Innocents' celebrations, as well as the badge of their successes. The following night mock charges are brought against the Master of Revels, charges which ironically celebrate the appropriateness of the play to its festival occasion: "And Lastly, that he had foisted a Company of base and common Fellows, to make up our Disorders with a Play of Errors and Confusions; and that that Night had gained to us Discredit, and it self a Nickname of Errors" (p. 23). Discredit is credit in the topsy-turvy Kingdom of Purpoole. The reason, of course, is the centuries-old tradition of beginning the Feast of Fools on Childermas or Innocents' Day. Until the time of the *Spectator,* Innocents was considered for this reason "the most unlucky day in the calendar"; it certainly is so to the inhabitants of Ephesus. Even the abundance of ass and ass-head jokes in the play may have had elusive connections to the festival tradition. In the culminating ceremony of the Feast of Fools, on 1 January, the ass was sometimes led in honor up the aisles of the cathedral. This tradition recalled, of course, the ass's close association with Christ's humility in Bethlehem as well as Jerusalem. Although the Feast of Fools was more common in France than in England, and although it was fairly well suppressed by the middle of the sixteenth century, its survival in the revelry at Gray's Inn suggests that it had not yet been completely forgotten.[17]

In a similar spirit, but ultimately more serious, the general pardon of the night before the play indicates how completely acknowledged and celebrated human error dominates the entire Gray's Inn festivity. Ostensibly a universal pardon, it contains so many legalistic exceptions as to exclude everyone present from its clemency. Those excluded from the pardon include:

slanderers of the mock prince or his court (everyone?); anyone later to be publicly employed in any capacity (all lawyers?); everyone who in any way may "entertain, serve, recreate, delight, or discourse with" any lady or gentlewoman without absolute courage, who try to convey said woman into his power, or slander her, or make forcible entry; all who use "any common house" (that takes care of the nongentlewomen); or recreation (such as bowling, hunting, fishing, pricking, etc.) (pp. 14–19). Because these categories include everyone who is even vaguely human, they implicitly establish and celebrate a spirit of universal guilt and shared absurdity. One exclusion is particularly important for our understanding of the festive and even communal spirit of this earliest recorded performance of *The Comedy of Errors*: "all concealed Fools, Idiots, and Madmen, who have not admitted their folly to the prince" (p. 17). Only the admission of folly gains pardon, as only the admission of sins gains forgiveness in the analogous context of Christian communion. Exclusion is universal during the feast of fools unless common humanity be joyously acknowledged. Shakespearean comedy in general seems to have absorbed the essence of this festive spirit which celebrates the ultimate wisdom and joy of acknowledged human imperfection. Our understanding of *The Comedy of Errors,* generally considered so superficial a play, is thus partially enriched by its festive context, as it could also have been for the Gray's Inn revellers. The subsequent performance of the play at Whitehall before James I on Innocents' Night 1604[18] reinforces the intimate association of the play and its festive occasion.

A glance at the liturgical tradition of Innocents' Day makes it even less likely that mere nostalgia or coincidence explains the dual performance of the play on that religious festival.[19] The repetition of *nativitie* in the final lines of the play seems to suggest a general awareness of the Christmas season. More specifically, as soon as we read the "proper" Lesson prescribed for Holy Innocents' Day in the *Book of Common Prayer,* we are struck by relationships to the framing story of Egeon and Emilia, Shakespeare's unique addition to his sources. Jer. 31:1–17, like the framework of *The Comedy of Errors,* is about the dispersal and reunion of families. In fact, from such other prescribed passages as Bar. 4:21-30, Matt. 2:13-18, Rev. 14: 1-5, and Isa. 60, we realize that this theme was a central motif of the liturgical festival.

Dealing as it does with the Lord's promise to reunite the dispersed and weeping families of Israel, Jeremiah 31 is insistently parallel to the first and final scene of *Errors*. After the Lord's several promises to gather the remnant of Israel from the coasts of the world, verses 15-17, on the ultimate deliverance of all innocents, seem particularly close to the situation and the sensibility of Egeon and Emilia, parents of their own lost children:

15 A voice was heard on hie, a mourning and bitter weping, Ra[c]hel weping for her children, . . . because thei were not.

16 Thus saith the Lord, Refraine thy voice from weping, and thine eyes from teares: for thy worke shalbe rewarded, saith ye Lord, and thei shal come againe from the land of the enemie.

17 And there is hope in thine end, saith the Lord, that thy children shal come againe to their owne borders.

In the other prescribed passages the theme remains the same: innocents have been scattered or displaced by their enemies, but they will eventually be returned home, even if that home is with the Lamb in heaven. Such strong parallels in narrative, theme, and tone suggest that Shakespeare expected his audience to perceive and appreciate the similarities as part of their dramatic experience.

Robert Nelson's *Companion* again adds focus to these parallels. The emblem of the children stresses that humility necessary to salvation: "*That* to be true disciples of *Christ*, we must become as little Children in the Frame and Temper of our Minds, without which we cannot *enter into the Kingdom of Heaven*. . . . The Emblem of little Children . . . consists in *Humility* and Lowliness of Mind, in total *Submission* to the *Will* of God" (pp. 106-7). It also urges our acknowledgment of weakness and folly: "In the true Knowledge of ourselves, and the understanding of our weak and sinful Condition, taking to ourselves the Shame and Confusion due to our Follies" (p. 107).

That the lords of Gray's Inn had just been absolved of their own guilt by the prince of Purpoole, thus becoming themselves mock-innocents and fools, may have heightened both the absurd and the serious dimensions of the parallel. They could hardly have hoped to see a more pertinent entertainment on the night of 28 December.

In addition to the correlations between *The Comedy of Errors* and Holy Innocents', one extant play of the other two recorded may have slight ironic relationships to the festival. *Cupid's Revenge* contains an innocent young prince who is miraculously delivered from an undeserved execution. But at the end of the play his mother stabs and kills him, Medea-like. An innocent sister dies likewise. If the courtier recognized the Innocents' tradition operating here, it would have to be through Herod's play rather than Rachael's. For this whole family, far from being delivered or reunited, is finally destroyed by the vengeful mother. It may be worth noting that two of the lost plays for Innocents' have titles that would suggest a similar relevancy. *A historie of the crueltie of a stepmother* (1578) could be in the tradition of *Cupid's Revenge*. And *Effiginia* (Iphiginia) is the Greek legend of the miraculously delivered, innocent daughter of Agamemnon and Clytemnestra, who was replaced by a stag just moments before her commanded sacrifice, like Isaac and the Ram, or Higgs's *Philomela*. However interesting these early parallels might seem, they are finally, of course, inconclusive without an actual play.

Table 6

Correlations of Innocents' Performances

None	Slight	Moderate	Extensive
The Northern Lass (1638)	*Cupid's Revenge* (1624)		*The Comedy of Errors* (1604)

Table 7

New Year's Performances

Dates	Titles	Authorities
1584	*Campaspe* (?)	Chambers, 4:100
1588	*Gallathea* (?)	Chambers, 4:103; title page (1592)
1600	*The Shoemaker's Holiday*	Chambers, 4:112
1604	*A Midsummer Night's Dream*	Chambers, 4:118
1605	*All Fools*	Chambers, 4:119
1609	*A Trick to Catch the Old One*	Chambers, 4:123
1611	*Oberon*	Chambers, 4:125
1613	*Cupid's Revenge*	Chambers, 4:127
1616	*Mercury Vindicated*	Chambers, 4:130
1622	*The Pilgrim*	Bentley, 7:42
1623	*The Alchemist*	Bentley, 7:46
1624	*The Lovers' Progress*	Bentley, 7:51
1625	*1 Henry IV*	Bentley, 7:57
1634	*Cymbeline*	Bentley, 7:90
1637	*Love and Honor*	Bentley, 7:105
1639	*Beggar's Bush*	Bentley, 7:114

Because the New Year's festival was often raucously secular in the Renaissance[20] and also because its primary religious connotation—circumcision—hardly seems propitious for dramatic purposes, one would expect little correlation between the plays and this holy day. But one would be wrong. Fully two-thirds of the recorded New Year's plays evidence obvious thematic correlation to either the secular or the religious strands of the festival, to a degree that warrants a fairly extensive discussion. In fact, the secular and the religious strands are often inseparable.

The first, which is primarily secular, is the Feast of Fools. This Saturnalian revelry has already been mentioned in connection with Innocents' Night and *The Comedy of Errors*. Its foolishness culminated on New Year's Day with a wholesale celebration of man's universal folly, his profound asshood. Such a celebration was probably as therapeutic in the social sphere as John Hollander has suggested it to have been in the theater. But it was, of course, not simply a secular observation. Roy Battenhouse has just recently reminded us of the rich Christian tradition that underlies the folly of such a character as Falstaff, who may in his grotesque absurdity and in more subtle ways as well become a Fool for Christ. The Rabelaisian, Erasmian, and Pauline celebrations of folly had certainly become a well-established Christian tradition by the Renaissance.[21]

The strictly liturgical content of the New Year's festival also bears important relationships to the folly tradition. The Collect in Queen Elizabeth's Prayer Book, for example, reveals that this circumcision signifies spiritual purification, the mortification of all worldly and carnal lusts: "graunt us the true Circumcision of the spirit, that our hartes, and al members, beyng mortified from al worldly and carnall lustes, may in al thynges obey thy blessed wil" (p. 64). Several of the prescribed passages for the day, most notably Colossians 2 and Romans 2 (p. 25), and Anglican fathers like Henry Bullinger, Hugh Latimer, and Thomas Becon also equate circumcision with the purification of the heart and the spirit, a cleansing from original sin, an avoidance of that "surfeiting and drunkenship" that lead to still profounder sins.[22] It is because the Feast of Fools, the parade of folly, is a manner of mortification that the secular and the religious traditions coincide in the New Year's festivities. Its celebrant either parades our grotesque folly before us in social ritual until we surfeit of it, Hollander's concept of "the morality of indulgence"; or he acknowledges worldly and carnal lusts, the sins of the flesh and the world, in order that they might be mortified and purged through religious ritual.

New Year's thus seems the festival most amenable to plays depicting the purging of worldly and carnal excesses, vices clearly embodied in such Lords of Misrule as Shakespeare's Falstaff and Jonson's Sir Epicure Mammon. However, the plays for at least three other festivals, Twelfth Night, Candlemas, and

Shrovetide, will have their share of such figures and themes as
well. A familiar comment by Bishop Edmund Grindal on these
Lords of Misrule explains why such dramatic figures and themes
were associated with Elizabethan ecclesiastical and sociological
traditions of the general Christmas season, rather than a single
festival:

> In the feast of Christmas there was in the Kings house, wherever he was
> lodged, a Lord of Misrule, or Maister of merry disports: and the like
> had they in the house of every nobleman or honour or good worship,
> were he spiritual or temporal. . . . These Lords, beginning their rule on
> All-hallow Eve, continued the same till the morrow after the Feast of
> Purification, commonly called Candlemas; in which space fine and
> subtle disguises, masks and mummeries, with playing of cards for
> counters, nayles, and points in every house, more for pastimes than
> gaine.[23]

How many connections are drawn for us by these words. The
Lords of Misrule, present in noble houses through Candlemas,
also entertain the court in the drama—the masks and mum-
meries—for such festivals. Falstaff, Toby Belch, Epicure
Mammon, and the rest all live in a drama that copies and
perpetuates the role of their social prototype in the court. In
the liturgical tradition they are shriven on New Year's, for it is
the feast of the mortification of the flesh. They are shriven
again on Candlemas, the feast of purification, for Lent is
coming. They are shriven again, finally, along with the beasts
and fools that embody their excesses, during the Shrovetide
performances, for Lent is at hand. In the social tradition they
wax during the Christmas festivities and wane after Candlemas.
In the noble houses and in the plays that entertained them such
figures were strictly governed and even generated by traditions
of the English church year.[24]

It is no wonder that the few New Year's and Candlemas
masques will seem so similar to the more fully developed
Epiphany and Shrovetide masques, which predictably oppose
carnival excess, misrule, and asshood, against a decorous revelry,
antimasque against masque (see chaps. 3 and 4). The conflict
derives from a common sociological and liturgical heritage. It
is embodied by a walking emblem in noble houses and on the

stage as well. Such cross-patterning is not contradictory but complementary in the English church year and this dramatic tradition that sometimes embodies it.

John Donne's homiletic comments help us connect the achievement of spiritual circumcision with the dramatic strategies of many New Year's plays:

> the proper use and working of *purging Physick,* is, not that that Medicine pierces into those parts of the Body, where the peccant humour lies, and from which parts, Nature, of her selfe, is not able to expel it: the substance of the Medicine does not goe thither, but the Physick lies still, and draws those peccant humours together; and being then so come to an unsupportable Masse, and Burden, Nature her selfe, and their owne waight expels them out. Now, that which *Nature* does in a naturall body, *Grace* does in a regenerate soule, for *Grace* is the *nature* and the *life* of a regenerate man. [6:198]

Falstaff's bloated body seems its own purging physic; the assortment of humourous fools in *The Alchemist* need a physician like Face to draw them together for eventual purging. But in one way or the other, many of the New Year's plays depict a similar anatomy and purging of worldly and carnal lust and folly, for the "pastimes" and "gaine" of their festival audience.

In this context, several of the New Year's plays are immediately and profoundly apposite to the festival. *1 Henry IV* is the best example. It is a feast of fools, with Falstaff the grand master of misrule, the finest emblem of carnality in English comedy. Even his first words in the play, asking, "Now Hal, what time of day is it, lad?" (1.2.1), [25] and the joking which follows about Falstaff's debts to time are significant on both the religious and the secular festival of New Year's. As Nelson suggests, New Year's reminds the Anglican communicant of "the great Value of Time" (p. 118). In fact, his catechism on the subject of New Year's would have been quite useful to Falstaff, who has his own irreverent catechism on honor later in the play:

> *Q.* How ought we to employ our Time, that it may be improved to the best advantage?

A. We ought to redeem that which we have misspent, by lamenting the Follies which have consumed so precious a Treasure.

[P. 119]

We need only the gentlest reminder to recall Hal's two most pithy and pertinent comments in this same regard. His last words in this same scene, their first in the play, define his redemptive role in terms of time: "Redeeming time when men think least I will" (1.2.205). His first speech in the play upbraids Falstaff in similar terms: "What a devil hast thou to do with the time of the day?" (1.2.5 ff.) Renaissance preachers also speak urgently of time in connection with New Year's. Donne, for example, at the end of his New Year's sermon, admonishes "a diligent and present dispatch." "Doe not thou say, *Cras Domine,* to morrow, some other day. . . . Come therefore to this Circumcision betimes, come to it, *this Day,* come *this Minute.* . . . Doe this to day; as God this day gives thee a New yeare" (6:203–4). And Becon, in his homiletic dialogue called "A New Year's Gift," concludes on a similar, traditional, note of urgency: "While ye have time, do good unto all men. . . . Now is the time of grace, now is the time of health. Therefore neighbours, stand not idle all day, work manfully in the Lord's vineyard."[26] How richly this central motif of the New Year's liturgical tradition could have reverberated forth as *1 Henvy IV* was performed at court on New Year's.

Hal's being of "all humours" may suggest from yet another perspective that purging, cleansing process he must perform to purify his bloated kingdom, though of course it must be his father who carries its excesses "wild into the grave." The concluding mock death of Falstaff, that "manningtree ox," "that father ruffian," "that vanity in years" (2.4.430–33), the old year and old age plagued with its creditors and bloated with its carnal excesses, is equally relevant to the associations of mortification on this holy day. As his fellows in worldly folly and debts to time, the Percies, especially Hotspur, might be Falstaff's appropriate thematic counterparts. Although its characters and actions far transcend mere thematic embodiments, *1 Henry IV* contains, and eventually mortifies, both worldly

and carnal lust, in the best tradition of its festival day. Barber
has already shown how intricately these dramatic motifs are
intertwined with their social festivals. The liturgical tradition
obviously lies behind them almost as forcefully.[27]

Frank Manley's introduction to the Regents Renaissance
Drama edition of *All Fools* makes it clear that this play is also
especially rich in worldly and carnal folly. Gostanzo thinks
himself a "crafty, Machiavellian man, provident, experienced in
the ways of the world," but he is really an old fool, "whose
sense of value is based on money alone":

> Love nothing heartily in this world but riches,
> Cast off all friends, all studies, all delights,
> All honesty, and religion for riches.[28]

Manley continues, "no one in the play is entirely free from
Gostanzo's flaw." In fact, the horn joke at the play's conclusion draws "the age at large and all men in it" into its community of carnal as well as worldly folly. "All the characters
in the play undergo a similar humiliation in the midst of their
finest triumphs." But the final spirit of this humiliation is more
Shakespearean than Jonsonian. "There is no sharpness, no
bitterness, no desire to change mankind, only a warm-hearted,
large-minded acceptance of our foolish humanity" (pp. xi–
xvii). As the *Prologus* tells even the audience, *"Auriculus asini
quis non habet?"* (1. 35). Who indeed? On the day that celebrates the ass in all of us on the steps of the cathedral, this is
an apt festival inscription.

Two masques and a play by Ben Jonson might also have
struck their court audiences as fitting New Year's performances.
The parade of gulled fools, worldly and carnal, in *The Alchemist* reads like a roll call for the Feast of Fools: Ananias,
Tribulation Wholesome, Drugger, Face, Surly, Dapper, Epicure
Mammon (a splendid combination for the day), Kastril, and
Dame Pliant. The wonderfully ludicrous situations in which
most of these characters eventually find themselves are equally
relevant to the festival's celebration and exposure of worldly
and carnal folly and excess. All are allowed to vent their unique

folly and to be mortified for it. *Oberon* is also especially pertinent to New Year's. As Jonson himself reminds us of one of its Saturnalian characters, "Silenius is everywhere made a lover of wine, as is *The Cyclops* of Euripedes and known by that notable ensign, his tankard."[29] In addition, Lyaeus is "a name of Bacchus" (p. 550). The antimasque of five drunken and lecherous satyrs contains six or seven pages of splendid *carpe diem* lyrics. They catalogue for us in vivid images and brilliant trochaic and iambic couplets a bevy of carnal lusts. The eventual morality of this overindulgence finally becomes obvious when the masque of Vertues follows. After this surfeit of lust, even such abstractions as Majesty, Glory, Wisdom, Knowledge, and Piety are welcome relief. With the masquers and the masque we too have been "mortified" and are, at least briefly, made pure. Moderately relevant to the festival in complementary ways is Jonson's other New Year's masque, *Mercury Vindicated from the Alchemists at Court.* As *Oberon* purges the carnal lusts of its antimasque, so *Mercury Vindicated* mortifies the worldly lusts of the absurd alchemists Vulcan and Cyclope, their "adultery and spoil of Nature" (1. 110). Taken as a pair, the two masques thus mortify the two traditional New Year's sicknesses. This close relationship of the masque to the festival may be explained by the fact that both masques were written for New Year's performances. But because Jonson's plays characteristically purge such follies, we should also see the natural affinity of his plays to such festivals as Saint John's or New Year's.

Middleton's *Trick to Catch the Old One* shares with Jonson's *Alchemist* both a thematic direction and a cast of characters particularly appropriate to the New Year's festival of the mortification of worldly excesses. The dramatis personae are the perfectly named Pecunius and Mistress Lucre, Onesiphorus Hoard, and the fops Freedom and Moneylove. Witgood, the clever protagonist, opens the play lamenting his recent lechery, which has cost him his modest fortune. He resolves to win it back by gulling competitive usurers, Hoard and Lucre, into pursuing the hand and the fortune of a courtesan posing as a rich widow. After a variety of escapades illustrating the abundance of greed in the world, the play ends on a strikingly penitential note. Witgood and the courtesan defy their past errors and resolve to lead a new and better life, mortified of the sins of the world and the flesh. Witgood kneels with her to "confess [his] follies" and "disclaim" his gambling and his "sinful riots" of lust and gluttony.[30] With such a clear speech of mortification ending the performance, the attentive courtier could surely have caught the pertinency of this New Year's play to its religious festival.

Our discussions of Shakespeare's, Jonson's, Chapman's, and Middleton's extensively pertinent New Year's works make the examples of slight and moderate correlation easier to perceive. Among the plays moderately consonant with the festival, Beaumont and Fletcher's *The Pilgrim* is probably the most impressive. For it is increasingly a feast of fools as we approach the conclusion. Act 3, scene 5 parades emblems of folly before us: an "English madman," a "Heathen drunkard," a lecherous "she-fool," and a mad scholar, who sees himself as Neptune (5:191). Act 4, scene 3 is likewise full of Saturnalian emblems of folly, "fools, and Bedlams," "Owls, and Apes" (5:210). As the play concludes, the heroine Alinda, who has herself played the fool, directs a formal shriving of Roderigo, who is mortified and reformed by her advice (5:223–24). Her prideful father is similarly mortified in a penitential scene of confession, contrition, and prayer. The play's wholesale, joyous embracing of universal folly, its concluding general mortification, and its benedictory welcoming of the resultant happy new year of love ("Love's new and happy year" [5:229]) probably create a context rich enough in a variety of festival associations that they could have been noticed and enjoyed by the audience at court.

The least impressive of the other moderately consonant New Year's plays is *Gallathea,* which shares the repeated New Year's motif of alchemy with Jonson's works. The worldly absurdity of Rolph and Peter is mortified by their being cheated out of their silver, after which they wisely escape the alchemist's clutches. Diana's maidens also fall in love, for which folly of passion they are severely reprimanded; Cupid is given the penance of untying love knots. In its gentle parading of the follies of love and worldliness, *Gallathea* could also have evoked festival associations, but not so obviously as *The Pilgrim.* More obviously pertinent are *Cupid's Revenge* and *The Lovers' Progress.* Tragedies of illicit desires, both explicitly state a theme consonant with the New Year's liturgy: "These are the fruits of lust" (5:128), and "they that begin in Lust, must end in Blood" (9:256). *Beggar's Bush,* like so many of its predecessors on New Year's, also parades before us foolish mortals about to be mortified for their worldly and carnal lusts.

Among the three plays of slight correlation, *Cymbeline* hinges on a husband's foolish bet that his wife would stand firm against seduction. Posthumus's folly here is both worldly and carnal, and he will be profoundly humiliated for it. *A Midsummer Night's Dream,* like *Gallathea,* gently mortifies its foolish mortals in the woods outside of Athens. It also makes fun of the humbler variety of worldly pretension and court entertainment through Bottom's play. Finally, *Campaspe* at the end of act 2 has Diogenes confront Alexander with a long *contemptus mundi* speech, which helps Alexander subdue his passion for Campaspe as ill-becoming a godly man.

This discussion does not mean to imply that any of these works were instructional vehicles for the Anglican church. Delight outweighs instruction in all but one of them, as it will continue to do as we go on. The plays are far more complex than the festival motifs they could have suggested. It also does not mean to imply a greater interpretive precision than the material allows. New Year's has no monopoly on mortification as a festival motif; Shrovetide might have been an equally hospitable host for many of its plays. Furthermore, Renaissance comedies are so amply endowed with examples of worldly and carnal excess that many could entertain at New Year's with similar appropriateness. But even with such imprecision, these first plays are not unimpressively related in thematic and narrative affinity to the holy days of their performance. Of the nine recorded Saint Stephen's works, eight are persistently and explicitly enough interested in the Saint Stephen's virtues

Table 8

Correlations of New Year's Performances

None	Slight	Moderate	Extensive
The Shoemaker's Holiday (1600)	*Campaspe* (1584)	*Gallathea* (1588)	*All Fools* (1605)
Love and Honor (1637)	*A Midsummer Night's Dream* (1604)	*Cupid's Revenge* (1613)	*A Trick to Catch the Old One* (1609)
	Cymbeline (1634)	*Mercury Vindicated* (1616)	*Oberon* (1611)
		The Pilgrim (1622)	*The Alchemist* (1623)
		The Lovers' Progress (1624)	*1 Henry IV* (1625)
		Beggar's Bush (1639)	

of patience in adversity, martyrdom, and the forgiveness of enemies or persecutors for us to assume the probability of perceivable affective power. Three—*Measure for Measure, The Island Princess,* and *The Duchess of Malfi*—are extensively apposite. Of the eight plays for Saint John's one, *Olde Fortunatus,* shows the most extensive correlations of this entire group, and another, *Volpone,* is also quite fitting. The two performances of *The Comedy of Errors* on Holy Innocents' could have seemed especially rich in festival resonances. Of the sixteen New Year's performances, fourteen evidence some correlation, eleven either a moderate or an extensive correlation, and five—*1 Henry IV* and *All Fools* are most impressive—an extensive correlation. Thus the hypothetical courtier who saw all thirty-five of these court performances would probably have had his dramatic experience affected by the day's liturgical context in well over half of them; in nearly one-third the appropriateness of the work to the festival would have been almost unavoidable. In four-fifths of the cases it would have been at least possible for him to perceive parallels. Because such figures reflect a numerical translation of this reader's own value judgments, they are obviously subject to some modification, both up and down. But this early in the tradition, before we have encountered the more impressive parallels between the commissioned masques and their festival occasions, these plays already begin to testify to a vital tradition of pertinent festival performances at court.

CHAPTER 3

The Epiphany Masques

The masques of Ben Jonson have finally begun to receive their deserved critical attention. However, the two excellent recent discussions of their aesthetic and moral seriousness, by Stephen Orgel and John C. Meagher respectively, ignore without apology the persistent and inviting fact that almost half of the masques, thirteen to be exact, were written for performance on Epiphany, its eve, or the Sunday following.[1] The masques were intended to grace the culminating celebration of both the religious and the social festival of Christmas.[2] Only Shrovetide, at the very end of the Christmas season, exhibits an equally rich tradition of masque entertainment.

This oversight is symptomatic of the inherited critical consciousness of our age. It is still surprising, however, since Orgel's study is explicitly aware that many of the masques were written to be performed on a specific night for a relatively small and select court audience which had just attended the Epiphany Evensong en masse and observed its sovereign reenact the Magi's homage to Christ.[3] That surprise increases when we add Meagher's convincing contention that the masques frequently and informedly employ Neoplatonic symbolism in their portrayal of "The More Removed Mysteries."[4] It may finally be little more than a footnote to these two perceptive studies, but we owe it to Jonson, to his age, and to ourselves, to see if some of that aesthetic, moral, and even anagogical seriousness of Jonson's Epiphany masques is not more immediately derived than from the Florentine academy and its literary and dramatic progeny.

The Liturgical Context

Epiphany, the culminating festival of the Christmas season, is as prominent liturgically as it is central to the dramatic tradition at court. From the emergence of this tradition in the early sixteenth century through the last decade of repeated festival performances in the 1630s, Twelfth Day was the festival most often graced by dramatic entertainments at court. From 1605 through 1632 most of the Epiphany performances were the fifteen masques to be considered in this chapter. Before, and after, plays like those considered in the next chapter were the usual dramatic fare. The title of Shakespeare's comedy *Twelfth Night* is an obvious indication of the prominence of this dramatic tradition, especially among members of the Lord Chamberlain's or King's company; so is the large number of Epiphany masques. Because the liturgical tradition of Epiphany is shared by the plays and the masques, all of its essential details will be presented in this chapter and merely referred back to in the next. Such a procedure, though it might initially tax the reader's patience with a barrage of liturgical background, should finally make our consideration of the festival more coherent and more efficient and also clarify the relationship of the two different genres which graced it.

The festival of Epiphany celebrates the manifestation of Christ's godliness and God's love to the Magi, who represented all Gentiles in the Renaissance. It simultaneously celebrates the effects of that manifestation, the enlightenment and purification of mankind into humility, peace, and concord. The Collect for the day and most of the prescribed biblical readings reveal Christ's deity and predict its effects primarily through the imagery of glorious light.[5] In the Collect, God, "by the leadynge of a starre, diddest manifest [his] onely begotten sonne to the Gentiles" (p. 64). Both Lessons for the day, Isaiah 60 and 49, also stress the light of Christ's manifestation, and its agency in man's seeing. The more famous is the passage Handel interpreted in the *Messiah* prophesying the coming of Christ:

1 Arise, o Jerusalem: be bright, for thy light is come, & the glorie of the Lord is risen upon thee. . . .

2 For beholde, darkenes shal cover ye earth, and grosse darkenes the people: but the Lord shal arise upon thee, and his glorie shalbe sene upon thee.[6]

The Gospel reading is the familiar narrative of the journey of the Magi, led by the bright star of Bethlehem to the manger of the Christ child. Again, its central image is that of the light in darkness, which frees man from his imprisonment, the impure blackness of his ignorance and sin.

This Epiphany of the bright mystery of godhead is associated with the love of Christ and the ultimate, macrocosmic manifestation of that love and its power, the creation of the world.[7] One of Donne's Epiphany sermons explains why creation and Epiphany are so closely connected. Both are means to accommodate the immensity of God's love to man's limited faculties.

The *reason* therefore of Man, must first be satisfied; but the way of such satisfaction must be *this*, to make him see, That this World, a frame of so much harmony, so much concinnitie and conveniencie, and such a correspondence, and subordination in the parts thereof, must necessarily have had a workeman, for nothing can make it selfe.[8]

That workman is revealed in the Scriptures, and in Christ (3:358–62). Epiphany is the festival of manifestation. The virgin birth of Christ and the creation of the world are the two most brilliant manifestations of God's power and love. They lead man's natural faculties to supernatural thoughts, and these thoughts are among the lights of Epiphany: "a love of the *outward beauty* of his house, and *outward testimonies* of this love [incline] your naturall faculties to religious duties" (3:375). Each of these primary associations with the liturgical and homiletic and biblical traditions of Twelfth Day will be shown to be repeatedly used by Jonson in his Epiphany masques.

Light, of course, was the first creation in Genesis. It also drew the wise men to Christ. But he was a child, not a king; he was in Bethlehem, not Jerusalem; and he was in a manger, not a palace. Thus, in the midst of these images of Christ's exaltation we are during Epiphany simultaneously made aware of his profound lesson of humility. For one of the great paradoxes of incarnation is this humiliation, Christ's, God's condescension to become man, to assume flesh and form, that He might become manifest. As Donne says, "hee suffered his *Divine nature* to appeare and shine through his *flesh,* and not to swallow, or annihilate that flesh" (3:354). To realize the benefits of this great light, man must both humble himself before His brilliance and accept the paradox of His humility. Only, Donne says, "If with that little candle [Scriptures] thou canst creep humbly into low and poore places, if thou canst find thy Saviour in a *Manger,* and in his *swathing clouts,* in his humiliation, and blesse God for that beginning [are his blessings available]" (3:360).

Robert Nelson and Lancelot Andrewes are equally emphatic in presenting this paradox of Epiphany. The latter inspired T. S. Eliot's "The Journey of the Magi" in a sermon which deals extensively with the potential difficulty of accepting this part of the lesson. In fact, humility is the most persistent theme in Andrewes's Christmas sermons: "Humility then: we shall find Him by that sign, where we find humility, and not fail; and where that is not, be sure we shall never find Him."[9] The theological and psychological reasons both lie in the first fall:

> Man was to be recovered by the contrary of that by which he perished. By pride he perished, that is confessed. Then, by humility to be recovered according to the rule, *Contraria curantur contrariis.* So He to come in humility. The pride was high, *eritis sicut dii*; the contrary as low, *factus est sicut jumenta,* "as low as they," he in their cratch. [1:206]

These passages, and there are many more like them, reflect a widespread tradition associating Epiphany with the abject humbling of God (incarnate in a child in rags in a manger) and the purification of mankind humbly observing that incredible manifestation of God's love and humility. Horton Davies summarizes the tradition for us: "At the heart of Anglican piety there was the awed wonder at the condescension of the God-man, sheer adoring amazement at the humility of the Incarnation."[10] This motif will prove much more important to the Epiphany plays. But because the revellers at the conclusion of many of the masques exhibit precisely this abject wonder over the brilliant manifestation of truth and the mysteries of creation, it is also slightly pertinent here.

Finally, the gloss to Ephesians 3 in *The Geneva Bible* makes it clear that the over-all spirit of Epiphany was closely analogous to the predominant form and spirit of Jonson's Epiphany masques, Shakespearean comedy, and indeed most of the romantic comedy of the Renaissance. Unlike Jonson's usual comic thrust of punishment, scorn, and separation, his Epiphany masques, like the festival itself, celebrate the movement from bondage to freedom, from discord to concord, and from plurality to unity.[11] The marginal gloss finds this meaning in the Epistle for Epiphany, Ephesians 3: "The Church being gathered of so many kindes of people, is an example, or a glasse for the Angels to beholde the wisdome of God in, who hath turned their particular discords into an universal concorde, & of ye Sinagogue of bondage, hathe made the Church of fredome."[12] But if light can symbolize this Epiphanic concord, so, according to the marginal gloss, can musical harmony. All discord becomes concord on Epiphany. Such imagery becomes explicit in Jonson's early masques in celebratory lines like "What harmony is this?" (1. 293) in *Hymenaei* and in a major character called Harmonia in *The Masque of Beauty*. But it is also implicit throughout the masques in their concluding revels, which celebrate new order and new peace through music and dance, constant dramatic and liturgical equivalents of the cosmic dance above. Because Epiphany also celebrates the harmonious espousal of Christ and his church it is also a prime occasion for court weddings.[13] Jonson's *Hymenaei,* in fact, was one of them in 1606. In this one dramatic mode which Jonson explicitly designed for the festival of Epiphany, he thus seems to have accommodated his usual satiric vision to the reconciliatory spirit of the Christmas season. Such a possibility becomes more likely after we have seen how frequently Jonson's Epiphany masques reflect other, more tangible qualities of the Epiphany festival.

The Epiphany Masques

Since the careful studies of Orgel and Meagher, students of Jonson are far more receptive to suggestions of the high aesthetic, political, moral, and even mystical seriousness of his masques: "In the masques, Jonson epitomized the ideals of his time, creating a symbolic vision designed to teach and to inspire, for, like Beaujoyeulx, Jonson desired his spectator to rise a wiser, and a better, man."[14] According to Meagher and James P. Lucier, that symbolic, allegorical vision was basically Neoplatonic and filtered down to the masque tradition along with the classical, mythological figures who traditionally embodied the allegory. The greatest technical legacy of this tradition of Neoplatonic mythography was its ability to embody virtues and abstract truths in the forms of gods.[15] That this principle of embodiment is also at the center of the festival of Epiphany suggests another interesting general connection between the masques and the festival. But the more convincing relationships are specific and tangible ones which can probably be best understood if we look at the Epiphany masques one at a time, and in approximate chronological order.

The first of the Epiphany Day masques, *The Masque of Moores* (Blackness), was performed at Whitehall in 1605. It begins with the image of the river Niger mixing with the sea, a mixing which is supposed to suggest the mixing of the pure, immortal soul with mortal bodies.[16] But though this image already suggests incarnation, the part of the masque which seems unmistakably associated with Twelfth Day concerns the heavenly visitation of Niger's twelve daughters:

> As they sat cooling their soft limbs one night,
> Appeared a face all circumfused with light.
>
> [L1. 158-59]

Their visitor instructs them to travel to a land of light, where the sun never rises or sets; the light embodies, naturally enough, the eternal light of the author of all beauty, God:

> [The sun] leaves that climate of the sky
> To comfort of a greater light
> Who forms all beauty with his sight.
>
> [L1. 168-70]

Table 9

6 January: Epiphany Masques

Dates	Titles	Authorities
1605	*The Masque of Moores*	Chambers, 4:119
1606	*Hymenaei*	Chambers, 4:120
1608*	*The Masque of Beauty*	Chambers, 4:122
1611	— *Love Restored*	Chambers, 4:125
1615	*The Golden Age Restored*	Orgel, p. 484; Chambers, 4:130 (1616)
1616	*Mercury Vindicated*	Orgel, p. 484; Chambers, 4:130 (1615)
1617	*The Vision of Delight*	Bentley, 7:22
1618	*Pleasure Reconciled to Virtue*	Bentley, 7:26
1619	*The Inner Temple Masque*	Bentley, 7:30
1622	*The Masque of Augurs*	Bentley, 7:42
1624	*Neptune's Triumph*	Bentley, 7:52
1625*	*The Fortunate Isles*	Bentley, 7:57
1631*	*Love's Triumph*	Bentley, 7:77
1632*	*Albion's Triumph*	Bentley, 7:81
1638*	*Britannia Triumphans*	Bentley, 7:108

Source: Steven Orgel, ed., *Ben Jonson: The Complete Masques,* is cited when he offers variant dates. E. K. Chambers, *The Elizabethan Stage,* and Gerald Eades Bentley, *The Jacobean and Caroline Stage,* remain my chief authorities.
*Five of these masques were performed on the Sunday after Epiphany, "Epiphany Sunday."

Then Cynthia, the white and silver moon, "crowned with a luminary, or sphere of light" (ll. 188–89), leads them to Britannia, the promised place of lights: "O see, our silver star! / Whose pure, auspicious light greets us thus far!" (ll. 194–95), and urges, "show the place / Which long their longings urged their eyes to see" (ll. 199–200). Like the star of Bethlehem which led the three wise men to the Christ child in the Gospel for Epiphany (Matt. 2:12), so this metaphoric "silver star" has led Niger's nymphs to their Bethlehem. It is Britannia, "this blessèd isle," the seat of refinement, fruitfulness, fertility, education and purity. As the courtly audience was surely expected to have appreciated the flattering association of Britannia with Bethlehem, so also would it probably have perceived and enjoyed the other light but pointed parallels to the imagery and the narratives of the Epiphany tradition. Such associations would have been almost unavoidable on Twelfth Day.

Between *The Masque of Blackness* and its intended sequel, *The Masque of Beauty,* comes *Hymenaei,* Jonson's best-known wedding masque. As with most of the wedding masques performed on Epiphany and Shrovetide, the subject of matrimony is far closer to the surface of the masque than the holy day.[17] Still, Epiphany was a prominent time for court marriages because it celebrates the espousal of Christ and his church. Further, Jonson encourages us to look closely when he promises in his prologue: "Though their voice be taught to sound to present occasions, their sense or doth or should always lay hold on more removed mysteries" (p. 76). Let us see if some of these mysteries lie in evocations of the festival of Epiphany.

After celebrating the marital union with white vestments and flaming torches, Hymen asks an intriguing question of the festival audience and the masque:

> What more than usual light,
> Throughout the place extended,
> Makes Juno's fane so bright!
> Is there some greater deity descended?
>
> [L1. 72-75]

The answer, occurring on Twelfth Night, the eve of Epiphany, and prefaced by Jonson's promise of "more removed mysteries," sounds too much like Christ to be entirely coincidental. Who is this greater light, who graces union even more than Juno? "The king, and priest of peace!" (1.81). Orgel correctly assumes that the king and empress referred to here are James I and his queen. But few in Jonson's Twelfth Night audience could have missed this allusion to the Christ child, the eternal king, the light of the world, the Prince of Peace. In a sermon about the incarnation's paradoxical combination of glory and humility, Donne advises this same James that his glory and his light are analogous to the glory and light of the eternal king (3:207). He tells him in the same sermon, "God hath given glory . . . to glorify him" (3:224), and in another, several years later, "Kings are blessings because they are Images of God" (7:357). The compliment to their majesties the king and queen would have been all the more impressive because of this connection, but would not have obscured it.

    Epiphanic images of light and darkness continue to characterize the language and the spectacle of the masque after this especially fitting moment. Their significance is heightened by Juno's Neoplatonic symbolism. For she is not only a patroness of marriage but also an anagram and symbol for cosmic unity or oneness, as is Christ on Epiphany (Iuno = Unio = One) (1. 209). In musical and visual imagery which we also customarily associate with Epiphany, her "glistening state and chair enlightened all the air." Her "charming tunes do beat / In sacred concords 'bout her seat" (ll. 212–13). When the eight powers of Iris join hands to form a chain on the stage, the masquers themselves explicate the symbolism in terms that parallel the blessing of Epiphany:

> Here no contention, envy, grief, deceit,
>   Fear, jealousy have weight,
> But all is peace and love and faith and bliss.
>   What harmony like this?

[L1. 290–93]

All of this universal unity, harmony, and concord culminates in the single image most readily associated with Twelfth Day, the bright star: "See, see! The bright Idalian star" (1. 319). As in *The Masque of Blackness,* this is not systematic allegory but a clever refraction of some of the more prominent images and themes of Epiphany through a Neoplatonic prism and a wedding masque. Jonson is careful to tell us in his notes that this is Stella Veneris, Venus or Phosperus, called Lucifer or the light bringer when it rises before the sun (pp. 87, 521). But with so much of the preceding imagery prompting us in another direction, it may suggest the star of Bethlehem as well as the star of Venus, heavenly as well as earthly love. In such subtle but persistent ways is that greater love, that greater light, that greater principle of universal harmony and concord, brought into the classical context of this Epiphany masque. Certainly the elusive parallels are not meant to teach but to delight, much as Pico and Ficino enjoyed the many parallels between Christian and Platonic symbolism in their own writings. The sophisticated Jacobean audience would hardly have stood for anything in the heavily didactic mode of earlier English drama. But they might have been delighted with Jonson to see these persistent if elusive refractions of the Epiphany festival. Jonson only rarely disappoints their expectations. Already we can see how much richer the quality of correlation becomes in these specially commissioned masques. Their festival genesis seems to be influencing their images, narratives, and themes.

In Jonson's third Epiphany masque, *The Masque of Beauty,* the festival manifests itself in different ways. The most striking is the culminating song of creation, an adaptation of Hesiod's legend about the creation of Eros, Love, out of Chaos.[18] As Meagher suggests, the masque again follows the allegorical tradition of Christian Neoplatonism. What he does not notice is the degree to which such a tradition, especially in this festive context, suggests Epiphany. Translating this classical legend into its common allegorization of the birth of Christ and the manifestation of his godhead in brightness, beauty, concord, and the act of creation reveals how dramatically Jonson's lines could evoke central traditions of the religious festival:

When Love at first did move
From out of chaos, brightened
So was the world, and lightened.
. . . .
So beauty on the waters stood
When Love had severed earth from flood!
So when he parted air from fire
He did with concord all inspire!

And then a motion he them taught
That elder than himself was thought,
Which thought was, yet, the child of earth,
For Love is elder than his birth.

[Ll. 236-38, 265-72]

In the allegory, the song celebrates Harmonia, the crowning characteristic of Beauty and of created, manifested order and peace. But in its persistent evocation of Genesis 1, the story of the first days of creation ("Let there be light"; "let the waters be gathered together"; "let the dry land appear") and in its naming of the principle of that creation as *Love,* we also have inviting allusions to the Epiphany context.

For the Christ child is not only the agent of creation in Ephesians 3; he is also the son of earth and heaven, yet "begotten of his father before al worldes, God of God, lyght of lyghte." Meagher explicates the traditional anagogical connection between Love and its manifestation in creation: "Love is, to the Neoplatonists, the primary force by which the cosmos is organized." This ordering love or $\epsilon\rho\omega\varsigma$, embodied in the Celestial Venus, "is plainly an emblematic expression of the highest love." In fact, we know further from Frank Manley's work that this Celestial Venus is often identified and/or confused with Christ himself in Christian Neoplatonism.[19] John M. Rist also discusses this confusion in his *Eros and Psyche*: "Certainly Origen's $\varphi\iota\lambda\alpha\nu\theta\rho\omega\pi\iota\alpha$ (philanthropia) is more than the Plotinian $\epsilon\rho\omega\varsigma$, in that it implies not merely cosmic love of self manifested in creation [the emanations of plenitude], but the love of a Saviour. Nevertheless it includes the cosmic $\epsilon\rho\omega\varsigma$." It is hardly gratuitous in this context to argue, then, that a Neoplatonic description of the creativeness of the Celestial Venus might also suggest Christ's agency in creation. As Meagher and Rist both remind us, Christ is preeminently the Christian embodiment of the overflowing love of God.[20] As a result of such identifications, suggests Robert Ellrodt, the contemplation of the beauty of creation, "the visible fabric of the universe," was commonly understood by Christian Neoplatonists to be "the means of beholding the beauty of the Lord." Christ, the creation, and the Celestial Venus (beauty as well as love) were thus all associated as well with biblical Sapience, upon such patristic authority as that of Augustine in *De Trinitate* (chaps. 1, 6-8). Thus, "the contemplation of God in his handiwork ultimately leads to the vision of the divine Sapience," or of Christ himself. Both Augustine and Edmund Spenser in representative Christian and Neoplatonic commonplaces "describe the upward flight to God through the degrees of the Creation. Both behold the beauty of the Lord, shining out in the beauty of his works."[21] The grandeur and the humiliation of such apprehensions are obviously close, in imagery as well as theme, to the liturgical celebration of Epiphany. They are also among the most characteristic events in Jonson's Epiphany masques.

The next masque, *Love Restored,* continues to blend images and themes of the Neoplatonic and Epiphany traditions. At the same time it combines with them elements of the other equally vital if contradictory Saturnalian side of the Twelfth Night revelry. For if Twelfth Day culminates the religious festivals of Christmas, Twelfth Night, its eve, rivals Candlemas eve, New Year's eve, and the eve of Lent (Shrovetide) as the time of greatest misrule of the holiday season.[22] Jonson begins to experiment with blending these warring festival traditions as early as his first Candlemas masque, *The Masque of Queens,* in 1609. But though the experiment continues in *Love Restored* two years later, it is not continued again until *Pleasure Reconciled to Virtue* in 1618. Thereafter his masques intensify the structural blending of antimasque and masque, the movement from the riotous shouting, dancing, and singing of the Saturnalia to the decorous, wise celebration and the symbolic songs and dances of the revels. Their precarious balance between pleasure and virtue occurs more often and is liturgically more appropriate in the Shrovetide masques we will discuss later. There, carnival and Lent are constantly in aesthetic and thematic combat, with a rich heritage in art and theology. It is thus no coincidence that *Pleasure Reconciled to Virtue* graces both festivals. This blending of masque and antimasque, saturnalia and decorous festivity, is an important mark of the maturation of Jonson's art.[23] It is also a vital contribution to the developing tradition of festival masques. *Love Restored* marks its first achievement.

We notice immediately that three-fourths of *Love Restored* is comic antimasque, written in excellent prose dialogue. This is in stark contrast to the elevated poetry of the previous three masques, more in the Saturnalian genre of *Christmas His Masque*. But in *Christmas His Masque* almost everything is low comedy and misrule. In contrast, *Love Restored* contains a rich system of contrasting perspectives. First, the carnival rioters have a Lenten, puritanical opponent in the antimasque itself. Then, the revels of the formal masque heals this discord by combining Neoplatonic and Epiphanic images and themes and portraying the decorous revelry of the sophisticated court. In *Love Restored* we are clearly approaching a more complex aesthetic structure, one intimately related to the warring traditions of the Christmas festivity. The fact that it is a first attempt may well explain its obvious and persistent relationship to these traditions. For as Jonson gains greater control over this material, its heritage in liturgical and social festivals becomes more subtle.

The antimasque opposes Plutus, a puritanical, Lenten figure in the fashion of Malvolio or Zeal-of-the-Land-Busy, against Masquerado, an empty-headed carnival drunkard like Toby Belch. But the third party is Robin Goodfellow, a good-natured spirit who seems to embody wholesome fun and imaginative vigor, as did another Puck in *A Midsummer Night's Dream*. Although Plutus cannot distinguish between the two revellers, we perceive quickly that Masquerado's wanton dissipation is far from Puck's creative revelry. This distinction is going to become a vital one later in the masque.

Plutus immediately brands himself as extreme a humour as Masquerado when he exorcises the rioter in unmistakable Puritan jargon: "Away, impertinent folly" (l. 21): "I will have no more masquing; I will not buy a false and fleeting delight so dear. The merry madness of one hour shall not cost me the repentance of an age" (ll. 31–33). But Plutus, without discrimination, has precisely the same message for Puck, who will lead us and Plutus to significant enlightenment later in the play:

"Away, idle Spirit" (1. 134): "'Tis thou that are not only the sower of vanities in these high places, but the call of all other light follies to fall and feed on them. I will endure thy prodigality nor riots no more: they are the ruin of states" (ll. 135–39). This sounds like the Lord Chief Justice upbraiding Falstaff in the tavern, or like Malvolio chastising Sir Toby in Olivia's house in *Twelfth Night*. Falstaff parodies this mood in his own ironic upbraiding of Hal as the misleader of his youth. It captures the archetypal confrontation of carnival and Lent. But there is a significant difference. Puck is no drunken mortal; he is instead a spirit capable of perceiving and articulating true festive joy on the one hand, and the limitation of Plutus's Puritan perspective as well as Masquerado's Saturnalian one on the other. In denying all license and all folly, even the innocent pleasure of the festival season, Plutus is denying all human complexity. Love would be swept out with lust; wise festivity with drunken riot. This explains Puck's counterepithets for Plutus, "A reformed Cupid," "Anti-Cupid" (ll. 155, 161), "usurping all those offices in the age of gold which Love himself performed in the Golden Age" (ll. 166–68): "'Tis you, mortals, that are fools, and worthy to be such, that worship him [Plutus]; for if you had wisdom, he had no godhead" (ll. 177–78). Plutus's love-denying position is as great a folly as Masquerado's carnality, and we are greater fools if we follow such an anticupid.

Puck's promises to reveal real love contain more obvious Epiphany overtones: "I'll bring you where you shall find Love, and by the virtue of this majesty, who projecteth so powerful beams of light and heat through this hemisphere, thaw his icy fingers and scatter the darkness that obscures him" (ll. 180–84). In this barrage of imagery reminiscent of Shakespeare's *Twelfth Night* and relevant to the common festival context, we see Plutus, like Malvolio, his anti-Epiphanic, antifestive counterpart, locked in the gross darkness of his own ignorance.[24] What Puck is suggesting is that instead of naysaying, Plutus and the audience should try to walk festively and humbly in the glory and brightness of love, that our hearts might be astonished and enlarged. Of course, this love is Cupid, not Christ, as Plutus is anticupid, not antichrist. But the twisting of that famous

Renaissance phrase for all things false, plus the festive context of Epiphany, the night of light and of the birth of love lying in a manger, visited by the wise men, makes the identification natural enough. Puck, like Feste in *Twelfth Night,* is guiding characters and audience alike out of the darkness of Lenten or carnival excess and presumptuous pride into the light of festive joy. The festival's overtones are certainly intriguingly similar in both works.

They are enhanced in *Love Restored* by Cupid's appearance. His own words could evoke images of Christ in a cold manger:

Love feels a heat that inward warms
And guards him naked in these places,
As at his birth, or 'mongst the graces

[L1. 209-11]

He later refers to Epiphany as his night of festivity: "I now am lord of mine own nights," and to himself as "a godhead's form divine" (ll. 215, 219). He has also worked a little miracle, one that the subsequent Epiphany and Shrovetide masques will never work better; he has transformed Plutus by his love into an ally of decorous revelry. In fact, Plutus is now delighted to enjoy a night of festivity free from "barbarous Mammon," one in which "your sports may proceed, and the solemnities of the night be complete without depending on so earthly an idol (ll. 185–87). Carnival and Lent are thus miraculously if precariously joined through the intervention of Love.

As always in Jonson, the parallels to the religious and the social festival are neither systematic nor extreme. But they unmistakably suggest Twelfth Day. In his first attempt to combine carnival and Lent in an Epiphany masque, Jonson has achieved an ingenious if tenuous union. As we look at the later Epiphany masques which attempt a similar union, and then beyond them to the Shrovetide masques with similar interests, we will come to realize that this first attempt is one of the most successful in the tradition. Carnival and Lent are too naturally opposed for frequent or lasting jointure, as we hear in Plutus's stilted language of joy, and see in Brueghel's painting. But occasionally, with the unifying spirit of the imagination and the unifying power of love, with a Puck and a Cupid, they can coexist in peace and festivity.

Because *Pleasure Reconciled to Virtue* is performed with some revisions on both Epiphany and Shrovetide and seems apposite to both traditions, it will not be discussed until chapter 6. In its parallel blending of carnival and Lent, sensuality and ethereality, body and soul through the characters of Comus and Daedalus (cf. Toby Belch and Orsino), the masque is at least moderately relevant to the festival of Epiphany. For in that festival is celebrated the analogous paradox of incarnation, the incredible humiliation of divinity made flesh. That Renaissance man saw himself perpetually in "a middle realm, existing somewhere between the extremes of the antimasque's misrule and the revels' order, but including both as possibilities,"[25] heightens the complexity of such a festival association in these Epiphany masques and plays. The title of the masque suggests its interest in this precarious blending.

Another masque of the same period, Middleton's *Inner Temple Masque,* continues this emerging tradition of opposing holiday revelry against holy day restraint in the Epiphany masques. Many of the characters and dancers in the masque are actually days and seasons of the year, with characters of riotous excess like New Year's and Shrovetuesday opposed to characters of somber restraint like Lent and Fasting-Day. A quarrel between one Plumporridge, the equivalent of a Comus or a Masquerado in the other masques, and Fasting-Day, the Lenten, Plutus figure, occurs because none of the days of this year want to host fasting. But just as carnival excess seems about to overwhelm all human order and dignity, the decorous masque succeeds the clamorous antimasque, and Harmony succeeds discord. As Harmony promises, "Time shall be reconciled." The masque then ends with flames of light signifying the rebirth of "Virtue's eternal spring."[26] Like Jonson's *Pleasure Reconciled to Virtue,* this masque by Middleton is more closely associated with another festival. Also intended for a Candlemas performance, it even contains as a central character one "Candlemas." But with such thematic and structural affinities to the previous two masques, *The Inner Temple Masque* is at least moderately fitting as Epiphany entertainment. For it embodies once again the conflict between the raucous sensual misrule of Twelfth Night and Epiphany's more decorous if ethereal celebrations.

Unlike the three previous masques, Jonson's next Epiphany masque, *The Golden Age Restored,* contains no Saturnalian elements and no conflict of carnival and Lent. It does, however, depict the miraculous restoration of a golden age which is again reminiscent of that analogous age ushered in by the birth of the Prince of Peace: "Now Peace / And Love / Faith / Joys / All, all increase; / / And Strife / And Hate / and Fear / and Pain / All cease" (ll. 138–39). Its most impressive echoes of Epiphany, however, are reserved for the conclusion. There Astrae seems to praise the power of God in terms that are almost certainly evocative of the Epiphany season:

> Of all there seems a second birth;
> It is become a heav'n on earth,
> And Jove is present here.

[L1. 213-15]

Again, as always in these festival masques by Jonson, a classical god is addressed, not the Christian one. And James is being flattered in no uncertain terms. But Christ is at Epiphany the heaven on earth, and God is present in and through him. Charles Wesley's familiar eighteenth-century hymn of Christ's birth and incarnation contains strikingly similar imagery. Christ is "Born to raise the sons of earth, / Born to give them second birth."[27] This is the mystery of the incarnation, the major source of Epiphanic awe. Astrae goes on:

> I feel the godhead! nor will doubt
> But he can fill the place throughout
> Whose power is everywhere.

[L1. 216-18]

This power is most manifest in the creation of the world and its subsequent salvation by the Son of God. As before, Orgel is correct to note for us that "Justice fled from earth when Saturn's reign was overthrown" (p. 232 n) and that she (Astrae) returned when Jove took control. But is it not equally fitting to

hear echoed in this classical myth something of the parallel
Christian mystery which Epiphany celebrates? Jonson characteristically does not insist on both possibilities. But he persistently makes them available to his audience through these
refractions of various patterns from the festival of Epiphany.
Jonson's *Vision of Delight* is more moderate in its relationships to the religious festival.[28] Again there is celebrated the rebirth of nature and the coming of peace and praise for the god
who caused such effects (ll. 176, 189–92). When the masquers
are urged in conclusion to "do your this night's homage in a
dance" (1. 203) to this god, we can hardly ignore this night,
Epiphany Night, and Christ, to whom the Magi did their homage. Aurelian Townshend's only Epiphany masque, *Albion's Triumph*, is also only moderately refractive of the festival. Most
impressive is the moment when the chorus sings a very appropriate hymn about incarnation: "Happy, thrice happy, is that
houre / Wherein a God descends" (p. 61). The masque also ends
with the predictable hymn to peace and unity (p. 74). Less impressive than most of Jonson's Epiphany masques, these two
would still probably have seemed pertinent in their festival
context.

More impressive is Jonson's *Fortunate Isles*, which uses its
antimasque for some clever comic exploitation of the Epiphany.[29] Merefool has devoted serious effort (seven days) to
Rosicrucian mysticism (1. 25), and yet has had no mystical experience, no epiphany. His unseen auditor is Johphiel, according
to the Magi the intelligence in Jupiter's sphere, sent to Merefool
by Father Outis (Nobody). Here then we have Epiphany with a
comic vengeance: "The good father [Outis] / Has been content
to die for you. . . . / He would not live because he might leave
all / He had to you" (ll. 63–64, 71–72). Merefool has become a
comical Faustus. Would you "Know all their signatures and
combinations, / The divine rods and consecrated roots" (ll.
435–37). He asks after this impassioned lament to see manifested some of the worthies of the past: Zoroaster, Hermes
Trismegistus, Pythagoras, Plato, Archimedes, Aesop. Unfor-
tunately, the only vision he is vouchsafed is intercourse with
John Skelton and Henry Scogan, apparently two of the most

obscure and least imaginative English poets Jonson could conjure up. Finally, Merefool is chased away, and chastened to remember that he has seen only masquers, not the true light. Audaciously, Jonson then follows this antimasque with one of his most lyrical efforts in the genre. He presents a formalized vision of the fortunate isles, a Sidneian golden world through the inspired poetical and musical eyes of Anacreon, Linus, Arion, and Stesichorus, who appear before the king and his court. Such a juxtaposition of ludicrous and profound, grotesque and ideal, delusion and vision approaches Shakespeare's audacious aesthetic combinations in *As You Like It* and *A Midsummer Night's Dream.* This juxtaposition also reminds us of the culminating structural achievement of *Love Restored* and *Pleasure Reconciled to Virtue.* Jonson has portrayed opposite epiphanies, absurd and profound, in this Epiphany masque. But he has avoided more pointed references to the religious festival.

The last of Jonson's Epiphany masques, *Love's Triumph,* contains in condensed form the richest variety of Epiphany imagery and themes. It has lost, however, the creative tension of the middle masques between flesh and spirit. Its premise is that Euphemius, a person *boni ominis,* of good omen, is sent down from heaven to Callipolis to teach or reveal true and false love. It is almost certainly pertinent that Lancelot Andrewes's only extant Epiphany Sunday sermon is on almost precisely this same topic, the consideration of true and false knowledge.[30] Following yet another Neoplatonic rendering of the birth of Love (cf. *The Masque of Beauty*), Euclia sings a hymn to love and creation. It contains the expected Epiphany images of light and seeing, but adds to them other traditional Neoplatonic symbols of the creation: order out of chaos, the shaping ideas of wisdom, goodness, and beauty, and the emanations from the plentitude of God. Such associations in the verse strongly suggest prominent facets of Christ's Epiphany.

> *Euclia.*   So Love, emergent out of chaos, brought
>   The world to light!
>   And gently moving on the waters, wrought
>   All form to sight!

> Love's appetite
> Did beauty first excite,
> And left imprinted in the air
> Those signatures of good and fair,
> *Chorus.* Which since have flowed, flowed forth upon the sense,
> To wonder first, and then to excellence,
> By virtue of divine intelligence.
>
> [L1. 135-45]

If this bombardment of Neoplatonic and Epiphany images and themes is not enough, the Celestial Venus, referred to in the middle lines above, later speaks explicitly of her incarnation and its effects. Recalling again that the Celestial Venus is in the Neoplatonic system one of the manifestations of God's love, and is even sometimes identified with Christ,[31] the pointedness of her speech becomes especially noteworthy:

> And therewith I descend
> But to your influences first commend
> The vow I go to take
> On earth for perfect love and beauty's sake.
>
> [L1. 175-78]

Like the rose and the lily in the final twelve lines, and like the presence of this suggestive material throughout Jonson's Epiphany masques, the allegory here is far more than Christian and far more than Epiphanic. It may suggest a union of England and France; it obviously alludes again to Hesiod's legend of creation. But it therefore inevitably also suggests Venus's Christian counterpart in this legend, Christ, the rose of Sharon, and his salvation of the lily for whom he became incarnate, erring man.[32]

Although he never mentions the Epiphany that celebrates man's awareness of this central incarnation, Meagher nicely articulates the ultimately Christian import of these analogies for us, and their visibility to Jonson's contemporaries:

Through the visible light of the masque and through the poetic image of light which defines and sustains its implications, the masques not only allege but demonstrate that one becomes splendid by relating oneself properly with the powers of heaven, with nature, with virtue, with wisdom, with love, with the divinely instituted and perfecting order of the king. And through the light thus acquired, men may, as the masquers do, resemble the heavens whose order they imitate. . . . The brightness of virtue and beauty is beheld, and its sources known.[33]

Of course, as Thomas Fuller reminds us from his perspective as a Renaissance churchman, secular poets have never very successfully portrayed the joys of heaven: "Heaven indeed being *Poetarum dedecus,* the shame of Poets, . . . falling as farre short of truth herein, as they go beyond it in other Fables. However, the sight of such glorious earthly spectacles advantageth our Ladyes conceit by infinite multiplication thereof to consider of Heaven."[34] Masques, which Fuller obviously if reluctantly enjoys, can hardly represent the joys of heaven, but they can as Meagher suggests "resemble the heavens whose order they imitate." Such high praise by a Renaissance, Anglican divine indicates that Welsford is surely correct when she argues that though amusement was the masque's primary purpose, some moral, religious, and philosophic edification was not completely alien to its experience in the Renaissance.[35] Not even to our Lady in Fuller's Holy State, however idly she be attending its message.

There is no need to think that Jonson is trying to teach his audience any doctrine through these varied connections between the images, themes, and narrative strands of the Twelfth Day liturgical and social experience and his Epiphany masques. From what we know, his audience would have been quite adequately informed about the doctrine and the liturgy without his help. What is fascinating is that he has chosen this way to entertain his courtly audience with a variety of suggestive parallels between the liturgical festival and the masques. If anything, the familiar liturgical patterns of light, harmony, creation, reconciliation, and similar manifestations of God's love and power would have helped explicate the Neoplatonic imagery of the masques, not the other way around. And the carnival rioters juxtaposed against the decorous revellers would have suggested from another perspective the entire festival context and made its specific manifestations all the more visible. Since Neoplatonic discussions were evidently "a constant theme for

Table 10

Correlations of Epiphany Masques

None	Slight	Moderate	Extensive
Mercury Vindicated (1616)		*The Vision of Delight* (1617)	*The Masque of Moores* (1605)
The Masque of Augurs (1622)		*Pleasure Reconciled* (1618)	*Hymenaei* (1606)
Neptune's Triumph (1624)		*The Inner Temple Masque* (1619)	*The Masque of Beauty* (1608)
Britannia Triumphans (1638)		*Albion's Triumph* (1632)	*Love Restored* (1611)
			The Golden Age Restored (1615)
			The Fortunate Isles (1625)
			Love's Triumph (1631)

discussion among the ladies" of the Caroline court, the liturgical patterns and their symbolic equivalents would have been especially available to this uniquely homogeneous audience.[36]

Only four of these Epiphany masques seem totally unrelated to their festival occasion, and three of them celebrate specific and purely secular political occasions. The fourth, *Mercury Vindicated*, was really written for New Year's, a festival to which it is much more amenable. Seven of the fifteen are extensively pertinent to Epiphany. That this ratio is far greater than we found in the festival plays discussed in the previous chapter is almost certainly attributable to the fact of their festival genesis. Four others evidence a sufficient enough correlation to the festival for us to assume that such resonances could well have been perceived by the audience and were also probably exploited by the playwright as he wrote the masque for its Epiphany performance. Such frequent and intense correlations (over 70 percent) would, of course, enhance affective possibilities of other festival performances on Epiphany and elsewhere. The audience's expectation of refractions of the festival might also explain their pleasant elusiveness in Jonson's masques. But such elusiveness is in the best tradition of Neoplatonism and of court masques. That these are sometimes "removed mysteries," as Jonson promised, should certainly not deter us from sharing them with his Renaissance audience.

CHAPTER 4

The Epiphany Plays

Most of the critics who have discussed *Twelfth Night* in terms of its festival namesake have concentrated upon Leslie Hotson's intriguing but generally unaccepted thesis about one particular performance before Don Virgilio Orsino on 6 January 1601.[1] But in their interest in topical exactness, these critics have left relatively unexplored the thematic, narrative, and imagistic patterns shared by the play and the religious festival. If Hotson's careful re-creation of place and time at Whitehall does not convince us of his particular thesis, it does suggest how closely the religious and the social traditions of the festival would have been related. According to his study, the chapel in which the Epiphany service would have been celebrated and in which Elizabeth would have delivered the traditional offering of gold, frankincense, and myrrh to the altar, was right next to the great hall where the subsequent play would have been performed. The audiences would also have been almost identical.[2] C. L. Barber and John Hollander have argued convincingly that the play invites comparison with some social aspects of Twelfth Night, the eve of Epiphany, especially its Saturnalian form and spirit. Prominent features of this Saturnalian tradition in the play include "a Festus or 'Lord of Misrule' to preside over the maskings, interludes, music, song, and other merrymaking."[3]

Two critics, however, Marion Bodwell Smith and Barbara Lewalski, have recently looked beyond the topical and social concerns of the eve to begin to demonstrate some of the thematic, narrative, and imagistic patterns which might be shared by the play and the festival. A brief summary of the ground they have already covered will save us time and help us focus our attention on other pertinent liturgical patterns in the play.

In Viola and Sebastian, Lewalski finds two miraculously delivered outside agents who will help to cure the flawed inhabitants of Illyria. Their flaws are basically two—ill will and self-love. Malvolio manifests both and is actually named for ill will. The self-love is manifested by an assortment of self-indulgences in the kingdom, including madness, drunkenness, preposterous postures and vows about love and grief, and excessive refinement and self-esteem. The central values in the play are the opposites of these flaws—good will and selfless love. Not coincidentally, they are also the basic values of the Christmas season, forgiveness and humility ("Peace on earth, good will towards men"). Since theologians tell us that men are naturally inclined toward the love of themselves, this selfless love must be learned.[4] Its chief teachers to Lewalski are Viola and Sebastian, who appear to her as light comic types of the incarnate Christ. While stopping short of their identification with Christ, this reader would agree that Viola exemplifies an exceptionally selfless love and that Sebastian inspires the same in Olivia (with Viola's considerable help). Together, these two characters lead Orsino and Olivia to the good will and the good willing of selfless love. To edify such prideful characters while retaining their good will is the main challenge of the comedy. It is also an appropriate endeavor for an entertainment named after the eve of Epiphany.[5]

Smith's fine chapter on *Twelfth Night* in *Dualities in Shakespeare* (1966) parallels several of Lewalski's suggestions. But his most important contribution to understandings of the relationships between the liturgical occasion and the play comes when he discusses their associations with the traditional feast of fools and its institutionalized praise of folly. Feste the Curate, for example, may be a clever comic variation of the role-reversals associated with the church's Feast of Fools:

Feste's impersonation of Sir Thopas may owe its inspiration to yet another traditional celebration of folly associated with Twelfth Night. The Church also had its Lord of Misrule, the mock abbot or bishop who presided over the Feast of Fools held in many of the cathedrals of western Europe including Lincoln and Berkeley. . . . Epiphany was most commonly chosen for this celebration. Feste, of course, reverses the rite: the fool plays the curate, not the curate the fool, but the transition, as his rapid alternation of roles indicates, is an easy one. [P. 115]

If the play has its mock priest, it also has many set pieces in praise of folly, another characteristic it shares with the festival day.

A set speech in praise of folly [like Viola's, 3.1.57-65] was a common feature of Christmas celebrations. . . . Feste . . . garners tributes . . . from almost everyone but Malvolio. However, Sir Toby's justification of his turning night into day, the Duke's glorification of his foolish love, Olivia's soliloquy of love for Cesario, and Malvolio's of self-admiration are also instances of the praise of folly by fools. [P. 115]

Even the hilarious duel between Viola and Andrew may refract prominent elements of the mummer's plays that also entertained the Christmas season: "Echoes of the mummer's plays may be found in the mock-combat which turns into a real one when St. George-Sebastian, restored to life, lays low the Turkish Knight Sir Toby, who then calls for a doctor, one of the stock characters of the folk play" (p. 116). These refractions of Epiphany are never obtrusive, but they are also never gratuitous.

Lewalski and Smith both focus their attention on the festival's motif of enlightenment and properly link that theme to the play's movement toward clarification. But neither critic gives enough attention to the secondary Epiphany theme: the humility of Christ and the humiliation of man. This theme lies close to the systematic humiliations that Olivia and Orsino must undergo to escape the bondage of their excessive self-love. Because Feste is so active and so self-conscious an agent of this liberating enlightenment, he deserves a closer look. Without question he represents the Christmastide spirit of good will that Lewalski and Smith attribute to him. But his awareness of his role as fool and curate in edifying the other fools in Illyria into a liberating humility suggests that he represents and facilitates a festivity far more profound than his merely Saturnalian name might suggest. Nowhere is this connection more persuasive than in his attempted "ministry" to Malvolio. Looking at Feste through the perspective of Epiphany will also suggest how closely the liturgical festival of humiliation and enlightenment might be related to the interest of all Shakespearean comedy in the benevolent edification of its most prideful characters.

Other connections can only be mentioned here. Images of musical harmony embody analogous thematic interests in the liturgical festival, Jonson's Epiphany masques, and Shakespeare's *Twelfth Night*. Also, it is hardly coincidental that on the festival day devoted to the renewal of the monastic vows of poverty, chastity, and obedience we have a play dramatizing three such clear if comic embodiments of those vows—Feste the begging fool, Olivia the cloistered virgin, and Viola, Orsino's perfectly obedient servant.[6] That Olivia is called *Madonna* eight times in her first scene in the play (1.5) must heighten the most important of these connections. Virginity is not prominent in the Epiphany masques. But its recurrence in several of the plays for Epiphany besides *Twelfth Night* and its centrality to *The Shepheard's Paradise*, which was evidently written for an Epiphany performance, encourages a closer look. Finally, the "Battle of Carnival and Lent" is as prominent in *Twelfth Night* as it is in some of the Epiphany masques. Its reappearance in two other plays for Epiphany, Middleton's *More Dissemblers besides Women* and John Lyly's *Campaspe*, prompts our continued awareness of its appropriateness to the liturgical as well as the sociological traditions of the festival. The structural juxtaposition of exaggerated ethereal and Saturnalian figures, like Orsino against Toby or Daedalus against Comus, and of killjoys against revellers, like Malvolio against Belch, will continue to interest us through the Shrovetide masques. There they seem to make the most sense in the light of the church year and its liturgical patterns. Some of these parallels are silly; others are profound.[7] But all might have been evoked by the festival title.

When Lewalski focuses upon Viola and Sebastian as agents of enlightenment, she must assume that the humiliating experiences of Olivia and Orsino are also directly apposite to the Epiphany tradition of edifying humiliation. That assumption is quickly verified. Both characters begin the play too fond of themselves. Olivia's pride takes the form of her excessive, self-indulgent posturing as a grief-stricken sister. Orsino's is embodied in his exaggerated, self-indulgent poses as a Petrarchan lover. The thrust of much of their comic action in *Twelfth Night* is designed to disabuse them of their amusing but ultimately antifestive attitudes, which are embodied in their extremest forms in Malvolio's pride and Toby's self-indulgence.

Olivia is soon proven a fool by Feste for her grief, and then her vow of celibacy is shattered by Viola-Cesario's first visit. Viola consciously ministers to her pride hereafter ["I see you what you are; you are too proud" (1.5.236)].[8] But as Lewalski suggests, her most effective ministry is unconscious, by accident and her own example of selfless love. Because of who she is, Viola must deny all of Olivia's suits, placing the charmingly haughty lady in the humiliating position of begging for the love of a page, not to mention another woman ["Love sought is good, but given unsought is better" (3.1.152)]. Her ultimate humiliation is public and painful. Viola-Cesario denies his new wife in favor of Orsino. And now Olivia must wonder what on earth she has chosen to wed. She is allowed to live with that humiliating uncertainty through much of the final act.

Orsino's edification into a regenerate humility is just as persistent; because of the immensity of his self-love, and the thickness of his mind, it cannot be as gradual, as charming, or as convincing as it is in Olivia. She smiles at the fool's first catechism of her folly; he misunderstands even his last. She suffers the repeated humiliations of Viola's rejections until she can embrace the miracle of Sebastian's acceptance. But Orsino is a slower study. Olivia rejects him again and again, yet still his self-esteem seems unaffected. His mind is truly a "very opal" (2.4.74). Feste tries several times to penetrate its darkness, but he cannot even insult Orsino, for Orsino cannot imagine an insult. Even when Feste tries to teach him the lesson of the play, that enemies are friends because they expose folly and that friends are enemies because they flatter them, Orsino completely misses the point. And then he curses Viola, the selfless lamb, the dove (5.1.124–25), who has loved and served only him throughout the play. He thus makes an absolute fool of himself in public and banishes forever from his sight the only person who could ever have loved the old Orsino. And so he proves himself a fool where Feste could not and stews in his own juice for a while.

But of course Olivia has not married an effeminate husband, nor has Orsino lost his Viola forever. Sebastian, miraculously alive, is waiting in the wings, and all will soon be well for both of them. The prideful Olivia will have learned through her humiliations, public and private, to embrace this final piece of good fortune and to know how little she deserves it. And even Orsino has been allowed to play the fool most grandly one last time in order that he might finally, belatedly, accept and embrace that folly and its paradoxical joy, along with the Viola who embodies it for him and for us. Jack will have Jill, and if he keeps his head on right, he might even be allowed to keep her happily and forever. Of course, no one deserves such joy, such grace. Knowing that and finding such joy nevertheless is a romantic experience of the first order. If it is an experience common to many of Shakespeare's romantic comedies, as it is, it is also an experience not irrelevant to the festival of Epiphany.

As is true of the systematic humiliation of Orsino and Olivia, so the role of Feste is richer when understood within the liturgical context of Twelfth Day. He does, as Lewalski suggests, represent the Christmastide spirit of good will. But far more important, he also persistently, consciously, and selflessly tries to mediate a humbling self-knowledge to each of the characters with whom he comes in contact, to lead them out of the bondage, the darkness, of false pride into the light of humble self-discovery. A glance at the religious background of the wise fool, the catechising that he directs to Olivia and Orsino, and the imagery and edifying intent the prison scene with Malvolio shares with the liturgy for Epiphany should suggest Feste's appropriateness within this liturgical context. His varied ministry reveals that the fool is no superficial curate in *Twelfth Night*. Toby is the only Saturnalian Festus in Illyria, and even he finally becomes something more than that.

Walter Jacob Kaiser in *Praisers of Folly* brilliantly explains for us the Christian elements in the medieval and Renaissance traditions of the wise fool. From the Pauline statements about the foolishness of preaching (e.g. 1 Cor. 1:21) derives a whole homiletic tradition, articulated by John Colet, William Fulke, and John Donne, among many others, that the curate is a "foole for Christ." He is a fool because of his own disdain for worldliness. More important, his exposure of the folly of others, and his awareness of his own, can lead them to his humility and therefore to grace.[9] Of all of the Renaissance commentators on this commonplace, Donne seems the most frequently interested in it. In a sermon on the subject, he asserts that a Christian must embrace his own folly, accept and celebrate it in a spirit of humble festivity, or he will never be spiritually whole, or even sane.

> *David* had such a zeale to Gods service, as that he was content to be thought a foole, for his humility towards the Arke. *S. Paul* was content to be thought mad; so was our blessed Savior himself, not onely by his enemies, but by his owne friends and kinsfolke. . . . And, if humility in the service of God here, be madnesse, I would more of us were more out of our wits, then we are; I would all our Churches were, to that purpose, Bedlams. . . . Humiliation is the beginning of sanctification. . . . Without humility, no man shall heare God speake to his soule, though hee heare three two-houres Sermons every day. [9:152–53]

Feste's spiritual ministry in *Twelfth Night* may suggest and parallel this homiletic tradition. As fool and as curate he repeatedly leads his victims to the acknowledgement of their folly that will ultimately free them to rejoice in the festivity of a greater wisdom.

Feste's catechising of Olivia (1:5) into smiling at her own folly begins her mending, a humiliation that will persist until she can finally love selflessly and joyously. His parallel cate-chizing of Orsino (5:1) is designed to lead him in the same direction, but typically, Orsino is too dense to distinguish be-tween true friends and enemies. Only his grotesquely humili-ating public misjudgment of Viola in the final scene will begin to lead him to a similar humility about his personal worth and judgment. We have to take his subsequent reformation on faith, but we have little trouble doing so.

Feste's efforts as Sir Thopas to enlighten Malvolio into humility represent his most extensive "ministry" in *Twelfth Night*. They also mesh nicely into other traditional associations with the religious festival. In fact, his opening words to his "parishioner" echo the *Book of Common Prayer's* Visitation of the Sick, "Peace be to this house." The Elizabethan would probably have known that the blessing of houses was traditional on Twelfth Day.[10] Feste first tries to make Malvolio distrust his physical senses, admit on that simple level his fallibility (with the festively pertinent dark-light puzzles), but to no avail. This predicts the eventual result of their long interview: like Maria, Feste makes a fool of Malvolio, but never makes him realize or admit that folly. Trickery produces numerous admis-sions. Twice the flawed man indicts his own wisdom, once when he declares, "I am as well in my wits, fool, as thou art" (4.2.86), once with "as any man in Illyria" (4.2.104). Feste then asks his quarry the impossible question, "Are you not mad indeed? or do you but counterfeit?" (ll. 110–11). But Malvolio will not reply with wisdom, humility, or humor. Malvolio even ironically calls for light. But while we laugh at these ritualistic admissions of his folly, we simultaneously realize that they are not like Olivia's earlier bout with Feste.[11] Malvolio will never laugh at himself as she did; he will never enact this comic equivalent of wisdom and salvation.

The darkness in which Malvolio finds himself is thus almost certainly related to the festival of enlightenment, Epiphany. *The Annotated Book of Common Prayer* complements our introduction to Jonson's Epiphany masques by stressing the amount of light imagery contained in the lessons and the epistles for that service. The Lesson, from Isaiah 60, is richest in this light imagery, as it invites man to see and understand the manifestation of truth:

> 1 Arise, o Jerusalem: be bright, for thy light is come, & the glorie of the Lord is risen upon thee.
>
> 2 For beholde, darkenes shal cover ye earth, and grosse darkenes the people: but the Lord shal arise upon thee, and his glorie shalbe sene upon thee.

The second Lesson, Isaiah 49, concerning the remaining prisoners in darkness, seems equally appropriate to *Twelfth Night*:

> 9 That thou maiest say to ye prisoners, Go forthe: and to them that are in darkenes, Shewe your selves. . . .
>
> 18 Lift up thine eyes rounde about & beholde. . . .

Finally, St. Paul in the Epiphany Epistle, Ephesians 3, paradoxically reverses this imagery. Paul, the "prisoner of Jesus Christ," tries, like Feste, "to make cleare unto all men what [is] the fellowship of the mystery" of Incarnation and humility. Malvolio's darkness and the jokes about his madness are thus partially explained, thematically and imagistically, by his alienation from the Christian enlightenment which the Twelfth Day festival celebrates. Although he finally escapes the literal prison, Malvolio's mind remains a black box of self-love, ill will, and blindness, in spite of Feste's attempted ministry. We mentioned in the previous chapter Epiphany sermons by Andrewes and Donne that stress humility as the message of Epiphany and the sign by which Christ is made manifest. As Andrewes elsewhere suggests, this mystery and this message are in part manifested "by the operation of [them] in us" (1:33).[12] A mystery signifies, like a ceremony; it also effects changes: "and work it doth, else mystery it is none" (1:41). Fortunately for the play's festivity, all its characters save Malvolio accept and manifest this mystery of humility in *Twelfth Night*. Feste's significant role in this process of humbling edification suggests that he is not coincidentally named for the Festus, the presiding spirit of Christmastide festivity; he gives that title a dignity its Saturnalian wearers never possessed. In some of the other festival plays, parallels in imagery and theme like these may well be coincidental. But in *Twelfth Night,* with the festival in the title of the play, the liturgical imagery and the dramatic imagery are too closely connected to be explained in that way. As many critics have shown, *Twelfth Night* is much more than an embodiment of Epiphany motifs. But with its fool for Christ, its little "Battle of Carnival and Lent," and its persistent theme of humiliating edification, it certainly rivals some of the parallels in Jonson's Epiphany masques.

Of the remaining seven Epiphany plays only one, *The Shepheard's Paradise,* deserves extensive discussion. Before we consider its connections to the festival for which it was designed, let us first glance at the slight to moderate correlations of the other six plays. Performed as they were on a night that so often hosted pertinent masques, the possibility of their affective power is increased.

Table 11

Epiphany Plays

Dates	Titles	Authorities
	Twelfth Night	A festival namesake
1584	*Campaspe* (?)	Title pages, 1584, 1591, 1632
1590	*Midas* (?)	Chambers, 4:104; title page (1592)
1624	*More Dissemblers besides Women*	Bentley, 7:52
1625	*Greene's Tu Quoque*	Bentley, 7:57
1633	*The Shepheard's Paradise*	Bentley, 7:85
1634	*The Faithful Shepherdess*	Bentley, 7:91
1642	*The Scornful Lady*	Bentley, 7:126

Source: E. K. Chambers, *The Elizabethan Stage,* and Gerald Eades Bentley, *The Jacobean and Caroline Stage,* are my usual authorities. However, because the title pages of the 1584, 1591, and 1632 editions of *Campaspe* mention an Epiphany performance at court, I have included it. This is my only deviation from Bentley and Chambers in this study.

The three least impressive plays all come late in the tradition, two after 1634. Two are by Beaumont and Fletcher. The first, *The Faithful Shepherdess,* contains the abstract and rather cold virtue of Clorin's virginity to remind us again that Twelfth Day was the traditional time for the consecration of virgins, since the festival celebrated the adoration of the Virgin Mary as well as her child.[13] As Andrewes says of Christ and Mary in a Christmas sermon: "And here are both. And where they meet, they make no less a miracle than *Mater* and *Virgo,* or *Deus* and *Homo*—even *fides* and *ratio*. And this, for *Virgo concipiet"* (1:139). Mother and Virgin, God and man. This is indeed a pair of equations to force the reason to submit itself to faith. As Andrewes says, "It is no sign or wonder, unless it be beside the course of nature" (1:137). Olivia in *Twelfth Night* also takes a vow of chastity she cannot keep. The duchess in *More Dissemblers besides Women* will follow their Epiphanic example. Clorin also alludes to the Magi in her reference to purification with "Frankincense and Mirrh."[14] On Epiphany this allusion at least would have been almost inescapable. The second play, *The Scornful Lady,* reflects two other Epiphany traditions we have found in Shakespeare and Jonson. In fact, it is probably based, like parts of the previous play, on Shakespeare's *Twelfth Night.* There is a battle of carnival and Lent, in which the Lenten figure, Saville, is easily overcome for possibly the last recorded time before the Restoration. There is also the humiliation of a prideful lady (Olivia's counterpart), who then falls in love with her humiliator. Donne and Andrewes have both discussed such benevolent humiliation as a hallmark of Epiphany, and *Twelfth Night* exploits it as a central romantic motif. Although *Greene's Tu Quoque* lightly shares this motif of humiliated, shared folly, its pertinency to Epiphany is too slight to be recorded. None of these three plays more than touches the surface of the festival. But the affective power of two, while not impressive, is possible on Twelfth Day.

Campaspe, perhaps the earliest extant Epiphany play (see Table 11 n.), contains a varied but elusive relevancy to its festival. Alexander's depiction conveys the play's persistent interest in man's precarious balance between God-likeness and bestiality, an interest shared by the structure of several Epiphany masques and Shakespeare's *Twelfth Night* and manifested also in the "Battle of Carnival and Lent."[15] Andrewes speaks of this "mystery of human and divine, humility and exaltation" in another of his Christmas sermons about the incarnation: "a cratch for the child, a star for the Son, a company of shepherds, . . . a choir of angels" (1:22). Alexander, obsessed by his god-likeness, provokes several philosophic discussions of this precarious blending of God and man (see, e.g., 1.3.85–86, 106–7). But as Hephestian suggests, it is in his longing for the virgin Campaspe that Alexander's pride, not to mention his god-likeness, is most vulnerable: "Alexander that would be a God, shew your selfe in this worse then a man" (2.2.72); "And shall it not seeme monstrous to wisemen, that the hearte of the greatest conquerour of the worlde, should be found in the handes of the weakest creature of nature? of a woman? of a captive?" (2.2.52–55). On Epiphany, the night the wise men found the Christ child improbably placed in rags in a cratch in the hands of a humble peasant woman in a manger, the court audience could have found in this warning unusual if elusive comic pertinency. Perhaps even more redolent of Epiphany are Apelles' descriptions to Campaspe of his paintings of gods and maidens who have begotten children on earth, offspring half-man and half-god, like Leda, "whom Jove deceived in likenes of a swan"; or "Alcmena, Unto whom Jupiter . . . begat Hercules"; or Danae, Europa, and Antiope (3.3). Now the God-man Alexander threatens Campaspe with a similar fate. In each of these light echoes—the motif of the God (and the beast) in man, the theme of the humiliation of greatness, and the catalogue of classical Gods who ravished maidens and begot incarnate God-men of them—we have narratives, themes, and images the Renaissance court audience might have associated with Epiphany. They are elusive associations; they are also too interesting to be ignored.

In contrast, Lyly's *Midas* contains one very obvious thematic relationship to Epiphany, the one most common to the Epiphany plays. Its central thematic value is the benevolent humiliation of greatness and pride and the festive acknowledgment of folly. In Shakespeare's *Twelfth Night* Olivia, Orsino,

Toby, and Malvolio have the most to learn in this regard. Here Midas is the ass who must come finally and festively to acknowledge his asshood. In *Twelfth Night* the emblem of asshood occurs in Feste's picture of we three in the midst of carnival revelry (2.3). The emblem of Midas's asshood—"the ears of an Asse upon the head of a King"—is his punishment for misjudging Apollo's heavenly strains (4.1.141). In Lyly's play as in Shakespeare's a decade later, to admit to having asses' ears is to lose their shame, by joining a joyous, universal fellowship of folly. For Midas the new humility, the "acknowledgment of folly and [the] profession of repentance,"[16] brings him to peace both with himself and with his enemies abroad (5.3.110 ff.). As Donne says in an Epiphany sermon, such reconciliation is one of the first fruits of the manifestation of God's love on Epiphany: "First then, there is a reconciliation of them in heaven to God, and then of them on earth to God, and then of them in heaven and them in earth, to one another" (4:298). The final hymn to Apollo, "the glittering Delian King" (5.3.144) who is a traditional Neoplatonic counterpart to Christ, is full of the light imagery of that other Prince of Peace who was visited by the wise men on Epiphany.

The last of the Epiphany plays of moderate correlation is Middleton's *More Dissemblers besides Women.* For the third time in plays for Epiphany, a seven years' vow of chastity takes a prominent initial position. Like Olivia in *Twelfth Night,* the duchess of Milan has promised "Ne'er to know love's heat in a second husband"; unlike her, she has kept the promise "To th' wonder of her sex, this seven years' day."[17] The virtue of chastity is, in fact, central to the whole play. The opening lines assert: "To be chaste is woman's glory, / 'Tis her fame and honour's story" (ll. 1–2). And the whole plot revolves around attempts to test the duchess's chastity, to feign its continuance after she almost falls, and then to celebrate its honorable if fortuitous preservation. Other characters feign chastity, praise it, test it, and abuse it during the play. Even the low comedy is lightly but persistently about lust, its opposite. Counterpointing this interest in chastity are parallel low comic moments of misrule which amount to mini-battles of carnival and Lent after the manner of other Epiphany and Shrovetide works. The first scenes of acts 4 and 5, in fact, frame with their overt misrule the more subtle forms of unchasteness among the "nobler" characters. This structural principle is especially reminiscent of *Twelfth Night*, where Viola is poised as the *via media* between the ethereal self-indulgence of Olivia and Orsino in 1.1 and the physical overindulgence of Toby and Andrew in 1.3. It also governs the title and the structure of Jonson's Epiphany masque *Pleasure Reconciled to Virtue*. As the play ends the duchess reaffirms her vow of chastity (5.2.196–204); this time she will keep it religiously. The uses of vows of chastity in *More Dissemblers* are sometimes more cynical than celebratory; nevertheless, with their echoes of misrule, they could persistently have suggested the festival of Epiphany.

W. Mountague's *Shepheard's Paradise* bears a unique relationship to this tradition. A play and not a masque, it seems to have been designed for a specific Epiphany performance at court. Queen Anne and her ladies acted in it on Epiphany Sunday, 9 January, at Somerset House. It was evidently intended for a repeat performance on Candlemas of the same year.[18] As might be expected of a play with so close a genetic relationship to the liturgical tradition, its pertinency to Epiphany (and Candlemas) and its relationship to these other festival plays is obvious and extensive.

In act 2 we arrive at the shepherd's paradise, where exists an order of chastity utopian in its democratic principles, its female rule, and its severe purity: "Both the Brothers and Sisters must vow chastity and single life, while they remaine of the Order; and the breach of this law is to be punished with death."[19] Again, as in so many of the Epiphany (and Candlemas) plays, the vow of chastity frames the romantic action of the play and is of crucial thematic importance. Both festivals are sacred to virgins, but Candlemas is actually the Feast of the Purification of the Virgin Mary. It celebrates the worshipper's purification through the light of Mary's example. The shepherd's paradise is thus a contrivedly appropriate festival setting. It encourages in its inhabitants purification and humility, and these festival virtues eventually lead to the union of its lovers and a general peace and order: "This is so heavenly a tradition," says one of the votaries, that the "order seemes a match betweene love, and honor, and chastity" (p. 27). Light imagery continually reinforces these festival virtues. The heroine Fidamora is even called *Gemella* in the paradise. In fact, she is a barely disguised Neoplatonic embodiment of faith and purity, emanating both light and selfless love. Her devotion for Agenor "is allready kindled in so pure a flame" that it focuses all its "light upon my thoughts, which shall be polished as they shall still answer one another with the reflex of my *Agenor's* image" (pp. 17, 14). Fidamora always talks and thinks like this. So do most of the others in this Neoplatonic paradise. When she is admitted to the society, for example, she is instructed, "Nature, Madam, hath by my humility lightened so the dark misfortune of my birth, as ambition, whose colour is my contrary, seems so unlovely to me" (p. 57). The lustful king, similarly purified by Gemella's example, would "undergoe a boundlesse pilgrimage," for "the expiation of my guilt to Basilino by the expiration of my selfe" (p. 58). Antenor reiterates the dominant leitmotiv of reflected light, swearing by "the reflex of that which lightt on her I loved" (p. 59). That Fidamora is disguised as a Moor only heightens the light image's impact.

The framework of all of these fitting festival images and themes is the Neoplatonic context in which they occur, a context as self-conscious as the images themselves. Long Neoplatonic discussions of the ladder of love (pp. 62 ff., 84 ff., e.g.) and a poem to spiritual love (pp. 94–95) naturally suggest the analogous Christian story of love revealed in the manger on Epiphany, the great light of the star and the child: "It is the essence of transcendental love" (p. 94). So do lines like "Blessed souls that coppied Heaven here so Together" (p. 109), or "Wonder of women on whose chastity / Heaven hath bestow'd such a posterity" (p. 108). Could the Renaissance audience miss the suggestion of Christ and Mary in these hymnlike words that conclude the fourth act? Finally, the Epiphany motif Andrewes stresses, love's humbling and elevating powers, is directly analyzed in act 5:

Love in that instant that it is let in, falls under our wills, and like an inundation, all it finds portable it raiseth up, and carrieth forward on it self, and love finds our wills so leight and so ascentive then; as it doth but take them up with this humility, and carries them along with it, and by the subjection of it self, raises them higher then they could e'er have got without it. [P. 132]

As infatuated as it was with Neoplatonic lore and discussions, and actually participating in this Epiphany play, Anne's court would have been even more likely to notice its appropriateness to the liturgical occasion.[20] Neoplatonism in England was, after all, a predominantly Christian phenomenon. All of the men are purified by this refined, spiritual love as it is embodied in the ladies of the court, made humble and selfless by it, and thus made men forever. Like Middleton's exemplary duchess, Fidamora will remain always chaste, her love "too pure for mortality" (p. 152). The men's humiliation is too abject and the ladies' purity too absolute for good drama. Uncharacteristically, doctrine here, liturgical and Neoplatonic, overwhelms the play's extensive, self-conscious pertinency to its festival context.

Table 12

Correlations of Epiphany Plays

None	Slight	Moderate	Extensive
	Tu Quoque (1625)	Campaspe (1584)	Twelfth Night (namesake)
	The Faithful Shepherdess (1634)	Midas (1590)	The Shepheard's Paradise (1633)
	The Scornful Lady (1642)	More Dissemblers besides Women (1624)	

After the persistent correlations between Jonson's Epiphany masques and the liturgical occasion for which they were designed, our consideration of the Epiphany plays has naturally been a bit anticlimactic. The over-all correlation is roughly equivalent to that of the works performed on the first four festival days. Shakespeare's *Twelfth Night,* with its inviting festival title, is especially rich in its reflections of the motifs of Epiphany, though they are not as obvious as the parallels between *Olde Fortunatus* and Saint John's. Only one other play, *The Shepheard's Paradise,* is also extensively pertinent. Since the former play was named for the festival and the latter designed for festival performance at court, we see once again the powerful influence a festival genesis has upon its dramatic works. That influence will culminate in the masques for Candlemas and Shrovetide.

CHAPTER 5

The Candlemas Masques
& Plays

Proportion and order both demand the consideration of the Epiphany and Candlemas works in separate chapters. Still, there would be some obvious advantages in discussing the plays simultaneously. First, they are consecutive festivals in this dramatic tradition, both of which look back to the joys of Christmas. They are also the last two major holy days before Shrovetide, which has its own rich and unique dramatic and liturgical heritage. More important, the two festivals share many imagistic and thematic patterns with their plays, most notably the imagery of light and the themes of humility, virginity, and benevolent purification or correction. But Shakespeare's *Twelfth Night* most obviously links the two festivals and encourages, almost demands, that we consider their connections even if we cannot discuss them simultaneously. For it is named after the eve of the first of these festivals, and recorded as twice performed on the second. Its inviting festival title has already led us to the play's many resonances of the social and liturgical context of *Twelfth Night*. Its two performances on Candlemas could also have been enriched by its repeated correlations to imagistic and thematic patterns of that festival.

On the other eight Candlemas performances at court, *Love Freed, The Masque of Queens,* and *The Inner Temple Masque* best portray the unique relationship most of the Candlemas works bear to the over-all festival tradition. Each is clearly about purification, also the central thematic motif of Candlemas. But possibly because there was never much of an established tradition of Candlemas masques, and possibly because Candlemas completes and summarizes the Christmas festivities and is liturgically so much like Epiphany, these Candlemas masques seem to reflect the general Christmas season as well as their particular festival. Middleton's *Inner Temple Masque* is typical. It is obviously apposite to its specific festival, having as an important character one "Candlemas," a very disgruntled and extremely worldly festival day. Further, the masque deals with his purification and that of the entire generation of plays and worshippers, a motif directly pertinent to Candlemas Day. But *The Inner Temple Masque* is also about the whole festival season, and it offers us important insights into its general traditions and their gradual decline in the seventeenth century. Not until *Coelum Britannicum,* which culminates the Shrovetide tradition, will we see another festival masque so self-consciously reflective of the traditions, specific and general, of its genesis.

Twelfth Night and King Lear

We know from a variety of sources that *Twelfth Night* was at least twice performed on Candlemas, 2 February, once at the Middle Temple and once at court. Its connections to this festival are not quite as impressive as those that have been demonstrated to exist between the play and its festival namesake.[1] But they certainly approximate the variety and the profundity of the relationships between *The Comedy of Errors* and Innocents'. The Marian characteristics of the festival ("purification of ye virgin Mary"),[2] two of the prescribed biblical passages for the day, Candlemas commentary in Nelson's *Companion,* and pertinent sections of two of John Donne's Candlemas sermons reveal extensive ties between this play and the holy day on which it was twice performed. They also remind us of the close affinities between the festivals of Epiphany and Candlemas which allow one play to have such relevancy to both days.

Like Epiphany, Candlemas is also associated with lights. Donne prefers to call the festival, in fact, *"dies Luminarium,*

Table 13

Candlemas Performances

Dates	Titles	Authorities
	Plays	
1588	*Endymion* (?)	Chambers, 4:103
1602	*Twelfth Night* (Middle Temple)	See J. M. Lothian and T. W. Craik, eds., *Twelfth Night* (London: Methuen, 1975), p. lxxix.
1605	*Every Man in His Humour*	Chambers, 4:119
1607	*The Devil's Charter*	Chambers, 4:122
1610	*King Lear* (Gowthwaite, Yorkshire)	See Kenneth Muir, ed., *King Lear* (London: Methuen, 1972), p. xl.
1612	*Greene's Tu Quoque*	Chambers, 4:126
1623	*Twelfth Night*	Bentley, 7:46
	Masques	
1609	*The Masque of Queens*	Chambers, 4:123
1611	*Love Freed from Ignorance and Folly*	Chambers, 4:125
1619	*The Inner Temple Masque*	Bentley, 7:30

Source: E. K. Chambers, *The Elizabethan Stage,* and Gerald Eades Bentley, *The Jacobean and Caroline Stage,* are my authorities.

the day of lights." According to Donne, the day's purification is the worshipper's as well as the Virgin's, a time for forgiveness and regeneration.[3] Thus the images of light and darkness so appropriate to Epiphany could be equally amenable to Candlemas, though they are obviously more coincidental. Also apposite are the persistent purifications into good will and selfless love that Lewalski finds central to the play.[4] Especially in Olivia's experiences can we see the painful, systematic purification of one virgin out of self-love. Feste, in fact, upbraids her pride with the frequent epithet of Madonna during their first meeting (1:5).[5] In Viola and Maria we see two other maids, one the whimsical namesake of the Virgin, mediating a curative grace to their erring but forgiven and finally regenerated lovers, Orsino and Toby. If these festival associations are pertinent to Epiphany, they also could have made *Twelfth Night* an appropriate play to be performed on the festival of the purification of Mary and the recipients of her grace.

Robert Nelson's commentary on Candlemas reveals the importance of humility, and humiliation, to Candlemas, Epiphany, and the whole Christmas season. According to him, the meaning of the holy day is "above all, to cloath ourselves with Humility, to be Meek and Lowly in Heart, that we may find Rest for our Souls." Vitally, Nelson finds this "Humility particularly a Christian Virtue," valued highly by neither "Heathen Philosophers" nor Jews: "Our Saviour first taught it in its greatest Perfection; and indeed his whole Life was but so many repeated Instances of *Humility* and wonderful Condescension for our Sakes: He begins his divine Sermon upon the Mount with this Precept, he lays it as the Foundation of our spiritual Building, without which we cannot discharge our Duty either to God or Man.[6] Among Renaissance dramatists, Shakespeare seems uniquely to have absorbed and reflected this value as the bedrock of his comic vision. The Lords in *Love's Labour's Lost,* all of the lovers in *A Midsummer Night's Dream,* Benedick, Beatrice, Claudio, and Pedro in *Much Ado about Nothing,* Bassanio and Gratiano in *The Merchant of Venice,* and most of the lovers in *As You Like It* all have to learn its painful lessons before they can approach their comic joy. Its significance culminates in *Twelfth Night,* with its systematic edification of most of the self-loving fools into this peculiarly Christian wisdom of humility. In most of the other Renaissance comedies, the prideful are humilated and exposed, but they are neither purified nor reconciled. In Shakespeare, with the usual pointed and instructive exception of a Malvolio or a Jaques, they are benevolently edified into humility. This crucial difference may underlie Shakespeare's unique compatibility with the whole festival tradition.

There is little of Nelson's Candlemas explication that does not help us understand parts of the action of *Twelfth Night*. Illyria is full of people whose estimations of themselves exceed reality. According to Nelson, "the Difficulty of this Virtue [humility] proceeds from that Self-love which is planted in our Natures, and when indulged will be too apt to deceive us in the Judgment we form concerning ourselves" (p. 149). Nelson's description of humility's exercise finds repeated positive and negative exemplification in the play. We think of Orsino never "avoiding to publish [his] own praises [2.4, e.g.] or to beg the praise of others," and of the repeated, humiliating rejections of his proffered love by the equally prideful Olivia. We think in contrast of Viola's maiden modesty and selflessness. We think of Olivia's persistently "bearing the Reproaches, the Injuries, and Affronts . . . with Patience and Meekness; the Reproofs of Friends with Thankfulness," as her humiliation by Feste and Viola progresses. And we think of Malvolio's inability to do so. We may recall above all the meanest of these characters, Feste the fool, who persistently and charitably accepts his humiliation, indeed wears it in motley, that he might be a mender of other fools, a botcher of souls (1.5; 4.2). Finally, the assembled festive company at the end of the play, particularly Olivia, is joyful and yet capable of compassion for the one man, Malvolio, who has missed the proffered secret of that joy—humility. As in the Epiphanic context, only the folly of pride is inimical to the profound spirit of this comic festivity.

Donne's Candlemas sermon about forgiving enemies and Nelson's *Companion* suggest another informative parallel to the play, one which further intensifies Feste's relationship to this pattern of purification and humility. In Feste's last catechism of Orsino, he proves to us if not to Orsino that a man's enemy is really his friend, and that he is "the better for my foes, and the worse for my friends" (5.1.10–11). This is Feste's explanation of the paradox: "Marry, sir, they [friends] praise me and make an ass of me. Now my foes tell me plainly I am an ass; so that by my foes, sir, I profit in the knowledge of myself, and by my

friends I am abused" (5.1.15–18). Donne, citing Seneca and
Plutarch, but also Saint Paul and Erasmus, also teaches that
the knowledge of one's folly is the beginning of wisdom.[7] The
abuse of an enemy can thus be turned to one's own good. As
Donne suggests, "Flatterers dilate a man, and make him live
the more negligently, because he is sure of good interpretations
of his worst actions; So a mans enemies contract him . . . and
make him live the more watchfully" (3:378–79). After all, the
coals of an "enemy's" fire can purify as well as punish; their
function depends entirely upon the nature of their recipient:
"If he have any gold, any pure metall in him, this fire of this
kindness will purge out the drosse, and there is a friend made. If
he be nothing but straw and stubble, combustible still, still
ready to take fire against thee, this fire . . . will . . . assure thee,
that he, whom so many benefits cannot reconcile, is irrecon-
cileable" (3:386–87). Orsino is finally stunned into humility
and true love by Viola's selfless turning of the other cheek and
the attendant miracles, not to mention the enormity of his own
folly. Olivia's extraordinary but humiliating love for the scornful
and unattainable Viola-Cesario finally leads her to embrace Sebastian with relief and happiness. Even Toby gives up drunkenness for the Maria who has forgiven him all of his Saturnalian
abuses. But as Malvolio himself has told them: "I am not of
your element" (3.4.116). Since Maria's element is gold ("My
metal of India" [2.5.11–12]), and since Viola's and Olivia's
must be equally rare and pure, this admission is another piece
of evidence that Malvolio is pitiable only in his irreconcilable
will.

Yet another of Donne's homiletic associations with the
Candlemas festival furthers our understanding of Feste's ministry to the impure people in Illyria. Its text is Christ's reminder
to the Pharisees in Matt. 9:12–13, that all men are impure to a
degree and that the business of the physician is therefore inevitably with the sick, not the well: "The whole nede not a
physicion, but thei that are sicke. . . . I am not come to call
the righteous, but the sinners to repentance."[8] Donne's gloss
reminds us of the festival of universal folly on Innocents' Night
and brings us again close to the center of the compassionate

yet strenuous spirit of Shakespearean comedy: "He that hates ill men, hates all men [Saint Augustine], for if a man will love none but honest men, where shall he finde any exercise, any object of his love?" (3:379). Feste's defense of the Fool's calling to Olivia must derive from this same tradition. Feste tells her that he is a mender, a botcher, of impure souls. He adds that we are all somewhat flawed, but that we are also capable of this mending: "Bid the dishonest man mend himself: if he mend, he is no longer dishonest; if he cannot, let the botcher mend him. Anything that's mended is but patched; virtue that transgresses is but patched with sin, and sin that amends is but patched with virtue" (1.5.40–44). This is the same humble equanimity with which Feste's Epilogue ends the play. The Fool brilliantly proves his point here by proving Olivia a fool in the sequel, and she good-naturedly applauds his "mending" as Malvolio can never do. Their diverse responses to this purifying or punitive "fire" of the Fool's mending predict nicely their future courses in the play.

Feste is far more successful with Olivia than he is with Orsino or Malvolio, partly because she is more willing to understand and profit from his reproofs. The stunning coincidence from the standpoint of this study, however, lies in the fact that in each of his two confrontations with Olivia and Orsino, both of whom need his purification, Feste almost directly anticipates Donne's homiletic uses of the Candlemas tradition. Donne and Shakespeare seem to have been operating within the same general festival tradition, one that has dealt persistently with the problems of human impurity and the means to purification, through the mediation of enemies as well as friends, and through the foolishness of preaching as well as the wisdom of the Fool.[9]

In *King Lear* as in *Twelfth Night* there appears a clown who sings snatches of the same song of stoical equanimity, "The Wind and the Rain," and who also tries to bring his masters to some acknowledgment of their folly. It is possibly less than coincidental, then, that these same two plays were also both performed on Candlemas night. Because *King Lear* was not performed at court but at Gowthwaite Hall in Yorkshire, it will not be included in the statistics of court performance.[10] But because it is so obviously appropriate a play for this Candlemas occasion, it is certainly worth a brief consideration here. Most of the critics of both *King Lear* and *Twelfth Night* would agree that they share Candlemas's central thematic motif of purification, though with the inevitable dissimilarities forced by their generic differences. Olivia, just as surely as King Lear, though much more gently, must experience painful humiliations in order to learn at last of her own human limitations and of the consequent wonder of the love she finally receives.

But it is only when we read one of the Lessons prescribed for Candlemas that we perceive how profoundly *King Lear* could have been associated with this festival day of its performance. Wisdom 9, obviously a central reading for the feast of purification, could almost be a text for the play as well, so often is it reminiscent of its structure and thematic interests.[11] Some of the most pertinent verses follow. Their relevance to the play is so startling as to require little interpretive comment. The passage begins:

1 O God of fathers, and Lord of mercie, which hast made all things with thy worde,

2 And ordeined man thorow thy wisdome, that he shulde have dominion over the creatures which thou hast made,

3 And governe the worlde according to equite and righteousnes, & execute judgement with an upright heart.

These first three verses articulate three major areas of medieval belief being undermined by Renaissance skepticism: the assumption that the universe was created for man's benefit as a personal manifestation of God's love, the assumption that man had been placed as microcosm and governor over this created universe, and the assumption that the political order is an inevitable reflection of the divine.[12] All of these assumptions are explicitly and strenuously questioned in *Lear*.

The next three lines plead for wisdom in a spirit of humility that Lear approaches only after he has plumbed the depths of personal and philosophical skepticism during acts 2 through 4:

1 Give me that wisdome, which sitteth by thy throne, and put me not
out from among thy children.

5 For I thy servant, & sonne of thine handmaide am a feble persone, &
of a shorte time, and yet lesse in the understanding of judgement
and the lawes.

In fact, from the assurance of truth and order in the first
three verses, as in the first scene of *Lear,* we travel almost full
circle by the final three verses of the chapter, into a nightmare
world of extremely doubtful epistemology:

14 For the thoghts of mortal men are feareful, and our forecastes are
uncerteine,

15 Because a corruptible bodie is heavie unto the soule, & the earthlie
mansion kepeth downe the minde that is ful of cares.

16 And hardly can we discerne the things that are upon earth, and with
great labour finde we out the things which are before us: who can
then seke out the thinges that are in heaven?

We recall the mad Lear apprehending the stench of mortality
as he talks with the blinded Gloucester. We think of both of
them beginning the play with epistemological illusions which
are dashed by uncertain forecasts and unclear perceptions. We
even remember how often our own conventional philosophic
and aesthetic expectations are systemically dashed as we share
their disillusioning tragic experience.

Lear's great moment of sanity and humility, when he
awakens with the angelic Cordelia above him, expresses his
strikingly analogous personal experience of the universe:

> Pray, do not mock me.
> I am a very foolish fond old man,
> Fourscore and upward, not an hour more nor less;
> And, to deal plainly,
> I fear I am not in my perfect mind.
> Methinks I should know you, and know this man;
> Yet I am doubtful, for I am mainly ignorant
> What place this is; and all the skill I have
> Remembers not these garments; nor I know not

Where I did lodge last night. Do not laugh at me;
For as I am a man, I think this lady
To be my child Cordelia.

[4.7.59-69]

Such absolute and controlled humility could never be taught by the comic fool alone. It requires the purgatorial purification of all of the assembled evil in the kingdom of man and all of the dignity and strength of Shakespeare's profoundest tragic protagonist to be assimilated and expressed. Lear is at last a whole man, mainly ignorant of what place this is, doubtful, fearful, old, and foolish, but accepting in a new place and time the oldest wisdom of man, his cosmic ignorance and impotence. But the love and forgiveness Lear shares with Cordelia elevates him at least momentarily above his frightening Old Testament wisdom and places him with his daughter in the new dispensation.

We cannot prove that Shakespeare thought of this parallel to the book of Wisdom while writing *King Lear.* It is reasonable, however, to suggest that someone in the Candlemas night audience, having just heard this biblical passage read earlier in the day, would have had his dramatic experience enhanced by perceiving its affective pertinency to the play's tragic vision.

The Other Plays

Almost as interesting as *Lear* in the Candlemas context is John Lyly's *Endymion.* On the night sacred to virgins, the night of the purification of the Virgin Mary, and in a court whose writers are constantly flattering their Virgin Queen, the story of Endymion's pure quest for Cynthia's favor is quite appropriate. Like Jonson a decade later (*Cynthia's Revels* and *The Mask of Queens*) Lyly must have seen a perfect chance to remind his queen of her overt analogies to classical deities and of her subtler connections to a prominent member of the Christian pantheon.

But the thematic and the theatrical connection is considerably closer than this. As Peter Saccio reminds us in his book on Lyly's "court comedies," *Endymion* embodies "the Christian allegory of the Four Daughters of God," Mercy and Truth, Righteousness and Peace. According to Saint Bernard, these four virtues debate the fate of man just after his fall in Eden. God then proposes Christ's guiltless sacrifice in response to their debate. The allegory has dramatic precedent in the Coventry mystery of the Salutation and Conception and in the Marian play *Respublica*. Lancelot Andrewes in a Christmas sermon deals with it too: "It is the day of Truth's birth," he says, when Mercy and Peace, Truth and Righteousness all meet. "They are not strangers, all four in the bosom of God from all eternity—attributes all four of His undivided Essence."[13] Such allegory in Lyly's play suggests that he is following a rich dramatic and liturgical tradition in portraying actions in heaven which culminate in the conception of Christ and the purification of the Virgin, mysteries central to Candlemas as well as the general Christmas season.

Saccio is fascinated throughout by the "shimmering," nonsystematic nature of the allegory in *Endymion*. But he is also perplexed by its absence of "a structure of common meaning": "Cynthia as the Moon, Cynthia as the Ideal Queen, Cynthia as Mercy: all these figures are there, and no explicit relationship among them draws them into a structure of common meaning save the fact that a single character suggests all three overtones" (p. 185). If we add a fourth overtone, the Virgin Mary, Queen of Heaven, Full of Grace, if we recall Saccio's own exposition of the Marian associations within the legend, and if we set all of this within the specific festival context of one particular Candlemas performance, we may have added delicately but significantly to that missing structure of common meaning in the allegory.

A few specific passages early in the play may enhance this identification of Cynthia and Mary. In the first scene Cynthia's waxing and waning is described as follows: "Coming out of thy royall robes, wherewith thou dazelist our eyes, downe into thy swath clowthes, beguiling our eyes."[14] It is hard to miss this possible echo of the Christ child's humble swaddling clothes (Luke 2.7, 12) as he descends from heaven to begin his "guiltless sacrifice." In the second scene Tellus describes his great love in hyperbolic terms that again suggest prominent images of the birth of the sacrificial Christ and the adoration of the Virgin: "Doth not Frankinsence & Myrrhe breath out of my nostrils, and all the sacrifice of the Gods breede in my bowels?" (3:24)

Finally, the play contains motifs of celibacy that were to appear much less seriously a decade later in another Candlemas play, *Twelfth Night,* and which might well have influenced it. We recall Olivia's seven-year vow and Orsino's fatuous feeding on the foods of love when Endymion asks Cynthia to "remember my solitarie life, almost these seaven years" (2.1.14). Typical of Lyly, these shimmering festival hues are quite subtle in *Endymion.* But they could probably have been perceived and enjoyed by members of the courtly audience.

The other two Candlemas plays are less impressively appropriate. *Greene's Tu Quoque* is the all-purpose play of our tradition, having already graced Saint John's and Epiphany with at least slight pertinency. Its correlation to Candlemas is greater because of its emphasis on the eventual purification of its bevy of fools, Will and Lionel Rash, Spendall, and Bubble, among others. All are purified, humbled, and forgiven by the conclusion. And Spendall, as he repents his former life and is humbled by his deserved afflictions, urges the audience to avoid his errors and live purely: "Let all avoid false strumpets, dice, and drink;/For he that leaps i'th mud, shall quickly sink."[15] Not idyllic like the other works we have studied, *Tu Quoque* is still moderately apposite to Candlemas. Slighter is the correlation of the last Candlemas play, *The Devil's Charter.* Its study of the impurity of the Borgias, "their faithless, fearless, and ambitious lives" could be pertinent to the Candlemas audience, if only as a negative example of impurities to be shunned.[16] So Alexander, called Antichrist, may like Spendall voice an appropriate Candlemas message in his final remorse: "Learne wicked worldlings, learne, learne, learne by me / To save your soules, though I condemned be" (sig. M2).

The Masques

One of Jonson's Candlemas masques, *Love Freed from Ignorance and Folly,* fits both the Candlemas motif of purification and the repeated, general festival motif of the "Battle of Carnival and Lent." It even contains like *The Masque of Moores* one suggestion of the bright star and the long journey of the wise men, Christmas motifs which might specifically apply to Epiphany. The priests are charged by Love

> To behold that glorious star,
> For whose love you came so far.

[L1. 263-64]

Its most insistent Candlemas motif lies in its purification of Love from a foolish, carnal principle into one of harmony, brilliance, and wisdom, from *cupiditas* to *caritas.* This dichotomy is paralleled in the structure of the masque, which displays "twelve she-fools," the follies of Love misunderstood, before the twelve priests of Wisdom inspire Love with their superior truth (ll. 210-66). As Jonson tells us, the initial antimasque, the dance of the twelve Follies or she-fools "shows that love's expositions are not alway serious till it be divinely instructed, and that sometimes it may be in the danger of ignorance and folly, who are the mother and issue; for no folly but is born of ignorance."[17]

The advice of the twelve priests of Wisdom, higher love, in the masque, is also glossed by Jonson: "Here is understood the power of wisdom in the muses' ministers, by which name all that have the spirit of prophesy are styled, and such they are that need to encounter ignorance and folly, and are ever ready to assist love in any action of honour and virtue, and inspire him with their own soul" (p. 182). Besides the characteristic flattery of James, the king-prophet of England, there is also the possible Neoplatonic reference to Christ, whose greater love purified man on earth from the ignorance and folly of his *cupiditas.* Ellrodt assures us that Christ was commonly identified in Neoplatonic symbolism with the same Wisdom whose priests reform Love in this Candlemas masque.[18] Surely Jonson's court audience could have enjoyed some of these suggestive Christmas parallels on Candlemas, the last festival day of the Christmas season.

Although designed for Epiphany, Jonson's *The Masque of Queens* was performed on Candlemas.[19] Given by this unusual genesis as well as the Candlemas tradition itself the special latitude of looking for parallels to either festival, it is hardly surprising that some moderate ones emerge. As Jonson suggests, the masque celebrates purification and embodies it in its structure. The antimasque of witches, "the opposites to good Fame . . . , a spectacle of strangeness" is replaced by a masque celebrating "honorable and true fame bred out of virtue" (pp. 122-23). Bel-Anna, England's queen and the queen of these virtues as well, is further imaged in fitting Candlemas or Epiphany garb:

> She this embracing with a virtuous joy,
> Far from self-love, as humbling all her worth
> To him that gave it, hath again brought forth
> Their names to memory; and means this night
> To make them once more visible to light
> And to that light from whence her truth of spirit
> Confesseth all the luster of her merit.
>
> [L1. 401-7]

Light, humility, gratitude for creation, and purification all figure forth in this final celebration of virtues attendant upon Epiphany and Candlemas, as well as England's queen. On its Candlemas occasion, this masque, like *Love Freed,* could have had moderate affective power.

Bentley relates the unique stage history of the last of the Candlemas masques to be considered in detail. *The Inner Temple Masque,* "which had been performed in the Banqueting House on Twelfth Night was intended to be repeated on Candlemas, but the Banqueting House burned on 12 January" (7:30). The incident suggests that this masque, like several other Candlemas works, suits Epiphany as well as Candlemas; we have found it to do so. In fact, it is explicitly about the whole church year we are discussing. However, since a central character in the masque is actually called *Candlemas,* this is the best festival for its full consideration, despite the Banqueting House fire. The masque's general relationship to the whole festival tradition enriches our understanding of that tradition; it also ties together many of the seemingly disparate strands of this day's dramatic works.

First, the entire masque laments the decline of a longstanding tradition of prescribed fasting and feasting associated with the church year. The characters and dancers in the masque are days and seasons of the year, like New Year's, Fasting Day, Candlemas, Shrovetuesday, and Lent. But to the disillusioned character Time, all of them—secular and religious days alike, feasting days and fasting days—are part of

> The rabble that I pity; these I've served too,
> But few or none have ever observ'd me.
> Among this dissolute rout Candlemas Day!
> I'm sorry to see him so ill associated.[20]

Time's sadness is surely increased by the fact that Candlemas should be associated with purification and humility, not dissolution and pride. But there is a more specific problem as well. Fasting-Day, unwelcome to any other day of the year, has been assigned to Candlemas by this New Year. But Candlemas, like the other days, wants no such somber company. Worse, he is jealous "because Shrove-tuesday this year dwells so near him" (ll. 161–62) and has come to complain to New Year about this encroachment upon his festivity.[21] As New Year responds, "You must be patient, Candlemas, and brook it."

The pervasive misrule of this season is accentuated by yet another allusion to the "Battle of Carnival and Lent," this one quite explicit. Fasting-Day, still patronless in the year, quarrels with Plumporridge; surely the former represents Lent and the latter carnival in this exchange:

> *Plum.* O, killing, cruel sight! yonder's a Fasting-Day, a lean, spiny rascal, with a dog in's belly; his very bowels bark with hunger. Avaunt! thy breath stinks; I do not love to meet thee fasting: thou art nothing but wind, thy stomach's full of farts, as if they had lost their way, and thou made with the wrong end upward. . . .

Fasting-Day. Why, thou whorson breakfast, dinner, nunchions, supper, and bever, cellar, hall, kitchen and wet-larder.

[L1. 37–46]

This is strikingly like analogous exchanges between Hal and Falstaff, even to the insulting epithets of excess.[22] When Dr. Almanak immediately reads Christmas's last will and testament, we realize how fully we are participating in seasonal, mythic games. Kersmas, father of festival misrule, bequeaths all of the carnival excesses of the season—the gambling, lust, and drunkenness—to his children the days of Christmas. Carnival seems to have overwhelmed not only Lent but all human dignity and order. In fact, Time almost concludes that the only way to purify the year is to bid it be impure, since misrule seems the rule of the time:

To bid 'em sin's the way to make 'em mend,
For what they are forbid they run to headlong.

[L1. 191–92]

But then the masque supercedes this antimasque, and "Harmony, with her sacred quire," purifies the New Year of these Carnival grotesques:

Time shall be reconcil'd.
Thy spring shall in all sweets abound,
Thy summer shall be clear and sound,
Thy autumn swell the barn and loft
With corn and fruits, ripe, sweet, and soft;
And in thy winter, when all go,
Thou shalt depart as white as snow.

[L1. 249–55]

Like Prince Hal "Redeeming time when men think least I will" (1.2.205), the seasons will be purified with this cleansing of the New Year. The masque concludes with flames of light imaging forth honour and virtue (ll. 270–73).

In an increasingly secular age, and from one of the last bastions of the old tradition, the Inner Temple, comes this first caustic and then lovely plea to observe again the festival year in all of its proper solemnity and beauty. The very festival days need purification, even Candlemas itself, which should be most pure. But if these heroic exemplars of virtue can be followed, then possibly there is still a chance for the redeeming of time, the reconciliation and purification of the days of the year, and the reclaiming of the society which supports and is supported by it. What better night than Candlemas for the attempt? And what dramatic vehicle would be more conscious of the observance and the breach of this festival tradition than a masque designed especially for Candlemas at court? Its lament testifies eloquently to the festival tradition that has preceded it as it plaintively predicts the Lenten excesses to come.

The degree to which the complementary Epiphany and Candlemas works correspond with their two festival occasions is thus quite impressive. For Epiphany nineteen of the twenty-three recorded performances, over four-fifths, show some correlation; sixteen, over two-thirds, evidence either a moderate or an extensive correlation, parallels probably perceived by the Epiphany audience. Nine of twenty-three, almost two-fifths, evidence extensive pertinency. For Candlemas, seven of eight evidence some correlation to the day and / or the Christmas season, six of eight either a moderate or an extensive correlation, and three of eight an extensive correlation. Including the

Table 14

Correlations of Candlemas Plays and Masques

None	Slight	Moderate	Extensive
Every Man in His Humour (1605)	*The Devil's Charter* (1607)	*Endymion* (1588)	*Love Freed* (1611) (masque)
		The Masque of Queens (1609)	*The Inner Temple Masque* (1619)
		Tu Quoque (1612)	*Twelfth Night* (1623)

two private performances of *King Lear* and *Twelfth Night,* half, five of ten, would almost surely have been capable of affective power on Candlemas night. Considered together over four-fifths of all recorded court performances on Epiphany and Candlemas might have been enriched by their festival context, and two-thirds would probably have been so affected. Forty percent are extensively pertinent.

Again, such ratios are offered only to indicate the tendencies of these masques and plays to be consonant with their religious festivals. As a numerical translation of this author's own value judgments, they are clearly subject to some downward or upward modification. Further, they emphatically do not "prove" anything. Only the collective weight of the individual, play-by-play analyses can carry the burden of proof. Three or four especially apposite plays or masques "prove" more than all these numbers. Such ratios are mentioned occasionally, and then tentatively, only to suggest in a general way some patterns within this emerging dramatic tradition. For example, the nineteen works named for or commissioned to be performed on one of these two festivals are significantly more appropriate to their occasion than the others. Fourteen of the nineteen, around three-fourths, evidence a moderate enough correlation for us to assume that the courtier could probably have perceived it. Eleven, over half, would almost surely have suggested their liturgical occasion, so richly do they contain festival motifs. This close affinity between the commissioned masques and their liturgical occasions will intensify in the Shrovetide works to be considered next.

CHAPTER 6

The Shrovetide Masques
& Plays

Poised as it is between Christmas feasting and Lenten fasting, Shrovetide is a unique and dramatic moment in the church year. Its distance from the clustered holy days of the Christmas season and its closeness to Lent in penitential spirit and calendar date sharply distinguish it from the Christmas festival days. Still, Shrovetide, the preparatory Sunday, Monday, and Tuesday before Lent, is also the host of carnival; Shrove Tuesday is also Fat Tuesday, Mardi gras, the last taste of Christmastide merriment. The tension between these interwoven if contradictory festival strands will have a significant influence upon the Shrovetide entertainments at court. Equally unusual, the Shrovetide liturgy celebrates a repeated thematic motif—shriving—but does not yoke it with a parallel narrative event. Thus, while it is among the most vivid of the festivals in its placement and thematic intensity, Shrovetide lacks the narrative strands that sometimes find their way into the other plays. As if to accentuate its uniqueness, Shrovetide is also a "movable feast," falling anywhere from 3 February to 9 March, depending on the date of Easter.[1] It is further a three-day festival, not a single holy day. However, because of its common liturgical motifs and customs, we can profitably consider all of the performances under the common rubric of Shrovetide. Just as unique as the festival is the intensity and frequency of correlation between its eight commissioned masques and its liturgical and sociological motifs. Jonson's Epiphany masques are impressively redolent of the festival for which they were designed, but the Shrovetide masques are even more intimately related to their unique festival occasion. Although several of the seven Shrovetide plays also have some affinities with their festival, only one, *The Merchant of Venice,* shares the masques's intense correlations. Because it is by Shakespeare, whose plays have proven most richly consonant with this whole festival tradition, and because it may have been chosen for its festival performance by King James himself, let us begin our discussion with that play.

The Merchant of Venice

The Revels Accounts for the court of King James I reveal that two performances of *The Merchant of Venice* were given during Shrovetide 1605. Since the second of these, on Shrove Tuesday, was expressly commanded by James himself[2] and since no records indicate court performances of the play on any other festival night, we are certainly justified in glancing at the liturgical tradition of Shrovetide to determine its possible relationships to Shakespeare's most perplexing romantic comedy.

Even the most cursory glance at the liturgical tradition reveals that Shrovetide shares with the play which twice graced it a mixture of incongruent qualities. As the name would suggest, Shrovetide, shriving-time, is a time for self-scrutiny, confession, penance, and absolution. *A Glossary of Liturgical and Ecclesiastical Terms* defines it as "the period between the evening of the Saturday before Quinquegesima Sunday [Shrove Sunday] and the morning of Ash Wednesday; i.e. that time when, preparatory to the Lenten season, the faithful were shriven."[3] In sharp contrast to this Lenten, penitential quality is the social tradition of high carnival. Shrove Tuesday is simultaneously a day of extraordinary license in Renaissance and Jacobean England, as it often still is today, the time called, in fact carnival, farewell to the flesh, because it hosts a final explosion of riotous misrule just before the somber restraints of Lent.[4] A. R. Wright succinctly describes this characteristic

Table 15

Shrovetide Performances

Dates	Titles	Authorities
	Plays	
1584	*Sapho and Phao* (?)	Chambers, 4:100
1605	*The Merchant of Venice*	Chambers, 4:119 (Sunday)
1605	*The Merchant of Venice*	Chambers, 4:119 (Tuesday, at the request of James I)
1622	*The Coxcomb*	Bentley, 7:43
1631	*Rollo; or The Bloody Brother*	Bentley, 7:78
1640	*Salmacida Spolia*	Bentley, 7:119
	Masques	
1613	*The Masque of the Middle Temple and Lincoln's Inn*	Chambers, 4:127
1613	*The Masque of the Inner Temple and Gray's Inn*	Chambers, 4:127
1618	*For the Honour of Wales*	Bentley, 7:26
1620	*News from the New World*	Bentley, 7:35
1631	*Chloridia*	Bentley, 7:78
1632	*Tempe Restored*	Bentley, 7:82
1634	*Coelum Britannicum*	Bentley, 7:92
1635	*The Temple of Love*	Bentley, 7:96

Source: E. K. Chambers, *The Elizabethan Stage,* and Gerald Eades Bentley, *The Jacobean and Caroline Stage,* are my authorities.

dichotomy for us: "For many centuries Shrovetide was the time for confessing and shriving, but its chief features were feasting and boisterous hilarity."[5]

The prescribed biblical passages for the season also reflect this persistent dichotomy, well known in another medium through Brueghel's painting *The Battle of Carnival and Lent.*

According to *The Prayer-Book Dictionary,* the prevailing mood
of the passages is one of rejoicing in "the grace of love." The
Collect prays for it; the Epistle (1 Cor. 13) is Saint Paul's
description of the superiority of love to the other Christian
virtues. The Gospel (Luke 18.31–43) shows Christ's love for the
blind man, even as He goes toward Jerusalem and certain death.
The Lessons reveal God's love to Noah (Gen. 9) and Abram
(Gen. 12), "while Gen. 13 contains a striking example of man's
self-denying love to his fellow man."[6]

However, the reason for this liturgical emphasis on the grace
of love, implicit in these same biblical passages and explicit in
one of Donne's Lenten sermons, is man's penitential awareness
of his need for that grace, his acknowledgment of his grotesque
but natural and universal imperfection. Genesis 9 is also about
Ham's "derision & contempt for his father"; further, it embodies allegorically the racial strife occasioned by Noah's subsequent banishment of Ham (Canaan) for mocking his naked-
ness and his drunkenness. The passage even embodies the
strikingly relevant mythic and legalistic passage forbidding the
eating of living flesh (9:4): "But flesh with the life thereof, I
meane with the blood thereof, shal ye not eat." The Geneva
note explains, "That is, living creatures and the flesh of beastes
that are strangled: and hereby all crueltie is forbidden." Shylock's cruel bond is not unrelated to this biblical context. Likewise, God's grace to Abram is tempered by Abram's moral
cowardice and distrust of God; further, Abram's kindness to
Lot is muted by the prediction that Lot's people and his inheritance will be destroyed. Even the Collect for the day, following
the lead of 1 Cor. 13, warns against the good works that are not
accompanied by the proper causative spirit of charity.[7] In fact,
a constant awareness accompanying this celebration of God's
grace is the danger of two sins in relationship to it, presumption
and despair: "The great souls are those who yield neither to
presumption nor despair, who know that the good they aim at
is too difficult for complacent human strength, but not beyond
the divine attainment."[8]

Donne's Lenten sermons are equally aware of this paradoxical combination of attitudes during the Shrovetide season.

Man should not be so overwhelmed by his Lenten meditations on his immense imperfection that he falls to despair; neither should he presume sufficient righteousness or sufficient grace. He should know that purity, like righteousness, can be vicious as well as virtuous, and strive therefore to blend during Shrovetide holy day and holiday, Lent and Carnival, feasting and fasting, as difficult as that blending is to achieve:

> All Lent is *Easter Eve*; and though the *Eve* be a *Fasting Day,* yet the *Eve* is *halfe-holiday* too. God, by our Ministery, would so exercise you in a spirituall *Fast,* in a sober consideration of sinne, and the sad Consequences thereof, as that in the *Eve* you might see the *holy day*; in the *Lent,* your *Easter*; in the sight of your sinnes, the cheerfulnesse of his good will towards you.[9]

This brief liturgical and homiletic background places us in a position to understand how *The Merchant of Venice* might have been thought relevant to Shrovetide by James I in 1605. It simultaneously helps to explain, though it cannot hope to resolve, the often dichotomous critical apprehensions of the play. For if the festive context is any index to our understanding of the play, it suggests that that understanding needs to follow the paradoxical lines articulated in Donne's sermon, rather than the simple polarities into which the critics have so often fallen.

First, there is inarguably an abundance of joy and festivity in the play, and there is nothing sinister about most of it. Most appropriately for Shrovetide, that joy is the joy of love's wealth, or of the grace of love. Bassanio exhibits it when he chooses aright; Antonio gives and hazards all for his friend, and Portia too loves so well that she hazards the casket plot and the wiles of Venice, and then even tries to convert Shylock to Christianity, to save his vicious soul. There is considerable love for these expliticly Christian characters to celebrate at the end of the play, and also some sense of grace. For they have all been delivered from their hazards and will, we must assume, live happily ever after. At least, the lovers will.[10]

But where are the Lenten aspects of the festival? What of penitence and imperfect charity; what of presumption and despair; what of "fasting, and sober consideration of sinne"? As

I have elsewhere argued and can here only briefly reiterate, it is the imperfect blending of this paradoxical other half of the Shrovetide perspective among the Christian and romantic characters of the play that separates them from all of Shakespeare's other major comic characters and that invites the ironic perspective to coexist with the romantic one.[11] These individuals inhabiting the most self-consciously Christian society in the romantic comedies are never invited to understand the inevitable imperfections of even their best-intended actions. The elopement, the forced conversion, the administration of a mercy and a justice that leaves many of us uneasy, Antonio's attempt to play Christ in a world that needs only one such sacrifice, his world-weariness and the self-righteousness that spits upon or brays at a sinner instead of forgiving or loving him—all of these may partially manifest the peculiar Shrovetide sins of presumption and despair. There is no wise fool in Venice or Belmont to lead the erring Christians to the wisdom of humility, no counterpart to Feste or the Feast of Fools.[12] The ring plot, its closest approximation, is at best a contrived, inorganic ritual of comic shriving and humiliation. The profounder Lenten awareness of the lack of deserving intensifies the festive celebrations of the grace of love in the other comedies. That awareness is absent in Belmont. As Donne suggests, it is "in the Lent that you see your Easter; in the sight of your sinnes, the cheerfulness of his good will towards you." If that paradoxical perspective is to enrich the festive experience of *The Merchant of Venice,* it is only because its absence among the festive celebrants forces the audience to understand and to celebrate, alone for once and therefore ironically, that profounder if more muted joy.

Of course, we should not judge the Christians too harshly. If Antonio and his company are somewhat presumptuous of their goodness and righteousness, Shylock completely embodies that Shrovetide sin in his self-assured pursuit of the "rightful" bond. As a result, a Renaissance audience preparing for the penitential rigors of Lent but still enjoying the masking and the carnival of Shrove Tuesday might well have been edified by both the facile joy in Belmont and Shylock's obdurate pride. They might have understood that Belmont's carnival is not sufficiently

Lenten, its feast a surfeiting of joy unmitigated by fasting, its holiday insufficiently holy.[13] Enid Welsford's descriptions of the mummery, the traditional Shrovetide observance involving public masking, parading through the streets, and dancing in neighbors' houses suggests that the play is set during Shrovetide and the Lenten month following. Such an additional coincidence also implies that Shylock's eventual scapegoating might have borne ironic resemblances to yet another Shrovetide custom—the sacrificing of the carnival fool.[14] The irony lies partly in his decidedly non-Saturnalian, antifestive associations and partly in the Christians' inability to bury their own carnival attitude, or to blend it with Lent in their final festivity. With this network of associations, it is at least feasible that the theologically and aesthetically aware James I, or one of his associates, would have noted the striking resemblance of the play to the holy season and commanded its repeat performance for the combined edification and entertainment of the court at Whitehall just before Lent. This festive context simultaneously suggests that the traditionally polar critical positions toward the play can be made complementary. In responding to *The Merchant of Venice* one properly celebrates the grace of love's wealth and accepts the severity of Shylock's shriving, but one simultaneously guards against the presumption that the grace is ever assured or deserved by maintaining something of an ironic distance from the attractive but still naïve revellers. Shrovetide richly encourages such a balanced perspective.

We have already established that while Shrovetide, or shriving-time, is a pre-Lenten period set aside for self-scrutiny, confession, penance, and absolution, it is simultaneously a time of carnival, of riotous merrymaking before the enforced abstinence of Lent. We need to broaden our understanding of this paradoxical "Battle of Carnival and Lent" before looking at the rest of the Shrovetide masques and plays. Let us look first at Brueghel's painting of the conflict, and then review its occasional embodiments in analogous masques and plays for New Year's, Epiphany, and Candlemas. For the antithesis lies directly behind their characters, emblems, and thematic interests and may have generated their common antimasque-masque

The Battle of Carnival and Lent (1559). *Courtesy of the Kunsthistorisches Museum, Vienna*

structure. Nowhere will the influence of the "battle" be more obvious or more extensive than in the Shrovetide masques.

R. H. Marijnissen, one of Brueghel's editors, highlights the painting's seasonal dichotomies for us:

> The underlying principle of the composition is antithesis. Carnival has its citadel in the Blue Ship tavern on the left, while the followers of austere Lent come streaming out of the church at the right. . . . Carnival is personified by a rotund Prince . . . riding on an enormous barrel on runners, which is being pushed along by his retinue. The Carnival fools are dressed in bizarre costumes draped with strings of eggs, waffles, or fritters. One of their duties is to make a racket with an extraordinary assortment of instruments. In the background Carnival plays such as *The Story of Ourson and Valentine* and *The Marriage of Mopsus and Nissa* are being performed. The boisterous fun spreads through the little town from street to street; even the cripples seem to be affected by it. The scene around gaunt, grim Lent is the opposite. Lent is a scrawny

old woman sitting on a straight wooden chair on a creaking platform, which is being pulled along by a friar and a nun. The weapon she holds is a long baker's paddle with two herrings on it. She wears an old beehive on her head; at her feet are meager Lenten foods. Her retinue is made up of good little girls and boys, poor people, pillars of the church and society, and almsgivers. Beside the fish tank her Lenten fare is being prepared.[15]

Carnival plays and a carnival parade or mummery are in progress. Carnival fools occupy center stage and a distant window. Carnival emblems of overindulgence and fasting, like the hog and the fish, lurk beside the well in the center and adorn Carnival's spear-spit and Lent's paddle as well. The complexities of these seasonal dichotomies are further emphasized when the figure holding up the bottle in Carnival's retinue seems to be a nun, and when Lenten figures with whips near the church seem to be mortifying the flesh but are actually spinning tops. In fact, Lent overflows into carnival and carnival into Lent all over the canvas, in spite of the apparent absoluteness of its division down the center. One would have to call both the revellers and the abstainers equally pathetic rather than equally attractive in their mutually grotesque overindulgence. Nowhere is this paradoxical similarity more obvious than in the unrelenting ugliness of bloated Carnival and emaciated Lent.

But though carnival and Lent are most obviously opposed during Shrovetide, other religious and social festivals, especially New Year's, Epiphany, and Candlemas, also uncomfortably oppose riotous celebrations against the theme of religious purification, holiday revelry against holyday reverence, overindulgence against fasting, misrule against rule. This battle of carnival and Lent has already been noticed as an influence on some of their festival plays and masques. On Candlemas, Middleton's *Inner Temple Masque* dramatizes an inconclusive quarrel between Fasting-Day and Plumporridge, clear Lenten and carnival opposites. On Epiphany, Jonson's *Love Restored* opposes the grotesque carnival rioters led by one Masquerado against the equally unattractive Puritanical, Lenten figure of Plutus. Shakespeare's *Twelfth Night* contrasts the Lenten Malvolio to the saturnalian Toby Belch. On New Year's Jonson's

Oberon opposes both the carnival figures of Silenius and Lyaeus and an antimasque of five drunken and lecherous satyrs against a concluding masque of virtues, and Shakespeare's *Henry IV* plays oppose both the Lord Chief Justice and Hal against Falstaff himself, the most notorious of all these carnival revellers. A much lighter portrayal of this conflict occurs in Dekker's *Shoemaker's Holiday.* This happy, gentle comedy contains so little of the "purging physick" of ugly, threatening worldly and carnal lusts that it was not considered a pertinent New Year's performance. But it is unquestionably pertinent to Shrovetide, even though it was apparently overlooked by the Master of Revels; it concludes with a Shrove Tuesday celebration of carnival proportions, and its title suggests that holiday. When the pancake bell announces the beginning of the first annual apprentices' holiday, as proclaimed by the new Lord Mayor Simon Eyre, one of the apprentices, Fiske, exults,

> O musical bel stil! O *Hodge,* O my brethren! theres cheere for the heavens, venson pasties walke up and down piping hote, like sergeants, beefe and brewesse comes marching in drie fattes, fritters and pancakes comes trowling in in wheele barrowes, hennes and orenges hopping in porters baskets, collopes and egges in scuttles, and tartes and custardes comes quavering in in mault shovels.[16]

This parade is as rich as Brueghel's canvas with traditional emblems of carnival's last gasp, but they are not nearly as sinister. Lacy is reminiscent of Prince Hal in his holiday excursion; both only appear dissolute. The Lord Mayor of London is reminiscent of Falstaff, but much healthier, in declaring a universal if brief holiday. When he is called "one of the merriest madcaps in all your land" (5.3.2), he recalls Hal's epithet, "madcap Prince of Wales" (4.1.95), not Falstaff's "swollen parcel of dropsies, that huge bombard of sack, that stuffed cloak-bag of guts, that roasted Manningtree ox" (2.4.430). Immediately the mayor is also called "serious, provident, wise" (1.7). Holiday is neither debauchery nor a permanent state of mind in this London; it is therefore not the sinister threat to order that it becomes in so many of the festival plays and masques. Ugly Lenten figures are similarly absent from this stage, though the two heavy fathers briefly play their life-denying, always-serious role. The king's final speech clearly suggests this lack of tension and ambiguity: "When all our sports and banquetings are done, / Warres must right wrongs which Frenchmen have begun" (5.5.190–91). Holiday has its place, but everyday is in complete control, in the Lord Mayor, in Lacy, in the kingdom, and even in the final closed couplet. Disorder lies abroad.

Unlike his happy, unambiguous portrayal in Dekker's New Year's play, the Rioter is usually quite ugly in his utter immersion in carnality. His opposite the Puritan can be just as unattractive in his self-righteous negation of all joy. As in Brueghel's painting, so in most of these festival plays and masques it is easy to tell them apart, but hard to prefer one over the other. In the complexity of their opposition we can see why such a conflict is most appropriate to carnival and most frequent in the Shrovetide masques. Usually the Rioter is all *carne*, the Puritan all *vale*. The Rioter is all despair of grace; the Puritan all presumption of election. The paired and unique sins of the Shrovetide season—presumption and despair—are thus embodied with such complexity in these opposed character types that the audience is uncomfortable with either extreme.[17] If anything, the Puritan seems even more threatening than the Rioter to the masque's goal of aesthetic, psychological, and sociological equilibrium. But pleasure must also be reconciled to virtue if society is to be made whole again.

The Puritan in this Shrovetide dichotomy obviously represents a rising social class in the Renaissance. The Rioter is sometimes his social opposite, a drunken knight like Falstaff or Sir Toby.[18] But the Rioter is also a social emblem transplanted into the drama from the court. For as the noble houses had a Christmas Lord of Misrule, so they had his Shrovetide equivalent, another "maister of merry disports" with his retinue of ragged revellers.[19] Here is a brief contemporary description of this lord in all his glory:

> But now stand off (my friends) give roome I say: for here must enter
> that wadling, stradling, bursten-gutted *Carnifex* of all Christendome;

vulgarly enstiled Shrove-Tuesday, but more pertinently, sole-monarch of the Mouth, high Steward to the Stomack, chiefe Ganimede to the Guts, prime Peere of the Pullets, . . . Protectour of the Pan-cakes, first Founder of the Fritters.[20]

The echoes of Hal's abuse of Falstaff, that supreme dramatic embodiment of this festival tradition, are obvious in the style of this abuse (cf. *1 Henry IV*, 2.4.267–77, e.g.). As C. L. Barber and Mikhail Bakhtin have both shown us, the social type and the dramatic type, so nearly identical here, both embody abuses of the liturgical festival they represent and disgrace. Thus both must be expelled, in the drama and in the society, when Lent finally begins.[21]

Beasts in the masques are as common as Puritans and Lords of Misrule. As obvious emblems of carnival license, they probably employed costumes that would have been used as well in the Shrovetide mummings. But their thematic significance in this festival, at least to ecclesiastical writers like Lancelot Andrewes and Stephen Batman, would lie in their embodiment of unrepented sins of the flesh, and their opposition to shriving and to fasting. Andrewes argues in a sermon on the subject, "To be born a man and to become matchable with beasts, that is our fault, our great fault" (1:349). We are beasts and worse than beasts if we do not repent our sins of the flesh and amend our lives. As "the professed enemies of fasting and of all abstinence" we are "the locust," "all belly," and "all for the belly" (1:376). In describing Bacchus and his associated emblems, Batman similarly explicates this Shrovetide imagery for us:

The Ape, the Hogge, and the Lyon, the Woolfe, and Dolphin, bewray the affections of the Dronken: for some playe the Ape in imitating every Thyng, some the Hog in returning to accustomed dronkennes, as filthy affections: some the Lyon in executing of cruelty: some the Wolfe in ravening and spoyling: some the Dolphin overwhelmed in Bacchus seas: the Ape looking in a glasse, they vaine flattery of deceivable folly.[22]

If Bacchus and his social and dramatic types the Lords of Misrule embody this general excess, the retinue of emblematic

Detail from the Battle of Carnival and Lent: Carnival and his retinue. *Courtesy of the Kunsthistorisches Museum, Vienna*

animals which traditionally surround him embody its particular sins. Such grotesquerie is particularly common in the Shrovetide masques.

But the marriage of these warring impulses of carnival and Lent is much harder to dramatize than their combat. As a result, none of the Shrovetide masques is more successful than Jonson's *Love Restored,* an early Epiphany masque with similar motifs, in blending carnival and Lent, despair and presumption, flesh and spirit, surfeiting and fasting, beast and angel. Symbolically, the marriage occurs in the revels, which dramatizes decorous revelry, song and dance in celebration of wisdom and virtue. But too often this part of the masque seems merely pasted on to the antimasque which preceded and precipitated it. Similarly, the Puritan and the Rioter usually find it equally difficult to enjoy or fit easily into the concluding festivity, for it transcends them both. Only when both figures can become wise and decorous, not excessive, can they fit comfortably into the final revels. It is hardly accidental that a similar aesthetic

Detail from the Battle of Carnival and Lent: Lent and her retinue.
Courtesy of the Kunsthistorisches Museum, Vienna

problem characterizes Shakespeare's *Twelfth Night*, with both
Malvolio and Sir Toby uneasy at the balanced festive conclusion. For they, like the excesses embodied in the Shrovetide
and Epiphany masques, have inevitably been superceded by a
wise, decorous festivity that neither of them can easily understand or enjoy.

These are the major liturgical and sociological motifs we
should expect to find in the rest of the Shrovetide plays and
masques. I would agree with Bakhtin and Barber that "sociological" and "liturgical" are virtually indistinguishable elements
at this crucial moment in the tradition. Along with the purely
liturgical themes of penance and shriving, the more complex
battles of carnival and Lent, despair and presumption, Rioter
and Puritan will occur with unprecedented richness and explicitness in the masques written expressly for the festival. So rich
are these parallels that one can safely assume, with even more
certainty than with Jonson's Epiphany masques or Shakespeare's
Twelfth Night, that most of the masques were created with the

major outlines of the festival season firmly in mind. In fact, the Shrovetide masque we shall consider in greatest detail, Thomas Carew's *Coelum Britannicum,* is almost certainly an allegorical dramatization, in the usual Neoplatonic mode of the masques, of most of the liturgical and sociological traditions of the season.

With the exception of *The Merchant of Venice,* however, the Shrovetide plays offer us only a moderate beginning. *Sapho and Phao* contains two brief but pertinent exchanges between Molus and Criticus about indulgence and Lent.[23] More impressive are correlations between *The Coxcomb* and *Rollo* (or *The Bloody Brother*), both by Beaumont and Fletcher, and the festival. In the former sensual excesses repeatedly cause remorse, repentance, and the intense desire to be shriven. The second act ends with Ricardo's shriving; the fourth with Mercury's. This placement suggests their thematic and structural importance. In the final act, Ricardo feels so sinful that he despairs of Viola's forgiveness. But after several confessions and shrivings, he finds peace and love.[24] *Rollo,* a tragedy, seems as insistently apposite to its Shrovetide occasion. Like *The Coxcomb, Rollo* contains a powerful central scene of remorse, confession, and shriving (4:308). Of his tears of shriving Rollo says, "Are they not drops of blood? / . . . They must thus drop, till I have drown'd my mischiefs" (5.2.80, 85). As La Fiske is shriven earlier, there is even a reminder of five of the seven deadly sins (4.2.23–28). With thematic patterns of shriving and repentance so close to the surface of these two plays, there is little chance that they would not have been noticed as appropriate by the Shrovetide audience.

The Shrovetide Masques

The first two Shrovetide masques, *The Memorable Masque* and *The Masque of the Inner Temple and Gray's Inn,* celebrate the marriage of Princess Elizabeth of England and Prince Frederick of the Rhine. Unlike the other wedding masques, these bear enough resemblance to their festival occasion to deserve some attention. For one thing, both contain the antimasques of Circean beasts, here baboons and asses, that will become so characteristic of later Shrovetide masques. John Chamberlain, an eyewitness of the first, describes "A dousen little boyes, dresst like babones, that served for an antimaske."[25] In the second an antimasque of a "Hee Baboone" and a "Shee Babone," a "Hee Foole" and a "Shee Foole"[26] again anticipates the grotesque emblems of human folly and carnality in later masques. Such emblems are vital penitential reminders during the season of shriving, in the midst of a celebration of the joys of marriage and carnival. Further linking the two masques to their festivals is an elaborate outdoor torchlight parade or mummery, much like the carnival parade of masked revellers outside of Shylock's house in Venice, with which each begins. Thus tantalizingly do both of these court masques hover between holiday festival and dramatic entertainment, with Lent an almost uninvited guest in the "lewde Musicke" and carnal beasts of the antimasques.

Compared to these Shrovetide works, and even compared to his own Epiphany masques, Ben Jonson's first Shrovetide contribution is surprising in its overt and extensive relevancy to the festival tradition. His successful Epiphany masque, *Pleasure Reconciled to Virtue,* is revised for Shrovetide performance as *For the Honour of Wales.*[27] The new antimasque of Welsh revellers persistently exploits the central dichotomy of the Shrovetide season, the battle of carnival and Lent. Added for this occasion, it contains several pages of songs in Jonson's best *carpe diem* style praising the pleasure of the world, the carnival delights of fine food, drink, music, and dance. This antimasque ends with a dance of goats, another traditional emblem of carnal excess.[28]

The original antimasque illustrates the inherent similarity between the structure and thematic focus of Epiphany and Shrovetide masques. For though in the Epiphany version the revellers are not Welshmen, they clearly embody similar carnival excesses. This time the songs praise the belly god, Comus, "the bouncing belly," "first father of sauce, and deviser of jelly" (ll. 10–11). Another antimasque of "men dressed as bottles and a cask" (1. 76), which vividly suggests Brueghel's painting, brings in Hercules, the Lenten voice of discretion, who severely upbraids the revellers. Now the battle of carnival and Lent is in full swing:

> (Help, Virtue!) these are sponges, and not men.
> Bottles? mere vessels? half a tun of paunch?
> . . . .
> Whose feast? the belly's? Comus'? and my cup
> Brought in to fill the drunken orgies up?
>
> [L1. 85-89]

Adding to the carnival notes of Circean bestiality and surfeiting (imaged here by swine), Hercules's potent Lenten voice continues to urge shriving and penance:

> Burdens and shames of nature, perish, die;
> Foryet you never lived, but in the sty
> Of vice have wallowed, and in that swine's strife
> Been buried under the offense of life.
> Go, reel and fall under the load you make,
> Till your swoll'n bowels burst with what you take.
>
> [L1. 92-97]

Almost exorcised by Lent's Herculean fury, these carnival figures vanish and are replaced by the refined maskers, Virtue and Pleasure. The battle is abruptly over; the reconciliation of carnival and Lent, Pleasure and Virtue is suddenly an accomplished fact. But what does it mean, and how has it occurred? Such questions will often arise in these Shrovetide masques and will usually be vouchsafed only elusive answers. Perhaps no other answers are possible. For Pleasure and Virtue, though they are considerably refined versions of carnival and Lent, can still be but strange bedfellows.

Daedalus is the interpreter of the revels common to both the Epiphany and Shrovetide versions of the masque. In fact, such explication seems his most important function in the work. To Daedalus the masque's decorous revelry blends pleasure and virtue just as surely as the antimasque's crudity and excess separate the two. With the proper people, and in the proper context,

> Grace, laughter and discourse may meet,
> And yet the beauty go not less;
> For what is noble should be sweet
> But not dissolved in wantonness.

[Ll. 280-83]

If this merging of pleasure and virtue is, then, a mystery of breeding and refinement (l. 201), of true nobility, it is also a considerable aesthetic trick. Even "Daedalus the wise / [Doth] in sacred harmony comprise / His precepts" (ll. 217-19). The masque can do no less.

Daedalus understands this paradox better than any of our subsequent interpreters of this Shrovetide tradition, so we had better attend his comments. The mysterious weaving of virtue and pleasure in the song, dance, and scenery of the masque is so curious a knot that "ev'n th' observer scarce may know / Which lines are Pleasure's and which not" (ll. 225-27). In dancing there is obvious pleasure. There is also measure, wisdom, and grace:

> For dancing is an exercise
> Not only shows the mover's wit,
> But maketh the beholder wise,
> As he hath power to rise to it.

[Ll. 240-43]

Scenic effects reveal the same paradox. Color, form, and proportion give delight to the senses, but they also edify the soul:

> Design and picture, they might boast
> From you a newer ground,
> Instructed to the height'ning sense
> Of dignity and reverence.

[Ll. 254-57]

As in love, "the subtlest maze of all" (l. 271), if these sensual props are delicately and wisely employed, "not dissolved in wantonness" (l. 283), they can reveal the "more removed mysteries" of the soul. Of course, one must learn "To walk with Pleasure, not to dwell" (l. 296). For "These, these are hours by Virtue spared" (l. 297); and "though / Her sports be soft, her life is hard" (l. 301). Remember that Bishop Fuller also thought that the masques could convey glimmers of the joys of heaven. [29] Perhaps this is the way. We will find no more sophisticated an attempt to resolve this unique festival dichotomy in the subsequent Shrovetide masques. Daedalus suggests how precarious the reconciliation of Pleasure and Virtue must remain, socially, morally, and aesthetically. For carnival and Lent, their seasonal counterparts, are usually at war, not at peace, during Shrovetide. But if its final equipoise is inevitably a precarious one, there should be no question that Jonson has woven central motifs of the Shrovetide festival into the fabric of this Shrovetide masque.

Jonson's other Shrovetide masque, *Chloridia,* is not as interesting in its use of the liturgical moment, possibly because the queen commanded "the invention of a new argument" (p. 462). Still, two connected motifs are probably evocative of Shrovetide. The first occurs in the antimasque. "A dwarf-post from hell, riding on a curtal, with cloven feet, and two lackeys" (ll. 95–96) is "no Mercury" Jonson tells us (1. 101), but his message still brims with Mercury's traditional Shrovetide truth.[30] Hell has become the setting for a carnival which is supreme and perpetual, without even the threatened torment associated with Lent: "Love hath been lately there [hell], and so entertained by Pluto and Proserpine and all the grandees of the place as it is there perpetual holiday, and a cessation of torment granted and proclaimed forever" (ll. 103–6). But Heaven is just as surely the site of refined revelry. Iris and Juno discuss, in a pointedly penitential spirit, the wisdom of humble prayer and the forgiveness of the gods, "If who offends be wise" (ll. 207–14). Cupid's carnival excesses in hell then require his subsequent shriving in heaven. Although such motifs would seem to have little to do with the prescribed subject of "Chloris . . . goddess of the flowers" (p. 462), they are comfortable enough in a Shrovetide context.

The next Shrovetide masque, Thomas Carew's *Coelum Britannicum,* is unique in the explicitness and the extensiveness with which it embodies its festival's images and ideas. The other commissioned works often refract motifs of their festivals in a rich variety of ways. But this masque practically dramatizes

Shrovetide's central thematic interests. One character, Momus, explicitly discusses his appropriateness to Shrovetide. If anything, these parallels are uncomfortably obvious. After all, the Renaissance audience hardly needed another Shrovetide sermon in the masque, however much it might have expected delicate refractions of the festival. But we, so far removed from this whole tradition, may need to be smashed by Carew's sledgehammer to feel Jonson's feather touch.

Given Carew's source, Giordano Bruno's notorious *Lo Spaccio de la Bestia Trionfonte* [The expulsion of the triumphant beast], such a close correspondence to Shrovetide is almost inevitable. Like Carew's masque, *Lo Spaccio* is set during an appropriate classical feast, the Gigantomachy, which celebrates the giants' expulsion from heaven by the first generation of reforming gods.[31] It also persistently reiterates the need to purify, purge, shrive heaven (and the Catholic hierarchy) of all of its accumulated sins of the flesh and the world.[32] As Bruno's editor suggests, "The Gods must first, according to Jove, cleanse their hearts and consciences through repentance . . . [and] destroy the physical vestiges of a life formerly motivated by inordinate desires." So after a formal ceremony of penance and shriving, they "purge heaven of all of the vices, which Bruno refers to collectively as 'the triumphant beast.'" (p. 28). The allegory of this beast touches many bases, of course. It attacks the old hierarchy of the Catholic church. It laments man's insatiable lust for wealth and power. It also reflects a philosophic skepticism as profound as Montaigne's. To some degree the Beast represents the ignorance, superstition, and prejudice which have always distorted man's reason. But as Jove finally realizes, only "those individuals . . . who are disposed to contemplation and study" (p. 26) are capable of correcting this distortion. Only the Lenten virtues of contemplation and fasting will lead anyone to be shriven of the errors of the past. One is not surprised at the dismay of the Catholic church over one direction of this allegory. But there could be no more apt a source for a Shrovetide masque directed to an Anglican audience.

Coelum Britannicum opens with a clever Shrovetide modification of Bruno, and a pleasant flattery of the Stuart court.

Where once Jove "acted incests, rapes, adulteries," now

> . . . in the Chrystall myrrour of your reigne
> He view'd himselfe, he found his loathsome staines;
> And now, [will] expiate the infectious guilt
> Of those detested luxuries.
>
> [L1. 84-87]

The "exemplar life" of King Charles and Queen Henrietta has led their court and heaven's to shrive themselves of their vicious excesses (ll. 62-72): "As yours doth here, their great Example spreads" (1. 73).

Mercury is again the Shrovetide messenger. But again he is interrupted, this time by Momus, who will become next to Daedalus our most important interpreter of the Shrovetide festivities. Momus addresses the audience in a way which offers two unexpected insights into the whole tradition of masques on Shrovetide:

> Know (gay people) that though your Poets who enjoy by Patent a particular privilege to draw downe any of the Deities from Twelfnight till Shrove-tuesday, at what time there is annually a most familiar enter-course between the two Courts [of heaven and earth], have as yet never invited me to these Solemnities, yet it shall appeare by my intrusion this night, that I am a very considerable Person upon these occasions, and may most properly assist at such entertainments. [L1. 126-34]

In interpreting his unique role as Lord of Carnival, Momus lends strong support to our thesis that there is an annual tradition of pertinent allegorical masques or other entertainments at court on Twelfth Night and Shrovetide.

As Momus, Greek god of censure and mockery, he goes on to explain to us and to remind the assembled Shrovetide audience why his spirit is always appropriately present, invited or uninvited, during each Shrovetide:

> My Offices and Titles are, The Supreme Theomastix, H[y] percrittique of manners, Protonotarie of abuses, Arch-Informer, Dilator Generall, Universall Calumniator, Eternall Plaintiffe, and perpetuall Foreman of the Grand Inquest.
>
> [L1. 135-39]

He is a "considerable person," who "most properly" assists at such occasions, because he plays the essential Shrovetide roles of exposing vice and absurdity, and discomfiting the complacent. Like his counterpart, the prince of purpoole in the Innocents' festivity at Gray's Inn, he is the grand accuser, the archagent of shriving. During carnival seasons, only his painful and persistent exposure of imperfection can usher in a more properly Lenten attitude, a penitential awareness of imperfection and unworthiness. His role even spans earth and heaven. For Momus can even "make *Jove* frowne, *Juno* powt, *Mars* chafe, *Venus* blush, *Vulcan* glow, *Saturne* quake, *Cynthia* pale, *Phoebus* hide his face, and *Mercury* here take his heeles" (ll. 152–55). As an exposer of human and divine viciousness and folly, Momus is unquestionably a proper and considerable person, in a Shrovetide masque or in the whole tradition of apposite festival performances at court.

Momus then describes Jove's new penitential attitude in cynical detail. Jupiter hath

> in a solemne Oration recanted, disclaimed, and utterly renounced all the lascivious extravagancies, and riotous enormities of his forepast licentious life and taken his oath on *Juno's* Breviary, religiously kissing the two-leav'd book, never to stretch his limbs more betwixt adulterous sheets.
>
> [L1. 199-204]

He has also instituted in heaven "a respective conformity in the severall subordinate Deities" (ll. 206-7):

> *Baccus* hath commanded all Tavernes to be shut, and no liquor drawne after tenne at night. *Cupid* must goe no more so scandalously naked, but is enjoyned to make him breeches though of his mother's petticotes. *Ganimede* is forbidden the Bedchamber, and must onely minister in publique. . . . *Pan* may not pipe, nor *Proteus* juggle, but by especiall permission. [L1.247-55]

Jove's heaven has become a Puritan's paradise. And Lent has clearly won this skirmish against carnival.

Appropriate Shrovetide motifs continue through most of the masque. Even "Venus hath confesst all her adulteries, and is receiv'd to grace by her husband" (ll. 262–63). Mars is again pacified by her love, smoky beard and all. Most obviously embodying this universal shriving and its resultant harmonies (ll. 262 ff.) is a series of seven antimasques, all representing excesses which must be purged in elaborate ceremony. First is the "Antimaske of naturall deformity" (ll. 305 ff.), the familiar emblems of bestiality that have so often been paraded and shriven in the other Shrovetide masques. In heaven, of course, they must be mythological: Centaur, Hydra, Goat-fish, Capricorn, Gorgon, and Sagittarius. "The second Antimasque is danc'd in retrograde paces, expressing obliquity in motion" (ll. 345 ff.). The third is like a late resurrection of the Seven Deadly Sins, an Antimaske of "severall vices, expressing the deviation from Vertue" (Flattery, Cowardice, Ambition, Avarice, Drunkenness, Rage, Calumny, and Ostentation [ll. 375 ff.). The fourth represents the rejection of wealth; the fifth of poverty; the sixth of Fortune (ll. 540–807). The seventh "Antimasque of the five senses" (ll. 808 ff.) represents Pleasure's expulsion. This long and elaborate ceremony illustrates how fully the structure and the thematic interest of the first two-thirds of *Coelum Britannicum* reflect the Shrovetide tradition.

As the instigator and the director of this penitential awareness and subsequent shriving in heaven, Momus's continued cynicism and mockery help keep the tone of the masque festive, joyous. For a while Carew thus rather ingeniously addresses the aesthetic problem of incorporating the Lenten attitude into the festive one. Momus is first amused and a little nervous over this reformation: "Heaven is no more the place it was; . . . a Monastery of converted gods" (ll. 228–29). But Momus will gradually let his Puritanical, Lenten tendencies take complete control over his masque, as he is infected by the reformers' zeal. In the exuberance of this wholesale shriving of imperfection, an excessive elegance and formality enters his rhetoric, especially during his first official pronouncement as the Protector of this newly shriven commonwealth. The courtly audience might have shuddered to glimpse in this change Carew's ironic prophesy of the successful Puritan uprising to come. Momus's speech is heavy with the *we's* and *our's* of uneasy royalty. It also reeks with that presumption of election or desert which can become so characteristic a failing of the Puritan mind.[33] To be sure, Carew will cleverly turn Momus's mockery against him, by turning him at the peak of his power into an absolute Puritan, a simplistic Lenten caricature like Jonson's Plutus, just as excessive and just as vicious as those seven antimasques he and Mercury have just dismissed. The concluding decorous but festive revelry would suggest that restrained, sophisticated carnival impulses have reemerged for at least a few more hours of Shrovetide celebration before Lent begins. But that celebration still occurs within a frighteningly prophetic context. Momus's proclamation, "Given at our palace in Olympus the first day of the first month, in the first year of the Reformation" (1. 465), comes less than a decade before 1642. If the milennium is indeed this close, the king and queen, their court, and even the theater and this tradition of festival performances,

> Yea, all which it inherit, shall dissolve,
> And, like this insubstantial pageant faded,
> Leave not a rack behind.[34]

All are teetering on the brink of Cromwell's power.

This threat of Momus's severely Lenten vision clearly takes its toll on the masque's conclusion. Unlike *For the Honour of Wales,* Pleasure cannot be reconciled to Virtue, for Pleasure has been exorcised in the seventh and final antimasque. All that remains then is virtue. And so the final third of the masque celebrates as joyously as it can Wisdom, Purity, Truth, and Concord with music and with dancing, rarefied remnants of the carnival tradition. Momus, like Plutus, like Mercury, like Antonio in *The Merchant of Venice,* has to be virtually invisible during the revels for them to have any thematic integrity at all. Aesthetically, a decorous revelry of wisdom and virtue, a merry, musical truth, is rudely stapled to the antimasque of severely shriven, indecorous falsehoods. Evidently in the Shrovetide masques, carnival and Lent can seldom be better reconciled than that.

Of the two remaining Shrovetide masques, the last, *The Temple of Love,* seems only slightly more relevant to the festival than the plays we considered at the beginning of the chapter. The antimasque again presents an array of fleshly, carnival revellers and asses, such as: "debosht and quarreling men with a loose wench amongst them"; "amorous men and women in ridiculous habits"; "drunken Dutch skippers"; alchemists, "witches, usurers, and fools." On the other extreme, there is at least one excessively Lenten figure amongst these carnival fools. He is just as clearly branded a fool in his Puritan excesses: "a modern devil, a sworn enemy of poesy, music, and all ingenious arts, but a great friend to murmering, libelling, and all seeds of discord."[35] Again this obvious exposure of carnival and Lenten excesses leads us as close as we can come to the unspoken but implied value system of the Shrovetide masques.

Tempe Restored, the last Shrovetide masque we shall consider, may help us understand the Shrovetide dichotomy between pleasure and virtue, and its eventual harmony, in a slightly larger philosophic context. The masque opens with Circe having transformed a young man into a beast (a lion).[36] This familiar carnival emblem is followed by an antimasque of Circe's other beasts, "Indians, and Barbarians, who naturally are bestiall, and others which are voluntaries, and but halfe transformed into beastes" (p. 87). The antimasque's procession contains other, more traditional Shrovetide emblems of the flesh, of carnival, such as hogs, lions, apes, and asses. The masque, in contrast, depicts the harmonies of Heavenly Beauty, the Celestial Venus, imaged among the eternal spheres. Townshend's explication of his own allegory is especially useful to us: "In the young Gentleman, . . . Transformed into a Lyon, . . . is figured an incontinent man,. that striving with his affections, is at last by the power of reason perswaded to flye from these Sensuall desires, which had formerly corrupted his Judgement" (pp. 96–97). Here then, clearly, the "Battle of Carnival and Lent," beast and angel, body and soul, occurs in one man rather than a set of opposing emblems. His reason's striving with his affections is precisely the equation that Bruno's *Lo Spaccio* postulates for the deliverance of man from the Triumphant Beast.[37]

However, with a sophistication reminiscent of *For The Honour of Wales,* Circe is not categorically negative in this allegorical equation. As "desire in generall" she is "mixt of the Divine and Sensible, [and] hath divers effects, Leading some to Vertue, and others to Vice." Carnival and Lent can thus be miraculously joined; desire, like pleasure, can be directed to spiritual joy, if only it will yield to the governance of reason. Circe can "voluntarily deliver her golden rod to Minerva" (pp. 97–98). As the "Battle of Carnival and Lent" culminates during Shrovetide, Townshend rather self-consciously depicts the eventual harmony of this discord, with the familiar symbolism of Neoplatonism. He prays at the end "that Corporeall *Beauty,* consisting in simetry, colour, and certaine unexpressable Graces, shining in the Queens Majestie, may draw us to the contemplation of the *Beauty* of the soule, unto which it hath analogy" (p. 99). We could hardly conclude our considerations of these Shrovetide entertainments at a better place. With the lavish praise of his queen, Townshend, like Jonson earlier, has also offered a direct aesthetic defense of his masque and of all of the masques of this season. Each of them ends with a tangible immersion in the delights of the senses, a revelry, which is at the same time a dignified celebration of spiritual truth. This final dichotomy is much in the manner of the festival season itself.

In retrospect, what seems inescapable by now is that these occasional commissioned entertainments, the Shrovetide and Epiphany masques, are the dramatic works which most persistently and elaborately reflect the liturgical festival which they are intended to grace. A play like *The Merchant of Venice* might have been chosen to entertain a festival on two occasions because of several profound if coincidental moments of relevancy. Others might rather, like *Rollo* or *The Coxcomb,* have refracted certain festival associations simply because of the affective context of their production. But these masques were written for one performance before a select court audience on a specific festival day, and they were commissioned well in

Table 16

Correlations of Shrovetide Masques and Plays

Masques			
None	Slight	Moderate	Extensive
News From the New World (1620)		*The Masque of the Middle Temple* (1613) *The Masque of the Inner Temple* (1613) *Chloridia* (1631) *The Temple of Love* (1635)	*For the Honour of Wales* (1618) *Tempe Restored* (1632) *Coelum Britannicum* (1634)

Plays			
Salmacida Spolia (1640)	*Sapho and Phao* (1584)	*The Coxcomb* (1622) *Rollo; or The Bloody Brother* (1631)	*The Merchant of Venice* (1605) S *The Merchant of Venice* (1605) T

advance of that performance. There are also various aesthetic explanations for the affinities of masques and festivals. For one, the masque's unique allegorical framework and its strong thematic bias are both well-suited to such occasions. This is especially true of an evidently traditional Neoplatonic symbolism, which so readily embodies the mysteries of the Christian tradition. The evident formal influence of the festivals on their celebratory masques is just as impressive. Only one masque, *News From the New World,* seems totally unrelated to the festival.[38] The other seven Shrovetide masques exploit as a basic structural principle the dichotomous nature of the festival night.[39] Comus is opposed to Plutus; the drunken and lascivious gods to Momus. And then an equipoise is reached wherein carnival becomes restrained, Pleasure reconciled to Virtue, and Lent thoughtfully festive, after the example of a Daedalus. This final truce is seldom completely satisfactory. But the principle of dichotomy, this "Battle of Carnival and Lent," is plainly a central structural motif in most of these Shrovetide masques. Such elaborate parallels to the liturgical festival must attest to a well-established tradition of pertinent festival entertainment at court. It may even explain the genesis of this traditional antimasque-masque structure.

CHAPTER 7

Easter Monday & Tuesday

Because the Easter Monday and Tuesday performances begin so late in this tradition and include no commissioned masques, one would not expect impressive correlations. To be sure, the most self-consciously appropriate works, the Shrovetide and Epiphany masques, are all commissioned after 1605. But that period also sees the dramatic calendar filled with secular dates between Epiphany and Candlemas and expanded back through Advent to All Saints' and then Michaelmas. There is even the brief invasion of the somber chamber of Lent by dramatic performances in 1612. Surely, then, the Easter Monday and Tuesday performances represent at best the reluctant concessions of Charles's queen to religious propriety. If she could not have her joyous Lent, at least on the day after Easter her play-starved court could finally end its dramatic fasting. Even the liturgical focus of the two days would seem to support this assumption. For how often could the joys of the Resurrection and the fears of forfeiting its chief benefit—eternal life—be celebrated in secular drama? Surprisingly, almost all of the seven Eastertide plays are directly and extensively pertinent to these central liturgical foci, not only thematically and imagistically, but even in narrative terms. As a result, the tradition of apposite dramatic performances that we have traced through most of the church year is given new life in these last Easter plays and receives in them one of its most direct and extensive expressions.

Both Easter Monday and Easter Tuesday celebrate the Resurrection of Christ and its blessed effects, forgiveness of sins and eternal life to all who believe in him. None of the festival days has a more persistent thematic and narrative focus. The Lessons, the Collects, and the commentaries on these two holy days reiterate again and again these two inseparable motifs: we should celebrate this "climax and completion of the Gospel of redemption," and we should take care not to forfeit the benefits of eternal life. For its alternative is eternal damnation. As *The Prayer-Book Dictionary* suggests, the prescribed New Testament readings, Luke 24:1–48 and Matt. 28:1–9, "bring before us in direct narrative the simple statement of the reality of the Resurrection." The Proper Lessons (Exod. 16, 17; Acts 3; 2 Kings 13:14–21; Ezek. 37:1–14) give us type and prophecy of the Resurrection, extending from Christ to all God's people" (p. 298). Such familiar biblical narratives as Israel's deliverance from Egypt by the parting of the Red Sea, the manna in the wilderness, and Peter's miracle in Christ's name emphasize our miraculous deliverance from sure death or destruction. Likewise, the narratives of the opened and empty tomb, Christ's appearance to his disciples on the Road to Emmaus, and the reminder of the prophecy that "it behoved Christ to suffre, & to rise againe from the dead on the thirde day" (Luke 24:46) confirm the reality of this miracle and relate its preaching to all the world.[1] Especially beautiful is "the mysterious love-song of the Canticles in which Christ is spoken of as the lover of the soul, the Bridegroom of the Church," and compared to rebirth in spring.

The Collects for both days stress the fact and the benefits of Christ's Resurrection, but they also remind the parishioner not to forfeit those benefits:

Almighty God, whiche through thy only begotten sonne Jesus Christe, haste overcome deathe, and opened unto us, the gate of ever lastyng lyfe: wee humbly beseche thee, that as by thy speciall grace, preventyng us, thou dost put in our mindes good desires, so by thy continuall helpe we may bring the same to good effect. . . .

Almighty Father whiche hast geven thy onelye sonne to die for our sinnes, and to rise again for our justification, graunte us so to put away the leaven of malice, and wickednes, that we may alwaye serve the in pureness of lyvynge and trueth, through Jesus Christ our Lorde, Amen.[2]

Similarly, Robert Nelson's *Companion* stresses both the joy and the fear implicit in these post-Easter festivals. We celebrate them "that we might have the leisure to confirm our Faith in the grand Article of our Saviour's Resurrection, and to exert our devout Affections in all those happy Consequences that are deducible from it." At the same time these days "should make us exercise ourselves to keep Consciences void of Offence both to God and Man, that we may not forfeit that blessed Immortality of our whole man, Body and Soul, which our Blessed Saviour hath promised to all those that persevere in his Service to the end of their Days." For the bodies of the wicked "shall [also] be immortal, that they may be fitted for that eternal Punishment they have drawn upon themselves, wherein they will always suffer without consuming: *Depart ye cursed into everlasting fire.*"[3]

Of the seven recorded performances for Eastertide, six are so richly pertinent to one or both of the thematic foci of the

Table 17

Eastertide Performances

Date	Title	Authorities
1618	*Twelfth Night* (Monday)	Bentley, 7:26
1618	*The Winter's Tale* (Tuesday)	Bentley, 7:27
1634	*Bussy D'Ambois* (Monday)	Bentley, 7:92
1636	*Arviragus and Philicia,* part 1 (Monday)	Bentley, 7:102
1636	*Arviragus and Philicia,* part 2 (Tuesday)	Bentley, 7:102
1638	*Bussy D'Ambois* (Monday)	Bentley, 7:110
1638	*The Lost Lady* (Tuesday)	Bentley, 7:110

Source: Gerald Eades Bentley, *The Jacobean and Caroline Stage,* is my authority.

festival as to suggest conscious selection. So much correlation is unprecedented in the earlier plays and rather surprising this late in the tradition. For it seems to evidence a self-conscious resurgence of apposite performances just before the demise of the whole tradition. At the very least, the affective power of these plays on Easter Monday and Tuesday would have been almost inescapable, especially at the end of a hundred-and-thirty-year-old tradition of festival performances.

The Blessing of Resurrection: Eternal Life

The Winter's Tale is so immediately and joyously relevant to the Easter context of the benefits of Resurrection that few among the Easter Tuesday audience could have missed its appropriateness. Hermione has been assumed dead since act 3, scene 2, by the audience as well as Leontes, struck down by the injustice of her husband's distrust and the death of her son. With Leontes, the audience finds this judgment of the gods an almost unbearable punishment. But also with him, we are asked to believe and bear it.

The intervening scenes in Bohemia, full of dance and song, youth and love, festivity and timelessness, help to soften this blow for the audience. And time has also begun to heal Leontes' grief and guilt, to a degree. Indeed, Perdita's emergence into womanhood and her love for Florizel is even a kind of rebirth, literal, symbolic, and mythic, of Hermione, of love, of concord, and of the earth itself, in spring. As the Canticles said: "For winter is now past, the rain is over and gone; the flowers have appeared in our land, the time of pruning is come. The voice of the Turtle is heard in our land: The fig tree hath put forth her green figs" (*Holy Bible* [Douay Version], 2:11–13). But even the joy we share with Leontes upon Perdita's return to Sicily is tempered by our continuing memory of his guilt, his grief, and Hermione's death, sixteen years before. Her statue embodies that mixture by keeping her regrettable death, as well as her exemplary life, so vividly before us. What is required for complete happiness, then, is more than Perdita alone can effect.

It is the almost inconceivable miracle of Hermione's resurrection and restoration to Leontes, who has finally suffered penance enough for his lack of faith in her.

And then, the statue moves. Hermione lives again. Bohemia's eternal springtime and this miracle of romance thaw Leontes' long Sicilian winter. That moment, with Paulina's words and Leontes', may be the most magical in all of Shakespeare:

> *Paulina.*   Music! Awake her, strike!
> 'Tis time; descend; be stone no more; approach;
> Strike all that look upon with marvel. Come,
> I'll fill your grave up. Stir, nay, come away;
> Bequeath to death your numbness, for from him
> Dear life redeems you. . . .
>
>   [*Hermione comes down*]
> *Leontes.*   O, she's warm!
> If this be magic, let it be an art
> Lawful as eating.[4]

Hermione has been redeemed from death, taken from the grave, by the natural magic of Paulina's own contriving, Perdita's growing up, and Leontes' sincere repentance and devotion. Shakespeare has even deceived his audience so that we might share the joy of this miracle with Leontes. But the moment is no less magical for these reasons, nor does its miracle diminish even after we know that it is coming. It is still a "holy" moment, an art "lawful as eating." And the miracle it celebrates is clearly analogous to the Resurrection of our Lord. This is not to say that the moment is simply allegorical. Memories of Ceres and Proserpina are surely evoked simultaneously. And "allegory" seems far too stiff and abstract a description of this very human and very theatrical moment. But on Easter Tuesday at court in 1618, what courtier could have missed perceiving and enjoying this second redemption from the grave, this second rebirth of love and life and spring, this holy, magical moment of romance?

Arviragus and Philicia, a two-part play performed in tandem on Easter Monday and Tuesday 1636, is just as obviously pertinent to its festival occasion. Not only are there several moments

like the end of *The Winter's Tale* when the audience as well as
the characters are led to believe Arviragus killed, only to learn
the contrary later and with great joy; but in addition, the motif
of blood sacrifice, other similar suggestions of Easter and communion, and further associations with the role of Christ on
earth and in heaven permeate the play with extensive associative
power on this festival day.

The first speech of the king would have rung immediately
with general liturgical significance, not only on Easter Monday
but throughout the church year: "My sonne, be better temper'd, and yeeld as I did t'necessitie; what wise, or loving father
wood have sent his onely sonne into an Armie fill'd with discon-
tent, and mutinie, where thou wert liker t'become a sacrifice to
please their high swolne rage" (sig. A5). What father, indeed,
but God himself, who sent his "onely begotten sonne . . . , who
for us men, and for our salvacion came doune from heaven . . . ,
and was crucified also for us, under poncius Pilate. He suffered
and was buried, and the thyrde day he rose againe accordinge to
the Scriptures, and ascended into heaven."[5] This familiar passage from the Nicene Creed is still recited during each communion service in the Anglican church. It describes the "ful,
perfect and sufficient sacrifice, oblation, and satisfaction" of
Christ for all the mutinous children of God.[6] The Easter sacrifice of Christ's death and Resurrection is thus commemorated
(or reenacted) during every communion service. Such an association could have been readily evoked in the Renaissance
audience by the king's first words in *Arviragus*. It is ironic that
the king should be analogous to God, for his thoughts, actions,
and words are most ungodly. Later, in fact, the king becomes so
jealous of Arviragus's military victories in his behalf that he
plots his treacherous death. His only son, Guimantes, though
Arviragus's childhood friend, encourages the plot. Both are
thus grotesquely unlike the heavenly father and son suggested
by the early echo of the Nicene Creed. Such ironies would have
been intensified by the festival occasion.

Arviragus is slightly analogous to Christ in both parts of the
play. Denied his rightful dominion over the country of his
father, Cymbeline, by the same treacherous king and his son,

Arviragus resolves to the "restoring of my captiv'd country" (sig. B7). A glance at Easter hymns reveals how commonly this metaphor of the deliverance of captives is associated with Christ on Easter: "many captive souls set free"; "break the weary prisoner's chain"; "O great O very sacrifice / Thy captive people are set free." Donne's Holy Sonnet 10 contains the same figure. The speaker's "reason . . . is captiv'd, and proves weake or untrue"; he is "like an usurp't town."[7] Arviragus could thus have seemed analogous in words and action to this Christ who delivered captive humanity on Easter; so the evil King could have appeared God's opposite in his unwillingness to hazard the life of his only son. The festival performance improves the chance of such connections.

The exemplary hero soon parts from his beloved Philicia and defeats Guimantes in fair battle. Then he forgives and pardons his treacherous enemy. Act 4, however, ends with the captain's news of Arviragus's bloody death: "Arviragus . . . was beaten from his horse, and pearc'd thorow with so many wounds that scarce his body cou'd be knowne after th'victory. . . . The souldiers tore it piece-meale, in revenge of all their kindreds blood that had been spilt" (sig. D1ᵛ). Philicia swoons at this horrible news of his death and dismemberment, and we share her grief. But almost immediately Arviragus is "resurrected" for us. The message we shared with Philicia was all "a prettie policy th' King us'd to know the certainty, by that terrible description of Arviragus' death," of Philicia's love. In fact, Arviragus has won the battle and slaughtered the king's troops. The first part ends, then, with Arviragus living still and still victorious.

The first two acts of the second part are equally rich in touches of Easter significance. The initial ironic comparison of part 1—the treacherous Guimantes and the sacrificial Christ—is opposed in part 2 by a positive comparison to Christ's sacrifice. Arviragus's noble brother Guiderius dedicates himself to "sacrifice" and to "expiate" just before the coming battle: "No sooner did he see the Armie move, and heard it was to charge Prince *Arviragus*, but fetching a deepe sigh, and looking up to heaven, as asking counsell there, he straight resolved to sacrifice his life to expiate our fathers fate" (sig. E2). Arviragus later repeats the crucial communion words *sacrifice* and *satisfaction* in promising his share of this "greater love" that would "lay down his life for his friend." He promises to "satisfie for both," because "no sacrifice can be so proper for the Danes as *Arviragus*" (sig. E7). Christ's death was "one sacrifice for sinnes" (Heb. 10:12), a "ful, perfect and sufficient sacrifice, oblation, and satisfaction." He was the sacrificial *agnus dei,* the "Lambe of God, that takest away the synnes of the worlde" (p. 57). Christ's "expiation" or "satisfaction" for our sins through his sacrifice on the cross is the cause of the Easter celebration and the center of the Eucharistic celebration.[8] Of course, Guiderius inevitably falls short of Christ's supreme example. He would die to ransom their captive kingdom and to expiate their father's fate. But both his proffered "sacrifice" and his "expiation" or "satisfaction" suggest revenge more than forgiveness. In fact, their bloody executions throughout the play clearly distinguish Arviragus and Guiderius from Christ. Still, the motif of sacrifice is so self-consciously reiterated, both visually and verbally, that the festival audience could hardly have missed its obvious pertinency on Easter Monday or Tuesday.

Twice more the noble Arviragus is rumored dead (sigs. E3, E11^v), but twice more he is also miraculously delivered from the threatened sacrifice. As Cleanthus says, "How much the workings of the heavens exceed our apprehensions, that when we thought destruction neere, their providence had so prepared, to make the Battles losse, the meanes of greater happines" (sig. F2). How typically Christian a paradox this is, and how appropriate to Eastertide, especially after two ladies, Philicia and Artemia, have been again lamenting the apparent deaths of their Lord Arviragus. The workings of providence and love have indeed miraculously delivered Arviragus from death and brought temporary peace to Cymbeline's distressed kingdom.

As drama *Arviragus and Philicia* is not particularly exciting. It is stiff, self-conscious thematically and structurally, repetitive, and simplistic with plot and character. And it alternates between the chasms of excessive dullness and excessive melodrama.

But from the standpoint of this study, its frequent correspondences to the liturgical focus of Easter Monday and Tuesday are valuable beyond all measure of the play's intrinsic worth. For they vividly illustrate how appropriately a basically "secular" Renaissance play could grace its festival occasion.

The next Easter Monday play, *The Lost Lady,* is a much better work per se, a tragicomedy with a nice blend of high and low action. It is also just as pertinent as *Arviragus* to its festival. Lysiscles, the romantic hero, has distrusted his beloved Milesia's honesty, much like Leontes. Also like Shakespeare's character, he has seemingly lost her to a mysterious disappearance and death. Nightly visits to the tomb of Onone attempt to expiate for this distrust and to demonstrate his undying fidelity to Milesia's memory. We are forced to wait for three acts with Lysiscles for a promised dramatization of Milesia's resurrection (sig. G1) and tantalized with him during that wait by references to her as a Phoenix who will finally rise out of the ashes of her dishonor and death.

Act 4 brings Lysiscles again to the tomb, this time to witness the play's first wonder of resurrection. "Milesia riseth like a ghost." Listen to Lysiscles' response to the event:

> Ha, what Miracle,
> Are the gods pleas'd to worke to ease affliction?
> The *Phoenix* is created from her ashes,
> Pure as the flames that made 'em: still the same,
> The same *Milesia*!
>
> [4.1.15-19]

Heaven has added to her "beauty / By making it immortall." But of course sixteen years have not passed as they had for Hermione. Lysiscles, still too reasonable, though earlier he tried to dismiss his reason (4.1.3-8), suggests doubting Thomas, Christ's apostle, when he asks to touch the risen hand:

> Let it be lawfull for thy *Lysiscles*
> To touch thy sacred hand, and with it guide
> My wandering soul into that part of Heaven,
> Thy beauty does enlighten.
>
> [4.1.22-25]

We can hardly help remembering here the breathless last moment of *The Winter's Tale,* with Leontes also wanting to touch the apparition, and yet not quite sure. But this is still the fourth act of a Caroline tragicomedy; all can hardly be well yet, and it is not. For one thing, the resurrection is still only an illusion, a show. Milesia (or the Moore) vouchsafed Lysiscles "the miracle of my reassuming / A mortall shape" (4.1.28–29), but not herself. As a result, her loss and its cause, his distrust, become so unbearable to him that he pledges vengeance upon all those responsible for his unrest and her death, especially himself:

I will prosecute [my revenge] till I have made
All that were guilty of my losse of peace,
Wash their impiety in their guilty bloud.
All places where I meete them shall be Altars,
On which I'le sacrifice the Murtherers,
To appease the spirit of my injured Mistresse:
And the last Victim I will fall my selfe
Upon her sacred Tombe, to expiate
The crimes I have committed in deferring
Justice thus long.

[Pp. 40–41, end act 4]

Revenging instead of forgiving; washing impurities in their guilty blood instead of the guiltless blood of the Lamb; sacrificing murderers on altars instead of an innocent on the Cross; expiating guilt by committing the sin of suicide—all these are inversions of the sacramental truth of Christ's sacrifice on Easter Sunday and its commemoration during each Communion service. Lysiscles' unexpected and melodramatic violence thus has interesting if ironic festival associations.

He promises that his first victim will be the "curs'd Magitian," the Moore. She is also, of course, his own disguised Milesia. And when we see her at the beginning of act 5, poisoned and dying her second death, we know that Lysiscles has been as good as his word. Milesia, for a moment at least, does seem to die: "Helpe, helpe, She dyes" (5.1.97). To our relief, "She does but swoone" (1. 100). As they chafe her temples to revive her, the blackness of her make-up is removed, and Milesia

reappears to them all for the second time: "My *Lysiscles*, I am
by miracle preserv'd" (1.121). But then she swoons again and
seems again to die. Notice here especially the particularly relevant Easter images of lilies and the rising day:

Irene. Sure she is dead: how pale she is!

Lyls. No she is white as Lillies, as the Snow
That falls upon Parnassus; if the Red were here
As I have seen't enthron'd, the rising day
Would get new excellence by being compar'd to her.

[L1. 163–67]

She stirs again, but says, "And therefore dying." And then,
"Like Semele I die, who could not take / The full god in her
Arms" (ll. 181, 188–90). And then again she seems to die, and
Lysiscles, more understandably now after all of these deaths and
resurrections, again contemplates suicide (ll. 195–96). But now
she lives again. She is restored. And he is saved from that ultimate act of despair.

And then Milesia tells that story of her miraculous deliverance from death, all of the lovers are reunited, and Lysiscles can
deliver his joyous epilogue. Surely, as in Arviragus's repeated
"deaths," the motif of resurrection is too persistent in *The
Lost Lady* for anyone seriously to doubt its affective power on
Easter Tuesday. However bathetic the play's conclusion, its
pertinency to the festival occasion is unmistakable.

The correlation of *Twelfth Night* to its Easter Monday
occasion is more moderate than that of these other plays. In
act 5 Viola and Sebastian celebrate the miracle of their mutual
deliverance from death in terms that might have suggested the
analogous Easter mystery. She thinks Sebastian to be a spirit
returned from the grave, like Christ on the road to Emmaus:
"If spirits can assume both form and suit, / You come to fright
us" (5.1.227–28). His response, that he is a spirit incarnate, is
also subtly reminiscent of our Lord: "A spirit I am indeed, /
But am in that dimension grossly clad / Which from the womb I
did participate" (ll. 228–30). There is also a mysterious, supernatural two-in-oneness about them. Sebastian calls it a "deity
in my nature / Of here and everywhere" (5.1.219–20). The

duke, amazed, "One face, one voice, one habit, and two persons, / A natural perspective, that is and is not" (5.1.208-9). All this might lightly suggest mysteries connected with the Resurrection, if only in the Eastertide context of this one performance. That the miracle of their deliverance is finally but a natural one, a benevolent accident of time and chance, does not lessen its pertinency here any more than it does in *The Winter's Tale.* On the other hand, the play's underlying assumption of life after death (1.5.66; 1.2.3-4), the benefits of Christ's death and Resurrection, paradoxically diminishes the power of this apparent miracle in the play. In the pre-Christian setting of *The Winter's Tale* the absence of a similar consolation gives much greater power to the final miracle of Hermione's resurrection.

The Torment of Resurrection: Eternal Damnation

The inevitable corollary to the celebration of the benefits of Christ's Resurrection, the gifts of eternal life, is the warning not to forfeit those benefits. Collects for both days warn against polluting that immortal body with lust, excess, malice or wickedness, and against sacrificing the immortal soul to everlasting damnation. As Robert Nelson's *Companion* suggests, the bodies of the wicked "shall [also] be immortal, that they may be fitted for that eternal Punishment they have drawn upon themselves, wherein they will always suffer without consuming: *Depart ye cursed into everlasting fire.*"[9] *Bussy D'Ambois,* performed in two parts on Easter Monday and Tuesday late in the tradition, is persistently and directly evocative of the liturgical theme. So is a subplot in *Arviragus.*

This is not to suggest that critical responses to *Bussy D'Ambois* are settled; nothing could be farther from the truth. The play has been interpreted as a Christian morality play pure and simple, but also as an existential tragedy, post-Christian in its ultimate vision. However, critics of neither opinion seem comfortable with such extreme views. On the one hand Ennis Rees argues that Chapman is a Christian humanist, outspoken in his belief in the moral, ethical, Christian, and humanistic assumptions and doctrines that serve as a foundation of much Renaissance literature. *Bussy D'Ambois* must be understood in the light of all of this tradition, he argues, for in it Chapman tries "to present examples of greatly gifted men who fail to set down virtuous decrees within themselves with which they may order their passions." To Rees, Bussy and Tamyra both lack freedom of will not because they live in a deterministic or imbecile universe but because they lack self-control and that "virtuous self-mistrust [humility] which is the true mark of the truest merit." Together they break all bonds of "manhood, noblesse, and religion"; thus they deserve their consorting with devils and the torments of eternal life so richly predicted for them in act 4 regardless of the dignity and passion with which they end the play.[10]

Just as persuasively, but with Rees's equally healthy sense of uncertainty, Nicholas Brooke takes the opposite side of the issue. Placing the play dead center within the morality tradition of *Dr. Faustus* and *King Lear,* Brooke perceives with Rees the clear context of hell and damnation in the thematically crude but theatrically effective act 4, scene 2. However, he derives from it quite another understanding. To Brooke, it is the universe that is absurd and Bussy who is heroic:

> The cumulative effect of points like this, together with the oracular futility of the foreknowledge Behemoth *does* provide, gives the scene a central place as an image of necessity: the devil's foreknowledge makes man's will anything but free, while the devil's own impotence makes his foreknowledge ridiculous. Monsieur and Co., plotting in a vision seen by the enemies that cannot touch them, have the diminutive absurdity of puppets.[11]

In fact, though "his body, mind, and soul have not fulfilled their apparent worth," sparks of Bussy's great humanity can transcend the abyss of creation. Bussy thus dies a noble, existential death, as a heroic man facing a meaningless universe.

Two other recent discussions of the play assume with considerable justice that the ambivalence of these responses suggests a dramatic vision that is flawed, one that can evoke and sustain both extreme responses, but that does nothing aesthetically to exploit or resolve that polarity. Robert Ornstein, for example, leans toward Brooke's position of a universe of diminished values and shadowed truths when he says: "From first tragedy to last [Chapman] dramatized a personal quest for values in an age when it no longer seemed possible to assent to established political, religious, and moral dogmas."[12] Yet this one play is severely flawed. Bussy is extremely heroic but he is also extremely immoral. And his roles as exemplar of vice and virtue are never adequately reconciled within the play. As a result, "one cannot imagine that Chapman was oblivious to the moral ambiguities which surround Bussy, Tamyra, and the Friar. For in the last act, he trembles on the edge of condemning all three and of turning his play into a moralistic exemplum of the wages of sin."[13]

This interpretive discussion reveals even in its diversity the pertinency of the Easter Monday occasion to a Renaissance court performance of *Bussy D'Ambois.* Even modern responses to the play's moral and structural confusion acknowledge that the play frequently reverberates with the Eastertide alternatives of salvation and damnation, the achievement of eternal reward or its equally eternal forfeiture. One wonders, however, how readily Charles's court would have affirmed an imbecile universe just hours after celebrating the Easter Monday Eucharist.

Another of the Easter Monday plays we have already considered, *Arviragus,* may also have a subplot with some relevancy to the threat of damnation contained in the liturgical message. Adrastus, the murderer of Arviragus's father Cymbeline, thus invokes the worldly blessings of the powers of darkness: "Guide me infernall powers, and let me be / Powerful on earth, this for eternity" (sig. E5). He seems as naïve as Bussy in his assumption that they will be kind and that he will be timeless. After consorting with various witches and devils, Adrastus watches the horrible death of a similarly self-deceived witch. Incredibly, he remains self-deceived: "By her death I reape a greater benefit, then what I came for, the knowledge of my end, no creature now can say, I kild the king, vanish all idle feare: since I had power to kill the Witch, I will contemne all danger" (sig. E9^v). So speak the damned, from Macbeth, to Bussy and Tamyra, to

Adrastus. In the dramatic tradition in England their hubris of foreknowledge, eternal life on earth, ceaseless power, and self-determination always produces an ironic forfeiture of the true freedoms of peace on earth and life after death. Adrastus's immediate arrest by two soldiers is vivid proof of his temporal naïveté, and a vivid reminder of the eternal imprisonment of his immortal soul. On Easter Monday and Tuesday these would have been powerful reflections of the other side of the Easter message of eternal life.

Although Easter Monday and Tuesday performances begin very late in this dramatic tradition, they are consistently among the most frequently and intensely pertinent festival plays. Even counting *Arviragus,* parts 1 and 2, and *Bussy D'Ambois* as two each, there are still only seven recorded performances. Of them, the correlation in six cases is so extensive that we can assume probable and extensive affective power. Even the seventh, *Twelfth Night,* had some chance to elicit festival associations. *The Winter's Tale, Arviragus,* parts 1 and 2, and *The Lost Lady* contain frequent and intense motifs of resurrection, miraculous

Table 18

Correlations of Eastertide Plays

None	Slight	Moderate	Extensive
		Twelfth Night (1618)M	*The Winter's Tale* (1618)T
			Bussy D'Ambois (1634)M
			Arviragus (1636)M
			Arviragus (1636)T
			Bussy D'Ambois (1638)M
			The Lost Lady (1638)T

deliverance from death, standing for sacrifice, and Holy Communion. *Bussy D'Ambois,* parts 1 and 2, and *Arviragus* portray characters who blindly and tragically forfeit those same benefits for the ephemeral joys of earthly bliss. In none of the other festivals have the plays, with their secular genesis, shown such extensive correlation to the spirit, the theme, the action, and the imagery of their liturgical occasion. While the tradition is faltering in quantity during its last two decades, with the commissioned masques and these Eastertide plays it is qualitatively still far from dead.

CHAPTER 8

Michaelmas, Hallowmas, & Saint Bartholomew's

The few recorded Michaelmas and Hallowmas performances and two more festival namesakes, Jonson's *Bartholomew Fair* and Middleton's *Michaelmas Terme,* form a minor but not irrelevant conclusion to this investigation. Deservedly last because of their late position in the church year, their absence during the first century of this dramatic tradition, and their relative paucity of plays, these days still have frequently and sometimes richly apposite performances. John Milton's *Comus* is one of the very few of these works to have been discussed before in the light of its liturgical occasion. For that reason, and because it is not performed at court but at Ludlow Castle, it is neither treated extensively here nor counted as a festival performance. But it is included for its obvious place in the entire tradition. Middleton's *Michaelmas Terme* is included because its title, like its Induction, invites our careful comparison to the festival. Two other plays were performed at court on Michaelmas, and four were recorded on Hallowmas; Jonson's comedy has the suggestive Saint Bartholomew's title. As has been so often true of the plays performed earlier in the church year and earlier in the tradition, the courtier's perception of these last plays could often have been affected by their festival context.

Michaelmas

We have only three Michaelmas performances, all of them during the 1630s. Sir William Davenant's *Unfortunate Lovers*

Table 19

Michaelmas Performances

Dates	Titles	Authorities
	Michaelmas Terme	A festival namesake
1630	*The Inconstant Lady*	Bentley, 7:74
1634	*Comus* (Ludlow Castle)	Bentley, 7:94
1638	*The Unfortunate Lovers*	Bentley, 7:111

Source: Gerald Eades Bentley, *The Jacobean and Caroline Stage*, is my authority.

and Arthur Wilson's *Inconstant Lady* were performed at court; Milton's *Comus* was written especially for its Michaelmas performance at Ludlow Castle. There is a fourth richly if irreverently appropriate festival namesake, *Michaelmas Terme*. Of the four, the masque and Middleton's play, with their common genetic relationship to the festival, predictably show the most pronounced affinity to it. But all four works could have had affective power on Michaelmas night.

As the Collect for Michaelmas suggests, this festival celebrates the order of the angels and their services to men: "Everlastynge God, whiche haste ordeined, and constituted the services of all Aungelles, and men, in a wondreful order: mercifully graunte that they whiche alway do the service in heaven, may by thy appoinctmente succour and defende us in earth, through Jesus Christe oure Lorde. . . ."[1] Such prescribed biblical readings as Genesis 32 (the angel wrestling with Jacob), Daniel 10 (his vision of the Archangel Michael), Acts 12 (Peter rescued from prison by an angel), and Revelation 14 (the angel-reapers) illustrate this angelic agency on earth.[2] Because their order and service is one manifestation of God's love for man, associated festival themes include catalogues in Ecclesiastes 39 of all of the blessings of the earth for the good man, and all of the curses for the wicked. Ecclesiastes 44 similarly praises certain holy men, including Enoch, Noah, Abraham, Isaac, and Jacob, who, through their goodness, enjoyed this great bounty. But also prominent among the biblical passages is the description from Rev. 12:7-12, of the war in heaven:

> 7 And there was a battel in heaven. Michael & his Angels foght against the dragon . . . & his Angels.
>
> 9 And the great dragon, that olde serpent, called the devil and Satan, was cast out, which deceiveth all the worlde. . . .
>
> 12 Wo to the inhabitants of the earth, and of the sea: for the devil is come downe unto you which hath great wrath, knowing that he hath but a short time.[3]

A second theme thus joins the celebration of the guardian angels and related blessings of the good man. For while these fallen angels would remind the Renaissance congregation of their allies in heaven, Michael and his company, they would also warn them of their hellish enemies and remind them to abjure the tempting impurities of this life in order to enjoy the angelic company in the next. As the Geneva marginal gloss suggests, the passage, "Wo to the inhabitants of the earth," refers specifically not to all men, but rather to the worldly, "them that are given to the worlde and fleshlie lustes." Thus a biblical passage associated with Milton's *Paradise Lost* has equally interesting affinities with his *Comus*.

From Matt. 18:1-10, another of the prescribed passages, and a very familiar one, we hear this stern warning to those who would undermine this heavenly ministration of the angels by perverting innocents:

> 4 Whosoever therefore shal humble himself as this litle childe, the same is ye greatest in the kingdome of heaven.
>
> 6 But whosoever shal offende one of these litle ones which beleve in me, it were better for him, that a mylstone were hanged about his necke, and that he were drowned in the depths of the sea.

Thus clearly are the battle lines drawn. Woe to the offender, and greater woe to the perverter of innocents.[4] We shall see the operation of each of these themes in the Michaelmas plays.

Milton's *Comus* is not a court masque, but its place in the tradition may warrant its inclusion at the end of this discussion. For of all the masques written to adorn a particular festival, it is among the most directly celebratory of its central liturgical patterns. Both in its benevolent governance by an attendant spirit who suggests a guardian angel and in its opposition of worldly excess and humble innocence, the masque is virtually a liturgical pageant. Its close relationship to its festival occasion suggests that Milton is self-consciously following a dramatic tradition that has by 1630 subtly graced court performances for one hundred twenty years.

"The attendant Spirit" of the published version of 1637 was much more suggestive of a guardian angel in the Michaelmas script. For in the 1634 manuscript he was called "a Guardian Spirit, or Daemon."[5] And though as in Jonson's Epiphany masques the heaven of *Comus* is Jove's and not Jehovah's, there is little question of the Christian heritage when the Spirit describes "all the company of heaven" in his opening speech:

> Before the starrie threshold of Joves Court
> My mansion is, where those immortall shapes
> Of bright aëreall Spirits live insphear'd.
>
> [L1. 8-10]

His role is also closely analogous to that of the angels: he protects such innocents as those who wander through "this dim spot / Which men call Earth" (ll. 11-12), particularly when they reach the "drear wood, / The nodding horror of whose shadie brows / Threats the forlorne and wandring Passinger" (ll. 44-46). For

> . . . here their tender age might suffer perill
> But that by quick command from Soveraigne Jove
> I was dispatcht for their defence, and guard.
>
> [L1. 47-49]

The adversary of these innocents is Comus, son of Circe, the enchanter of these woods of the world who causes so many men "To roule with pleasure in a sensuall stie" (1. 84). The cosmic stage is thus set. Innocents will now have to wander between earth and heaven, flesh and spirit, angel and beast, with only right reason and their attendant spirit to guide them aright.

In much the manner of the analogous Shrovetide masques, to which the structure and technique of *Comus* are so clearly indebted, the appearance of the Spirit is then followed by the antimasque of Comus and his transformed beasts. The unique vitality of his trochaic tetrameters announces a forbidden but attractive lewdness. Following his unchaste revelry, Comus senses a virgin's approach: "some chaste footing neere about this ground" (1. 160). We can almost feel his anxiety to lead another innocent into depravity. And we can clearly see how appropriate to its Michaelmas occasion his characterization could have appeared.

The Ladie then appears alone and afraid. But she is also secure in her Michaelmas faith in the potency of God and his angels to defend the pure. Of her momentary fear she says,

That he, the Supreme good, t'whom all things ill
Are but as slavish officers of vengeance
Would send a glistring Guardian if need were
To keepe my life, and honour unassail'd.

[L1. 232-35]

We have already met him and are assured of his ready succor and defense, in liturgy and masque alike.

So perfectly suited are these opening lines to Michaelmas and so central to the masque's action and meaning that we may observe here the clearest example of a masque "well fitted" to its holy day. Milton, of all writers, would have understood such significance and would probably have exploited it just this uncompromisingly. Thus writer, mode, and holy day all come together most obviously at Ludlow Castle on Michaelmas, 1634.

Similar parallels continue unabated throughout the rest of the masque. The last six lines rearticulate the festival's central liturgical message of the ministration of guardian angels to virtuous mortals: "Or if virtue feeble were / Heaven itself would stoop to her" (ll. 1073-74). In fact, Michaelmas so persistently influences the imagery, actions, and themes of *Comus* that further exemplification would be redundant. Recent criticism uniquely confirms this influence. James Taaffe argues that *Comus* may be considered a "translation" of the Michaelmas traditions of order and disorder into the ceremony of the masque as Milton conceived of it. . . . *Comus* is a ritualistic evocation or celebration of the recognition in Everyman of the need for self-government and guidance from above; it is also a topical and occasional entertainment deeply rooted in the traditions of the Michaelmas holiday.[6]

William B. Hunter, Jr. argues that the Michaelmas Collect and most of the prescribed biblical readings must have figured into Milton's creation of the masque and the audience's response to it. Among specific parallels he cites the passage in 1 Corinthians 13 on faith, hope, and charity and the Lady's first prayer; the cosmic struggle between Saint Michael and the forces of evil; the passage in Matthew 18 forbidding the temptation of children; and the prayers in Psalms 140 and 141 for deliverance from wicked men and the vain desires of the world.[7] Hunter concludes that Milton used these liturgical materials, "Knowing in advance that his actors and audience would all have them so recently in mind that they would immediately recognize them and appreciate the way in which the author had embellished them" (p. 15). Although more overt, this is precisely the kind of relationship we have demonstrated to exist between many of the commissioned masques and the festivals they were designed to grace at court in the Renaissance.

Unlike *Comus,* Davenant's *Unfortunate Lovers* was not written for Michaelmas but for public performance at Blackfriars. Also unlike Milton's masque, its affective power on Michaelmas does not celebrate the festival. Indeed, the performance tragically depicts the absence of attendant spirits and the destructive power of the wicked. Early in the play the defamed innocent Arthiopa naïvely compares her deliverer Altophil to a guardian angel, "lately come from Heaven"; then she tells him, "The angels if they had but leisure to / Descend would testify I am betray'd."[8] But the angels will not have such leisure in this late Caroline tragedy. Poor Arthiopa is desired and imprisoned again, by both the wicked prince of Verona and the barbarian Heildebrand. Once more freed, this time by the courageous Amaranta, Arthiopa is nevertheless finally defiled by the ruthless Heildebrand, who has also ravished Amaranta for her

attempted charity to his victim. Altophil's bitter response to
Amaranta's ravishment and suicide would have had particular
poignancy on Michaelmas night: "Where are our better angels
at such times as these?" (end act 4). As Altophil avenges both
innocents, his own disgusted charges ring with righteous fury:

> Look on the ruins you
> Have made of such a building! cherubims
> Would strive to dwell in it, but that they knew
> They then must dispossess a soul as good
> As they.

[P. 80]

But the Michaelmas audience is again reminded in these words
that even against this monstrous an enemy, the guardian angels
did not intervene. Bullinger, in a sermon "of good and evil
spirits," proclaims to his Renaissance congregation that the
angels worship God, love and spread the truth, watch for our
safety, and revenge the mischievous: "Moreover, they take upon
them the charge and defense of us, God so commanding: they
are our keepers, ready at hand watching over us that no adversity happen unto us, and do guide our ways."[9] Where were they
when Heildebrand ravished Amaranta and Arthiopa? The question gains immense power on the play's liturgical occasion.

The autobiography of Arthur Wilson, the author of *The
Inconstant Lady,* reveals that Michaelmas was a particularly
ominous day for him, especially when he was near the water.
His life was once threatened by a rough Michaelmas storm
during a channel crossing. One of his maids nearly drowned on
another Michaelmas occasion. And then an unruly horse carried
him into a pond on yet another Michaelmas.[10] The irony of
these incidents of ill fortune on this particular day was probably so obvious to Wilson's audience that he never has to spell
out the joke for them. The affective presence of Michaelmas in
The Inconstant Lady would have been similarly light; it is none-
theless visible for that. Quite simply, Cloris, Emilia's virtuous
sister, is often called a guardian angel by her lovers Aramant and
the duke. Cloris describes herself to the forsaken hero Aramant
as "a spirit / The genius of that love once dwelling in thee"
(p. 41). When he awakens from a charmed sleep he thinks he

has seen an angel indeed: "Sawe you no woman heere? . . . Why then it was an angell" (p. 46). The duke, Aramant's powerful rival, obviously agrees with him: "Me-thinks shee looks / Like a caelestiall figure, that hath borrowed / Mortallitie, to mock the world withall" (p. 54). Finally, Aramant finds her in prison, and exults,

> 'Tis faire Cloris!
> My angell guardian! How shall I appeare
> Before you, madame, to expresse a mind
> Thankful for all your mercies?
>
> [P. 77]

Cloris is thus persistently the romantic angel of the play. The connection, to be sure, never transcends insipid conventionality. But it would have had obvious resonance on the feast of all the angels.

The title of Middleton's *Michaelmas Terme* invites us to include it in our study, as it could have invited many Renaissance readers and viewers to consider its appropriateness to the festival season. Even more inviting, Michaelmas term and "the other three terms" are actors in the play, though not as central as Candlemas was in *The Inner Temple Masque*. But most inviting of all, Michaelmas Term himself promises us pertinency at the end of his Induction: "Why we call this play by such a dear and changeable title, *Michaelmas Term*, know it consents happily to our purpose, though perhaps faintly to the interpretation of many."[11] In looking for these happy if faint ways the play "consents" to the festival as well as the term of Michaelmas, we are even warned against assuming that the legal quarrels that permeate the play are the only parallels. We are also warned against going too far when the Induction ends, "*Sat sapienti*: I hope there's no fools i'th'house" (p. 218). Like Portia's leaden casket, "This rather threatenest than dost promise aught." But after Middleton's promise here and after the felicitous comic relevance of his Candlemas masque to the whole church year, we "must give and hazard all."[12] At the worst, what will be vented to the world for our ill-advised attempt but our own folly?

There are certainly enough echoes of the secular side of

Michaelmas term. As the editor A. H. Bullen tells us, the setting of the first scene, "the middle aisle of Paul's," was the place "where servants out of employment came to find masters" (p. 219 n). As mentioned earlier, Michaelmas term was the traditional time for such hirings and for the signing of contracts, the trying of lawsuits, the letting of chambers, and of course the harvesting and selling of crops.[13] Such suits and the inevitable haggling about fees that accompanies contracts of all sorts are mentioned by Michaelmas Term and the other three Terms in the Induction (pp. 215–18 passim). And as we go through the play we find a joke about a lawyer who died of too long a vacation before Michaelmas and who always wished for a fifth term to enhance his business opportunities (pp. 219–20). We hear of bills for chambers needing to be let (p. 255). We hear puns about lawsuits: "I would sue for your name, sir. / Your suit shall end in one term, sir" (p. 237). We are, in fact deluged with such pertinences and impertinences: "all my rent till next quarter" (p. 239); "you know 'tis term time, and Michaelmas Term too, this drapers' harvest for foot-cloths, riding-suits, walking-suits, chambers-gowns, and hall-gowns" (2.3.210–13). The fields do not provide the only harvest of the fall. Time is also ripe during Michaelmas term for drapers and for the well-suited lawyers who can afford to buy their suits and gowns.

But the play "consents happily" to liturgical purposes as well, "though perhaps faintly to the interpretation of many." On a term named for the feast of Saint Michael and all the angels, some of the gambling jargon in act 2, for example, could have been amusingly appropriate:

> *Lethe.* Tut, the dice are ours;
>   Then wonder not at those that have most powers.
> *Rearage.* The devil and his angels!
> *Lethe.* Are these they?
>   Welcome, dear angels! Where you're curs'd ne'er stay.
>   [2.1.58–61]

The pertinency is irreverent, to be sure. So is much of this cynical, worldly city comedy. But irreverence does not reduce affective pertinency; if anything, it increases it. Continuing this offbeat liturgical humor, Shortyard and Falselight, the dishonest cohorts of Quomodo the larcenous woolen draper, are called in the dramatis personae and throughout the play "his attendants; familiar spirits." Bullen's footnote at least touches the Michaelmas joke intended here: "Though Shortyard and Falselight are several times throughout the play termed 'spirits,' they exercise no supernatural power, and are knaves of the ordinary type" (p. 214). Is their quite ordinary knavery the point of another liturgical joke? Whenever these limited villains are called Quomodo's "disguised spirits" (or "excellent, excellent sweet spirits" [4.1.63]), we may be invited to remember, however fleetingly, the Feast of all the Angels that lies behind the title of the play.

A final ironic suggestion of the liturgical occasion occurs at the end of act 4. To test the fidelity of his son and wife, who both detest him, Quomodo plays dead. The son curses his niggardly and treacherous memory; the wife immediately plays him false with Easy, one of the gentlemen he has cheated. The couple have evidently hoped for this moment for a long time, and they take immediate advantage of it by getting married:

> *Thomasine.* Delay not now; you've understood my love,
> I've a priest ready; this is the fittest season.
> No eye offends us: let this kiss
> Restore thee to more wealth, me to more bliss.
> [L1. 78-81]

Their miraculous deliverance from this evil man suggests indeed that this is the fittest season, for contracts or for heavenly intervention. Easy encourages such an association when he replies: "The angels have provided for me" (4.4.82). Preposterous, of course. But if this allusion to the liturgical tradition behind Michaelmas is sly and even a little cynical, it is also clear enough. Its placement at the very end of act 4 accentuates the parallel. Then in the final act Quomodo really undoes himself: he carelessly signs away his property as well as his wife. We can hardly attribute this destruction of the villain to the company of angels, of course. They hover over the play only as bad puns and clever jokes. But innocence still prevails in the end, with the help of some hard-nosed shrewdness on the part of Easy and Thomasine and some overreaching by Quomodo. The Induction's promise is thus fulfilled with a feather touch. The play "consents happily" to the festival's secular and liturgical currents; however, it does so "faintly" as well, thus keeping Middleton's warning before us: *"Sat sapienti*: I hope there's no fools i'th'house."

Table 20

Correlations of Michaelmas Performances

None	Slight	Moderate	Extensive
		The Inconstant Lady (1630)	*The Unfortunate Lovers* (1638) *Michaelmas Terme* (namesake)

Table 21

Hallowmas Performances

Dates	Titles	Authorities
1604	*Othello*	Chambers, 4:119
1611	*The Tempest*	Chambers, 4:125
1614	*Bartholomew Fair*	Chambers, 4:130
1623	*The Maid of the Mill*	Bentley, 7:49

Source: E. K. Chambers, *The Elizabethan Stage,* and Gerald Eades Bentley, *The Jacobean and Caroline Stage,* are my authorities.

Hallowmas

Hallowmas (1 November) is All Saints' Day. Like Easter Monday and Tuesday and Michaelmas, it is without recorded dramatic performances before the seventeenth century. Like them also, it lies outside the Christmas season. It is hardly surprising, then, that the parallels between the four All Saints' plays and their liturgical festival are less impressive than most of the others we have considered. What may be more surprising is their evidencing of as much relevancy as they do. For two of the four, both by Shakespeare, could almost certainly have seemed appropriate to All Saints'. And both of the others might have.

The thrust of the Hallowmas liturgical festival concerns the righteousness and the persecution of the saints and martyrs of the church, and the rewards they can expect after their deaths. It also urges all Christian souls to follow the examples of these saints, anticipating the same rewards. The Collect for the day sufficiently summarizes these interests: "Almighty God, . . . graunt us grace so to folowe thy holy sainctes in all vertues and Godly living, that we may come to those inspeakable joyes which thou haste prepared for them that unfainedly love the. . . ."[14] The persistent theme of persecuted blessedness also characterizes the prescribed Gospel for the day, the Beatitudes (Matt. 5:1-12). It is shared by the prescribed Epistle, Heb. 11:33-12:6, giving us the clearest and the simplest of all these liturgical contexts.

Othello bears the most attractive similarities to the festival. The day's theme of martyrs and persecuted blessedness is quickly suggested by Desdemona's suffering for her blessedness' sake at the hands of an Othello who is himself ironically motivated by a strong though perverted sense of righteousness. Desdemona's whiteness of dress and skin, symbolizing her purity, even find their coincidental counterpart in the imagery of two prescribed readings from Revelation.

The first, Revelation 19, describes the righteousness of the saints in terms of clean white linen and white horses. The second, Rev. 7:2-12, also images the servants of God in white robes. The Lessons from Wisdom further these associations. Wisdom 3 is also reminiscent of Desdemona when it urges that a saint, however horribly she dies, goes to her reward. Wisd. 5: 1–14 suggests Othello, one of those who misjudged righteousness and must be punished for it. The whole concept of reward and punishment after death for the righteous and their persecutors is also shared by the festival and the play. Hugh Latimer's paraphrase of the Beatitudes in a Hallowmas sermon in 1562 further suggests how clearly Desdemona's tragic fate could have appeared fitting during an All Saints' performance: " 'Blessed be they that suffer persecution for righteousness' sake, for theirs is the kingdom of heaven.' Whosoever suffereth any thing for any manner of righteousness' sake, blessed is he. Blessed are ye when men speak ill of you. . . . Be merry, because your reward is great in Heaven."[15]

The same Hallowmas sermon by Latimer also suggests how the festival audience might have understood Iago's relationship to Othello and Desdemona as a painful negative *exemplum* of another of these same Beatitudes, "Blessed be the peacemakers":

> But I tell you, this law is not kept: for there be a great number of those which speak fair with their tongues, as though they would creep into a man's bosom, but behind his back, or before other men, they betray him; they lie upon him, and do all they can to bring him out of estimation. These whisperers be peace-breakers, and not peace-makers; for the devil bringeth his matters to pass through such fellows. [1:485]

Iago tells Roderigo in a direct definition of his villainy in the first scene:

> I follow him to serve my turn upon him.
> We cannot all be masters, nor all masters
> Cannot be truly followed. . . .
>   Others there are
> Who, trimm'd in forms and visages of duty,
> Keep yet their hearts attending on themselves;
> And, throwing but shows of service on their lords,
> Do well thrive by them. . . .
> And such a one do I profess myself.

> [1.1.42–55 passim]

Here, for once, Iago is honest, though he is about to break the peace of Brabantio's night. Latimer has described him perfectly in his Hallowmas sermon. To illustrate such peacebreakers, Latimer goes on to describe one Doeg Idumeus, who betrayed the priest's kindness to David by whispering of it to Saul. Saul's resultant jealousy caused all of the priests and their wives to be immediately slain. As *Doeg* and *Iago* are a fascinating pair of names in this context, so their parallel roles suggest an interesting connection to the festival.[16] It must be said, however, that while Desdemona's relationship to the festival is both central and obvious, Iago's remains peripheral. Without Latimer's Hallowmas sermon, one would never have thought of his role in terms of this festival.

In *The Tempest* both Prospero and Miranda seem to combine characteristics which are described in Matt. 5:1-12, the Beatitudes. The courtly audience could have perceived that they share humility, mourning, meekness, righteousness, purity of heart, peacemaking, and persecution with the blessed as they are described by Christ. Further, the regenerative action of *The Tempest,* directed by Prospero's forgiving love, is glossed by Heb. 12:6 as well as the homiletic commonplace which derives from it: "Whome the Lord loveth he chasteneth." The meek are indeed blessed, says Latimer in that same Hallomas sermon. Private vengeance is wrong.

> But there is a public vengeance, that is, the magistrates': they must see that wrong-doers be punished, and rewarded according to their misbehaviours. . . . They that have the Spirit of God, and to whom these blessings pertain, they will be charitable [to their debtors] and yet use the law when necessity shall require so; but they will do it with a godly mind. [1:481-82]

Of course the merciful are blessed with the meek, so this same administrator of public vengeance should be merciful both in admonishing sin and in forgiving it.

> There is a ghostly mercy, which is to admonish them that be in errors, to bring them to the right way. Item, to forgive them that do me wrong, this is a mercy, and a needful mercy. . . . Magistrates ought to punish sin and wickedness; but private men one ought to show mercy

unto another: that is, he ought to forgive when any man hath done him harm, and so he shall have mercy at God's hand. [1:484–85]

The Hallowmas audience could have perceived that Prospero ideally exemplifies both the private and the public dimensions of these commandments of the blessed as he deals with Caliban's depraved troop and Alonso's with justice and mercy.

Just as fitting to Ferdinand and Miranda but also to Othello and Desdemona is Wright's comment that Hallowmas was a "favorite time for testing the fidelity of lovers." *The Tempest* can refract that tradition romantically, and *Othello* tragically. We all know as well that on the mystic evening of the last day of October, Allhallow Eve, it was an ancient belief that supernatural influences prevailed, and spirits, visible and invisible, revisited the scenes of their earthly existence. Omens, spells, and all sorts of mystical practices were and still are therefore associated with the season of All Saints'.[17] They are certainly abundant too on Prospero's magical island. In this elaborate context of liturgical and sociological associations, *The Tempest* evidences a complex relationship to the festival.

The other two plays have only a peripheral relationship to the festival day. *The Maid of the Mill* celebrates Florimel's whiteness and innocence, and her trial by Otrante proves her righteousness and redeems him into following it. In *Bartholomew Fair* Zeal-of-the-Land-Busy clearly thinks himself one of the saints and believes himself persecuted for righteousness' sake, as in the Beatitudes. Like Othello's, however, his is a false righteousness; its comic punishment by Saturnalian agents causes his repentance, his humility, and his inclusion in the fellowship of folly that concludes the play. In each of the four plays, then, connections are present; in the first two instances, they are fairly extensive.

Bartholomew Fair and Saint Bartholomew's Day

Its similarity to the name of another religious festival, Saint Bartholomew's Day, suggests that Bartholomew Fair might also manifest some connection to its festival namesake. Much like

Table 22

Correlations of Hallowmas Performances

None	Slight	Moderate	Extensive
	Bartholomew Fair (1614)		*Othello* (1604)
	The Maid of the Mill (1623)		*The Tempest* (1611)

Hallowmas, in which context the play was once performed, Saint Bartholomew's Day celebrates the proper spirit of discipleship. In fact, it promises through the prescribed Collect, Epistle (Acts 5:12–16), and Lesson (Gen. 28:10–17) that true prophets will prosper and false ones die: "Graunte, wee beseche the, unto thy church, both to love that he beleved, and to preache that he taughte, throughe Christe oure Lorde."[18] This Collect is supported by Acts 5, in which the hypocrites Ananias and Sapphira are exposed and shunned ("why hathe Satan filled thine heart, that thou shuldest lie" [v. 3]), while the true apostles of Christ flourish in His truth: "the nombre of them that beleved in the Lord, bothe of men & women, grewe more and more" (v. 14). Instructions to parish priests in *Speculum Sacerdotale* intensify the connection between Saint Bartholomew's and the unmasking of false disciples: "St. Bartholomew reveals the Devil masking as a palmer at a great feast by questioning him about heaven and hell."[19] Finally, the Lesson, describing Jacob's true vision of the ladder of God's kingdom, again celebrates true prophets like Saint Bartholomew. The fair at Smithfield which Jonson depicts also commemorated this very liturgical tradition, in fact, by hosting theological disputations each year.[20]

Surely Jonson parodies this tradition in one of the most important moments of his play, when the puppets humiliate

Zeal by exploding his false theology of righteousness. However, Zeal, "confuted" by the puppets, gains from that humiliation not the punishment we normally expect of Jonsonian comedy but freedom from the narrow-minded bondage of his former self and inclusion both in the audience of the puppet show and in the final festivity. As he says, "I am changed, and will become a beholder with you."[21] The self-righteousness of Justice Overdo is likewise dealt its eventual share of edifying humiliation. But as with Zeal, his awareness of personal imperfection is a paradoxical blessing. It unites him with the society of flawed men, which is for one of the few times in Jonson also the society of all men. As a result of this new vision, neither Overdo nor Zeal is finally separated for satiric abuse; instead, Overdo invites all of the comic community to share his home and his hospitality in a festive conclusion to the play. Moral indignation and the exclusion of the flawed are thus replaced in this late Jonsonian comedy by forgiveness and communion, after the compassionate manner of Shakespearean comedy. As several recent critics have suggested, this "compassionate satire" is more Christian than classical, Anglican rather than Puritan in tone, a manifestation of the New Law rather than the Old. It therefore seems hardly gratuitous to impute this uncharacteristically compassionate festivity, at least in part, to some of the liturgical traditions which stand behind the play. Whether those traditions filtered their way into *Bartholomew Fair* through the fair or the liturgical celebration, false prophets experience an exposure and a regeneration that is both strenuous and profound, when understood within the play's liturgical context.[22]

After the intense and frequent correlations of the Easter Monday and Tuesday plays, the Shrovetide works, and some of the masques and plays for Candlemas and Epiphany, the works for these other festivals inevitably suffer in comparison. Still, these last three festivals, like the first four we considered together, seem to have attracted their share of pertinent plays. Excluding *Comus,* all eight works show some correlation; six either a moderate or an extensive correlation; four, half of them, extensive correlation. As we have observed before, such liturgical parallels are only one interesting dimension of these complex plays, and sometimes a minor dimension at that. But at the end of the tradition, such appropriateness is not unimpressive.

CHAPTER 9

Conclusion

We have known since the work of Chambers and Bentley that when dramatic performances entertained the English court from 1510 through 1640, they were very likely to occur on one of ten festivals of the English church year.[1] During Elizabeth's reign 88 percent of all recorded court performances (289 of 328), an average of all but one per year, occurred on one of the seven holy days between Christmas and Ash Wednesday. Even during the Jacobean and Caroline periods with their increased love of plays and masques at court, one-third of all court performances still occurred on these same predictable holy days, with periods, like 1621–25, of greater correlation. During the entire period of 1510 to 1640 when the dramatic tradition seems to have been in operation, 70 percent of all recorded court performances took place on these ten festival days. This represents an impressive quantitative correlation of almost 400 festival performances out of over 560 total performances at court.

The Renaissance court audience would, then, certainly have expected dramatic performances to occur on these repeated festival days of the English church year. Prompted by such knowledge, the present study has investigated the degree to which this same audience might have seen in these court performances thematic, narrative, and imagistic facets of their recurrent festival occasions. It has discovered frequent and extensive correlations between the plays and masques and the holy days on which they were performed. In fact, the self-conscious appropriateness of many of the commissioned masques gives strong support to the probability that the Renaissance court audience would have expected such apposite performances, and therefore looked for parallels. The frequent liturgical motifs in plays with festival titles strengthens this probability still further. So do the resonances that are demonstrable in a large majority of the plays of secular genesis, especially when they are viewed through the powerful affective context of their liturgical occasions. The inference that even these plays were sometimes selected for this appropriateness is reinforced by its frequency and intensity, as well as the testimony of Griffin Higgs and *The Stage Acquitted*. Having looked at the most interesting individual works in some detail, it remains for us to conclude with a summary and interpretation of the quantitative and qualitative dimensions of this whole tradition.

Of course, the tradition's most impressive evidence has already been presented. Its demonstration depends not on final statistics but on the cumulative weight of evidence in the many appropriate masques for Epiphany and Shrovetide, masques like *Coelum Britannicum* and *Pleasure Reconciled to Virtue*; Middleton's *Inner Temple Masque* about the whole tradition; the festival namesakes like *Twelfth Night*; the Eastertide plays; and the especially apposite festival plays of Shakespeare, Jonson, Lyly, and Beaumont and Fletcher. Such impressively appropriate works would also have shaped, to a greater or lesser degree, the occasion on which all of the others were performed. But because we have looked almost exclusively at individual plays and individual festivals, some concrete sense of the overall shape of this tradition might also prove interesting, especially if its nature and purpose are not misunderstood.

So complex a tradition of appropriate festival performances will obviously elude any precise statistical analysis and such an analysis is not intended here. The figures which follow are offered only as another way of understanding the larger patterns of this dramatic tradition, not as its final proof. Because they inevitably reflect a numerical translation of this author's own value judgments, the figures are subject to some modification, both up and down. Further, since there are almost as many shades of correlation as there are festival works, such distinctions as slight, moderate, and extensive correlation can only roughly approximate the differences in the amount and quality of a work's affinities to its occasion. The counting of plays is also imprecise. When a play is recorded as performed twice, it is counted twice in the statistics. But the second Innocents' performance of *The Comedy of Errors* and the second Candlemas performance of *Twelfth Night* are not counted because they did not occur at court. Neither is Milton's *Comus,* however pertinent it is to the tradition. When a play is named after a festival it is counted only once, though that counting also underestimates its weight in the whole tradition. What follows, then, is a rough attempt to fairly quantify the amount and the degree of correlation between these three festival namesakes and ninety-three performances and the liturgical character of the ten holy days with which they are connected.

Though these figures cannot reflect the variety and intensity of the correlations we have been discussing and though they are admittedly imprecise, they do attest, rather impressively, to the tendency of Renaissance drama to be consonant with its festival occasions at court. For the period 1585–1642, during which we have extant plays and a tradition of court performances on festival days, around 80 percent of the plays performed on liturgical festivals demonstrate at least "slight correlation" to their festival occasion. Close to 70 percent of all of these recorded plays show at least "moderate correlation," pertinencies to the festival that the court audience would probably have noticed. And almost 40 percent show "extensive correlation," parallels so central, so frequent, or so intense that they would almost certainly have been perceived on their liturgical night. This means that a hypothetical if unlikely courtier who attended all of these festival performances during this fifty-year period would probably have noticed that plays were apposite to festivals in seven performances out of ten and could have noticed parallels even more often. He could hardly have missed correlations in four performances out of ten.

When we consider only the commissioned masques and *The Shepheard's Paradise,* the three plays with festivals in their titles, and the five plays performed twice on the same festival,

Table 23

Summary of Correlations

Festival Day	At Least Slight Correlation	At Least Moderate Correlation	Extensive Correlation
St. Stephen's	8 of 9	8 of 9	3 of 9
St. John's	4 of 8	2 of 8	2 of 8
Innocents'	2 of 3	1 of 3	1 of 3
New Year's			
Masques	2 of 2	2 of 2	1 of 2
Plays	12 of 14	9 of 14	4 of 14
Total	14 of 16	11 of 16	5 of 16
Epiphany			
Masques	11 of 15	11 of 15	7 of 15
Plays	8 of 8	5 of 8	2 of 8
Total	19 of 23	16 of 23	9 of 23
Candlemas			
Masques	3 of 3	3 of 3	2 of 3
Plays	4 of 5	3 of 5	1 of 5
Total	7 of 8	6 of 8	3 of 8
Shrovetide			
Masques	7 of 8	7 of 8	3 of 8
Plays	5 of 6	4 of 6	2 of 6
Total	12 of 14	11 of 14	5 of 14
Eastertide	7 of 7	7 of 7	6 of 7
Michaelmas			
Plays	3 of 3	3 of 3	2 of 3
St. Bartholomew's	1 of 1	1 of 1	0 of 1
Hallowmas	4 of 4	2 of 4	2 of 4
Totals and Percentages	81 of 96 (84%)	68 of 96 (71%)	38 of 96 (40%)

including *Twelfth Night* and *The Comedy of Errors,* these correlations become much too impressive to be purely coincidental. Over half of them contain such extensive liturgical parallels that almost no one could have missed them. And well over 80 percent, almost all of them, demonstrate at least a moderate correlation to their festival, parallels that the court audience could probably have perceived. Such works appear, then, to have been written with the festival firmly in mind. This conclusion is reinforced by our knowledge that most of the masques were designed to be performed only this one time. Surely the Renaissance courtier would have been aware of a tradition of such scope, spanning over fifty years of Elizabethan, Jacobean, and Caroline court performances. That awareness would have made him all the more likely to have noticed, to have expected and sought, just the kinds of correlation we have recently found. In fact, with the medieval and early Renaissance proclivity for finding correspondences among most areas of human experience, and the Renaissance courtiers' proximity to the explicitly allegorical and moral drama of the sixteenth century, he would probably, like the author of *The Stage Acquitted,* have noticed and enjoyed parallels that we have missed completely. He would certainly have been unhampered by our hermeneutical scruples and our distance from the freshness and the frequency of his exposure to the Anglican liturgy.

Analyzed another way, these correlations can suggest the affinities of particular authors to this tradition. Table 24 tries to make some sense of the quantity and quality of correlation each dramatist's plays have evidenced. The most important facts are the number of times an author's plays are chosen for festival performance and the degree of correlation they evidence.

Some clear patterns emerge immediately from this analysis. The works of Shakespeare, Jonson, and Beaumont and Fletcher dominate these festival performances to an extraordinary degree. This is in part an index of their continuing popularity throughout the Jacobean and Caroline periods. But it might also attest to an unusual affinity between certain of their works and the liturgical currents of Renaissance England. For their works, especially Shakespeare's plays and Jonson's masques, are not

Table 24

Correlation by Authors

Author and Number of Performances	At Least Slight Correlation	At Least Moderate Correlation	Extensive Correlation
Jonson (24)	19 of 24	18 of 24	12 of 24
Shakespeare (14)	14 of 14	12 of 14	10 of 14
Beaumont and Fletcher (18)	16 of 18	11 of 18	1 of 18
Lyly (6)	6 of 6	4 of 6	0 of 6
Davenant (5)	2 of 5	2 of 5	0 of 5
Middleton (5)	5 of 5	5 of 5	3 of 5
Chapman (4)	4 of 4	4 of 4	3 of 4
Cooke (3)	3 of 3	1 of 3	0 of 3
Dekker (2)	1 of 2	1 of 2	1 of 2
Townshend (2)	2 of 2	2 of 2	1 of 2
Brome (1)	None		
Carew (1)	1 of 1	1 of 1	1 of 1
Carlell (1)	None		
Massinger (1)	None		
Mountague (1)	1 of 1	1 of 1	1 of 1
Webster (1)	1 of 1	1 of 1	1 of 1
Wilson (1)	1 of 1	1 of 1	1 of 1
Anon (6)	5 of 6	4 of 6	3 of 6

only more numerous than the others; they are also far more intensely appropriate. Jonson's works entertain these ten liturgical festivals twenty-four times, one-fourth of all the recorded performances. Twelve of these performances, half, are quite fitting. Eighteen, or three-fourths, would probably have appeared pertinent to his court audience. On the other hand, five of his works show no correlation at all. And most of the extensively apposite works are the specially commissioned masques, which we would expect to grace their festivals with some kind of pertinency. The courtiers would seldom have been embarrassed by the explicitness of the liturgical refractions of Jonson's masques. But they could hardly have remained oblivious to most of them. In fact the festival occasion may have played some role in making these Jonson masques less satiric and realistic, more optimistic and celebratory, than his normal dramatic works.

Shakespeare shows extensive correlations in ten of the fourteen plays. This correlation would increase to thirteen of seventeen if we included the three other known festival performances of *King Lear, The Comedy of Errors,* and *Twelfth Night.* In contrast to Jonson, none of Shakespeare's plays show no correlation to their festival occasion, though two are only slightly pertinent. When we remember that only one or two of Shakespeare's plays have any demonstrable genetic relationship to their festival occasion, their uniquely intense appropriateness is all the more impressive. The affinities are also usually more obvious and more profound than in the other dramatists. Shakespeare's repeated motifs of humility, good will, forgiveness of enemies, patient bearing of adversity, exemplary virgins, selfless sacrifice, benevolent edification out of self-love, the celebration of universal folly, the "morality of indulgence," and miraculous "resurrections" are also repeated motifs of these liturgical festivals and of the Christian consciousness. This intense and natural correlation of his plays to their festival occasions suggests that the Christian patterns recent critics have begun to attribute to Shakespeare's works were probably even more readily discernible to his contemporaries than they are to us today. Their festival context would have reinforced them.

With Beaumont and Fletcher the case is somewhat different. Numerically their works rank with Shakespeare's and Jonson's in this tradition. But in the intensity of relationship, the qualitative factor, they are not in the same class at all. Only one of their plays, *The Island Princess,* evidences extensive correlation to its festival, and that just barely. Eleven of the eighteen, however, evidence at least a moderate, readily discernible aptness.

Almost all evidence some correlation. Several factors seem to account for their differences from Jonson and Shakespeare. For one thing, Beaumont and Fletcher were not writing the commissioned masques like Jonson, the form where he demonstrates most of his extensive pertinency. For another, unlike Shakespeare, to whom a variety of Christian images and motifs seem quite characteristic, Beaumont and Fletcher seem to evidence these patterns of forgiveness, humiliation, virginity, providential deliverance, and the like rather as borrowings than as inherent qualities of their works. They seem copied from the successful master Shakespeare rather than generated from within. This superficiality, paradoxically, would account for a rather obvious if superficial affinity to these festivals. Because they occur so overtly and so self-consciously in many of the works, the parallels should have been immediately perceived by the Renaissance audience. They might well have led to the frequent choice of these plays as appropriate liturgical fare. But the sauce had little meat with it.

These four writers account for almost 60 percent of all the recorded performances. Such a high percentage of court performances is undoubtedly an index to their popularity at court and their connections with either the King's Men or the court masques. It might also persuade us that the works were not just coincidentally apposite to their occasions, but often were either selected because of special pertinency or commissioned to produce it. Lyly, more modestly, belongs in the same company. Only six performances of his plays grace these festivals. But all of them show correlation, and two-thirds evidence enough probably to have been recognized. His tonal affinities with Shakespeare's romantic comedies are evidently parallelled by shared thematic and imagistic affinities with this liturgical tradition. Perhaps we need to reassess the interrelationship of all these dramatists.

Leeds Barroll and Glynn Wickham have recently suggested one direction such a study might take. The licensing power of the Master of Revels and the formation of court companies like the Lord Chamberlain's and the King's Men near the start of this tradition might well have influenced, in their opinion, the style and content of popular drama.[2] Muriel Bradbrook made a similar observation about Shakespeare years ago:

> Many of Shakespeare's plays were of course given at Court before Elizabeth and James; and the playwright would probably have to reckon beforehand on the possibility of his play being given in a Court setting, for the players received short notice of a command performance, and usually gave an item from their repertory.[3]

The pressure of such a social tradition must have influenced Renaissance drama in many ways. One influence must be the observed affinities between the plays produced by the court company and the religious festivals on which they were still regularly performed well into the seventeenth century.

The only other writers with any important quantitative place in this tradition are Middleton and Chapman from early in the century, and Davenant near the end. Each has a unique relationship. Chapman, with only four recorded performances, has three intensely pertinent ones. One is a commissioned Shrovetide masque. The other three are sternly moralistic plays, two performances of *Bussy D'Ambois* and one of *All Fools*. They are so morally and tonally perfect for Eastertide and New Year's, respectively, as to suggest again conscious selection. This would be especially likely given the ancient age of *Bussy* when it is twice chosen for an Eastertide performance.

Middleton's works are equally apposite, but in somewhat different ways. His plays' characteristically ironic and worldly tone would be out of place on many of these festivals. In fact, of his two performed plays, one, like Jonson's *Alchemist* and Chapman's *All Fools,* adorns the festival of mortification to which it is almost solely pertinent, New Year's. But the play called *Michaelmas Terme* has rich and frequent affinities with the liturgical and sociological currents of Michaelmas, even though they are also irreverent affinities. Similarly, his one commissioned masque, *The Inner Temple Masque*, is about the whole festival tradition, if also in ironic ways. Oddly, it is Middleton's amused irreverence toward this whole tradition that makes his place in it so important.

If Middleton is uniquely irreverent, Davenant is uniquely irrelevant. For of his recorded works, only two have even a moderate correlation to their festivals, and one of those is characterized by ironic glances at the angels. Evidently Davenant's vogue as a Caroline playwright accounts for his rather frequent appearance late in the tradition, for his five plays are seldom appropriate to their festival occasions. In contrast, one masque each by Thomas Carew and John Milton, *Coelum Britannicum* and *Comus,* should illustrate to anyone's satisfaction that such a tradition of pertinent performances had been in existence for many decades and that it was still in operation in the 1630s. Both are clearly written for their respective Shrovetide and Michaelmas occasions. And both are repeatedly, intensely, and self-consciously redolent of those occasions. In commissioned works like these two and Jonson's, authors whose other works are seldom selected for festival performance due to thematic or generic irrelevancy, we sense the impressive influence of the whole tradition.

One could also consider the writers who are conspicuously absent, the fellows of Davenant and Middleton whose works may share too few of the pervasive liturgical motifs and too little of their spirit ever to have been chosen to grace them. The brooding chaos of Webster, the "inherently evil" world order of Tourneur, the "tumultuous confusion of thought and passion" of Marston, the microscopic focus of Ford, the uneasy skepticism of Greville are incongruent with the spirit of these liturgical festivals, and with their conventional Christian world view. That incongruity must partially explain the absence of their plays from this tradition. Chapman still presents with many Elizabethan dramatists a positive testimony to the "universe of the spirit." These other writers are usually united in negative testimony or obliviousness to that universe.[4] Wickham has discussed these two conflicting visions in Renaissance drama in his *Early English Stages.*

> What we are really confronted with is a conflict between an emblematic theater—literally a theater which aimed at achieving dramatic illusion by figurative representation—and a theater of realistic illusion—literally a theater seeking to simulate actuality in terms of images . . . , an

emblematic theater concerned with man's relation to God and society, [and] a theater striving to imitate actuality within the more limited terms of reference permitted by images of fashionable conversation and backgrounds of painted perspectives. [2.1.155]

It is probably not coincidental that the only Webster play with an "older," less dismal vision, *The Duchess of Malfi*, is the one represented among the festival plays at court. Similarly, what Brian Gibbons has called the "Jacobean City Comedy" of Jonson and Middleton appears just occasionally at court on these liturgical occasions, and then usually on the festivals of mortification, like New Year's. Only in their masques especially commissioned for these occasions do Jonson's or Middleton's works reflect some of the more conventional liturgical outlines. And even those are usually ironic reflections in Middleton, and fairly subtle ones in Jonson, refracted through the prism of Neoplatonism. Marston, the third of Gibbons's writers, is again totally absent from the liturgical calendar. If the unusual pertinency of the plays we have analyzed to their respective liturgical occasions suggests the likelihood of their conscious selection, then the omissions of these writers would argue a similar likelihood. Had the visions of their plays not seemed so inimical to the liturgical occasions, these popular playwrights would have made more festival appearances at court.

There should remain little reasonable doubt at this point of a fully developed tradition of apposite dramatic entertainment at court on selected festival days of the English church year. But as impressive as the quantity and quality of correlation already appears to be, there is still more of the tradition remaining to be pieced together. Momus suggests in *Coelum Britannicum* that there was an Epiphany and/or a Shrovetide masque or play every year. Our total of thirty-seven plays and masques for the two festivals confirms the richness of this tradition, but it also illustrates how few of the actual performances we know. The same is probably true of performances on the other festival days. Even as these gaps begin to fill in, we will still have those sixty lost plays from the sixteenth century, most of them coming at what could be a crescendo of the early tradition. But in the unlikely event that those lost plays are found,

and in the much likelier event that other dates of festival performance surface, the findings presented should be supported
by them.

As is often true of a study of this kind, several new research
opportunities have emerged that might be pursued. The most
obvious is an examination of the plays performed seasonally at
Oxford and Cambridge.[5] The "Battle of Carnival and Lent" as
an aesthetic, liturgical, and sociological motif in the Renaissance
may also deserve a book-length study.[6] One would probably
find a wealth of doctrinal commentary, paintings, and sculp-
tures other than Brueghel's, plays other than those mentioned
here, and other literary treatments. The mystery cycles might
also be reviewed in the light of this study. Do their portrayals
of some of the liturgical traditions herein discussed contribute
insights into both medieval and Renaissance drama? And is
their suppression by Anglican authorities and the simultaneous
rise of this tradition more than a chronological coincidence? In
a related vein, might not continental court drama of the Reformation evidence a similar tradition? The likelihood would seem
to warrant at least an exploratory investigation by someone
equipped to handle Renaissance Italian, German, and French
drama. R. G. Hunter has already suggested some connections
of this sort between earlier French drama and the English
"comedy of forgiveness" in the Renaissance.[7] The persistent
appropriateness of plays by Lyly, Chapman, Shakespeare, and
Beaumont and Fletcher to this festival tradition suggests affinities between all four canons that might also deserve further
study. Are all four dramatists part of a coherent school of
Renaissance comedy? Are they related more simply by their
responsibilities to the court audience? And is that relationship
definable in a major way by its unobtrusive but persistent
absorption and reflection of the liturgical tradition? Finally,
there might well follow demonstrations of other correlations
that this study has missed completely, after the lead of *The
Stage Acquitted*. Each of these topics could cast additional light
on the tradition of pertinent festival performances that the
present study has attempted to establish and analyze.

Appendix A

Primary Material Concerning the Festival Day

The following catalogue contains biblical and liturgical references pertinent to a study of each festival day. Most of these readings are either contained in or prescribed by *The Prayer Book of Queen Elizabeth 1559,* a standard sixteenth-century *Book of Common Prayer* with a few special devotions for Her Majesty. The few other sources for the supplementary biblical passages are mentioned in context. Page numbers in parentheses refer to *The Prayer Book.*

1. Saint Stephen's Day, 26 December
   Lessons: Prov. 28, Eccles. 4, Acts 6 and 7 (p. 25), Isa. 56
        (p. 40)
   Epistle: Acts 7:55–end (p. 62)
   Gospel: Matt. 23:34–end (p. 63)
   Collect: "to learne to love our enemies . . ." (p. 62)
2. Saint John's Day, 27 December
   Lessons: Eccles. 5 and 6, Rev. 1 and 22 (p. 25), Isa. 59
        (p. 40)
   Epistle: 1 John 1 (p. 63)
   Gospel: John 21:15–end (p. 63)
   Collect: "attaine to thy everlasting gyftes . . ." (p. 63)
3. Holy Innocents' Day, 28 December
   Lessons: Jer. 31, Wisd. 1 (Apocrypha) (p. 25), Isa. 60
        (p. 40) (Bar. 4:21–30: *The Prayer-Book Diction-*
        ary)

Epistle: Rev. 14:1-5 (p. 63)

Gospel: Matt. 2:13-18 (p. 63)

Collect: "the yonge Innocentes" have "shewed furthe" thy "praise" in "diyng" (p. 63)

4. New Year's Day, 1 January

Lessons: Gen. 17, Deut. 10, Rom. 2, Col. 2 (p. 25)

Epistle: Rom. 4:8-14 (p. 64)

Gospel: Luke 2:15-21 (p. 64)

Collect: "beyng mortified from al worldly and carnall lustes . . ." (p. 64)

5. Twelfth Day, Epiphany, 6 January

Lessons: Isa. 49 and 60 (p. 25)

Epistle: Eph. 3:1-12 (p. 64)

Gospel: Matt. 2:1-12 (p. 64)

Collect: "God . . . by the leadynge of a starre, diddest manifest . . ." (p. 64)

Sermons: Andrewes, *Ninety-Six Sermons,* 5:54 ff.

6. Candlemas, "Purification of ye virgin Mary," 2 February

Lessons: Wisd. 9 and 12 (p. 25)

Epistle: Col. 3:12-17 (pp. 86, 66)

Gospel: Luke 2:22-27 (p. 86)

Collect: "We may be presented unto the with pure and clean mindes" (p. 86)

Sermons: Donne, *Sermons of John Donne,* 3:379; 7:325-26; 10:65

7. Shrovetide, Quinquagesima, Sunday, Monday, and Tuesday before Lent

Lessons: Gen. 9 and 12 (p. 24); Gen. 13 (*The Prayer-Book Dictionary,* p. 749)

Epistle: 1 Cor. 13 (p. 67)

Gospel: Luke 18:31-43 (p. 67)

Collect: "powre in our hartes that moste excellent gift of charitie . . ." (p. 67)

Sermons: Numerous sermons by Donne and Andrewes were apparently preached during Shrovetide and Lent. See esp. *Sermons of John Donne,* 2:348; 7:73

8. Eastertide, the Monday and Tuesday after Easter
   Lessons: Exod. 16, 17, 20, 32; Matt. 28; Luke 24; Acts 3;
        1 Cor. 15 (p. 25)
   Epistle: Acts 10:34–43; Acts 13:26–41 (p. 72)
   Gospel: Luke 24:13–48 (pp. 72–73)
   Collect: "opened unto us, the gate of everlastyng lyfe"
        (p. 72)
9. Saint Bartholomew's Day, 24 August
   Lessons: Eccles. 25 and 29 (p. 25)
   Epistle: Acts 5:12–16 (p. 89)
   Gospel: Luke 22:24–30 (p. 89)
   Collect: "truely to beleve, and to preache thy woorde . . ."
        (p. 89)
10. Michaelmas, 29 September
    Lessons: Eccles. 39, 44 (p. 26)
    Epistle: Rev. 12:7–12 (p. 90)
    Gospel: Matt. 18:1–10 (p. 90)
    Collect: "graunt that they which alway do the service in
        heaven, may . . . defende us in earth" (p. 90)
11. All Saints' Day, Hallowmas, 1 November
    Lessons: Wisd. 3 and 5; Heb. 11 and 12; Rev. 19 (p. 26)
    Epistle: Rev. 7:2–12 (p. 91)
    Gospel: Matt. 5:1–12 (p. 91)
    Collect: "to folowe thy holy saintes in all vertues and God-
        ly living . . ." (p. 91)

Appendix B

Wedding Masques

Five wedding masques designed for festival performance are clearly written simply to celebrate court marriages and bear little resemblance to the festival day. Because of their obvious topicality and a close relationship to another liturgical tradition, they are excluded from the final statistics but included here for completeness.

1607. Epiphany. *Maske . . . Lord Hayes.* Chambers, 4:122
1608. Shrovetide. *The Haddington Masque.* Chambers, 4:123
1613. Shrovetide. *The Lord's Mask.* Chambers, 4:127
1613. Saint Stephen's. *A Wedding Mask.* Chambers, 4:128
1614. Epiphany. *The Mask of Flowers.* Chambers, 4:129

Notes

CHAPTER 1

1. E. K. Chambers, *The Elizabethan Stage,* vol. 4; Gerald Eades Bentley, *The Jacobean and Caroline Stage,* vol 7.
2. C. L. Barber has related Elizabethan social customs and festivals to Renaissance drama in *Shakespeare's Festive Comedy*; O. B. Hardison has studied *Christian Rite and Christian Drama in the Middle Ages.*
3. Chambers, *The Elizabethan Stage,* 1:159.
4. Chambers, *The Elizabethan Stage,* vol. 4, records the titles and dates of most of these lost plays. For the few lost plays after 1616, see Bentley, *The Jacobean and Caroline Stage,* 7:41, 46, 50, 77.
5. Chambers, *The Elizabethan Stage,* 1:21. Alvin Thaler, "The Players at Court, 1564-1642," *Journal of English and Germanic Philology,* 19 (1920):33, records an average of seventeen plays a year at James's court, twenty-six at Charles's. Three-fourths are by the King's Men.
6. Ten counts the three Shrovetide days and the two Easter days as one festival apiece, on the basis of their liturgical similarity. Easter, Michaelmas, and All Saints' Day are added during the Jacobean period as the court calendar expands.
7. See V. A. Kolve, *The Play Called Corpus Christi,* pp. 42-50.
8. Horton Davies, *Worship and Theology in England,* pp. 219-20.
9. Ibid., pp. 213-14.
10. Richard Hooker, *Ecclesiastical Polity,* 5:69-72; Robert Nelson, *A Companion for the Festivals and Fasts,* chaps. 10, 12.
11. See Lancelot Andrewes, *Ninety-Six Sermons,* 3:164; Hooker, *Ecclesiastical Polity,* 2:349-51.
12. Dorothy Gladys Spicer, *Yearbook of English Festivals,* p. 136; A. R. Wright, *British Calendar Customs,* 3:80, 88. The four terms were Easter term, after Easter; Trinity term, after Trinity Sunday; Michaelmas term, after September 29; and Hilary term, after Christmas (see *The Prayer-Book of Queen Elizabeth 1559,* p. 27). Davies, *Worship and Theology,* p. 211, reminds us that this was the standard and universal

Renaissance *Book of Common Prayer* until 1660. John E. Booty's fine
new edition appeared too late for me to use, though I have consulted it.

13. See Kolve, *The Play Called Corpus Christi*, chap. 4, "Principles
of Selection."

14. Spicer, *Yearbook of English Festivals*, pp. 181-83; "Feast of the
Holy Innocents," *Encyclopaedia Britannica Macropaedia*, 5:98.

15. Spicer, *Yearbook of English Festivals*, p. 20; Ethel Urlin, *Festivals, Holy Days, and Saints' Days*, p. 15; Leslie Hotson, *The First Night of Twelfth Night*, pp. 174-75, 190.

16. See Barber, *Shakespeare's Festive Comedy*, pp. 3-35. Mikhail
Bakhtin, *Rabelais and His World*, pp. 5-9; Stephen Batman, *The Golden Booke of the Leaden Goddes*, sig. 10^V-11; and Robert Nelson, *A Companion for the Festivals and Fasts*, p. 11.

17. *Vox Graculi*, p. 55.

18. Enid Welsford, *The Court Masque*, p. 151.

19. Griffin Higgs, *The Christmas Prince*, p. 46; subsequent references
are cited in the text.

20. *The Stage Acquitted*; subsequent references are cited in the text.

21. *Mr. William Prynn His Defense of Stage-Plays* (London, 1649),
p. 6; Richard Baker, *Theatrum redivivum, or The Theatre Vindicated 1662*, intro. Peter Davidson (New York: Johnson Reprints, 1972), pp. 1, 11-12, 36, 127-34; John Dennis, *The Usefulness of the Stage to Religion, and to Government* (London: Richard Parker, 1698), pp. 114-18.

22. Appendix A provides a catalogue by festival day of such pertinent
primary material, including its source when relevant.

23. Nelson's *Companion* has reached a nineteenth edition by 1748,
only forty-four years after the first edition.

24. Robert G. Hunter suggested this useful distinction to me.

CHAPTER 2

1. Robert Nelson, *A Companion for the Festivals and Fasts*, pp.
63-69, passim; subsequent references to this work are cited in the text.

2. *The Prayer-Book of Queen Elizabeth 1559*, pp. 25, 40, and 62.
See Appendix A for a full list of prescribed biblical readings. See also *The Prayer-Book Dictionary*, p. 341.

3. Matt. 7:1-2, in *The Geneva Bible*; subsequent biblical quotations
will cite Lloyd E. Berry's facsimile of the 1560 edition.

4. Donne, *The Sermons of John Donne*, 8:185-87; subsequent references to Donne's sermons are cited in the text. See also Latimer, *The Works of Hugh Latimer*, 1:388.

5. This often reiterated commonplace can be found in *Certaine Sermons or Homilies,* pp. 44-45; subsequent references are cited in the text.

6. Robert G. Hunter discusses this motif thoroughly in *Shakespeare and the Comedy of Forgiveness.*

7. Beaumont and Fletcher, *The Works of Francis Beaumont and John Fletcher,* 8:161; subsequent references to this collection are cited in the text.

8. Webster, *The Complete Works of John Webster,* 2:18; subsequent references to this collection are cited in the text.

9. *Arviragus and Philicia,* sig. E6-E7.

10. *The Prayer-Book,* pp. 25, 40, 63; see Appendix A for a full list. See also *The Prayer-Book Dictionary,* p. 341.

11. Ridley, *The Works of Nicholas Ridley,* p. 340.

12. Whitgift, *The Works of John Whitgift,* 3:584-85.

13. Alvin Kernan, ed., *Volpone,* p. 1; subsequent references are cited in the text.

14. Dekker, *The Dramatic Works of Thomas Dekker,* 1:120-23, 128-30, 135-36, 144-45, 166-67, 174-75, 190-91, 196-97; subsequent references to this collection are cited in the text.

15. *Gesta Grayorum,* ed. W. W. Greg, pp. 14-23, contains this account; subsequent references are cited in the text.

16. R. A. Foakes, ed., *The Comedy of Errors* (London: Methuen, 1962), p. xxxvi; Sidney Thomas, "The Date of *The Comedy of Errors,*" *Shakespeare Quarterly* 7 (1956): 380; James G. McManaway, "Recent Studies in Shakespeare's Chronology," *Shakespeare Survey,* 3 (1950): 24; John Dover Wilson and Arthur Quiller-Couch, eds., *The Comedy of Errors,* 2d ed. (Cambridge: Oxford University Press, 1962), pp. 83-84.

17. Urlin, *Festivals, Holy Days, and Saints' Days,* pp. 252-54, quotes an old Latin chant commemorating an ass: *"Adventanit Asinus."*

18. *Extracts from the Accounts of the Revels,* p. 204, reads, "By his Matis Plaiers. On Inosents Night the Plaie of Errors. Shaxberd."

19. *The Prayer-Book,* pp. 25, 40, 63; *The Prayer-Book Dictionary,* p. 730, adds the passage from Baruch.

20. Nelson, *Companion,* pp. 5-6, 15; Welsford, *The Court Masque,* p. 12; Wright, *British Calendar Customs,* 1:1.

21. Urlin, *Festivals, Holy Days and Saints' Days,* pp. 252-54; John Hollander, *"Twelfth Night* and the Morality of Indulgence," *Sewanee Review* 67 (1959): 220-38; Roy Battenhouse, "Falstaff as Parodist and Perhaps Holy Fool," pp. 32-52; Walter Jacob Kaiser, *Praisers of Folly* (Cambridge, Mass.: Harvard University Press, 1963).

22. Latimer, *Works of Latimer*, 2:133; Bullinger, *The Decades of Henry Bullinger*, 2:176-77; Becon, *The Early Works of Thomas Becon*, 1:323-24.

23. Stowe's *Survey*, p. 79, quoted in Grindal, *The Remains of Edmund Grindal*, p. 141 n.

24. See William Tyndale, *Doctrinal Treatises*, pp. 91-92, for a description of the Catholic feast of asses on 14 January.

25. William Shakespeare, *The Complete Works*, ed. Alfred Harbage; subsequent references to this edition are cited in the text.

26. Becon, *The Early Works*, 1:349. See also 1:321-22, 326-27.

27. C. L. Barber, *Shakespeare's Festive Comedy*, pp. 192-221, and chap. 2, contain his seminal essays on Falstaff and misrule.

28. Frank Manley, ed., *All Fools*, p. xi; subsequent references are cited in the text.

29. Orgel, ed., *Ben Jonson: The Complete Masques*, p. 548; subsequent references are cited in the text.

30. Middleton, *The Works of Thomas Middleton*, 2:351-52; subsequent references are cited in the text.

CHAPTER 3

1. Stephen Orgel, *The Jonsonian Masque*; John C. Meagher, *Method and Meaning in Jonson's Masques*.

2. Hotson, *The First Night of Twelfth Night*, p. 12; see also Welsford, *The Court Masque*, p. 12.

3. Orgel, *The Jonsonian Masque*, p. 62; Urlin, *Festivals, Holy Days, and Saints' Days*, pp. 15-16. Hotson, *The First Night*, pp. 174-75, 190.

4. Meagher, *Method and Meaning*, chap. 2, defends this proposition theoretically; the entire book demonstrates it as a central thesis. See also James P. Lucier, "The More Remov'd Mysteries: Neo-Platonic Epistemology in the Masques of Ben Jonson" (Ph.D. diss., University of Michigan, 1963), *DA* 24:1162.

5. *The Prayer-Book of Queen Elizabeth 1559*, pp. 25, 29, and 64; subsequent references are cited in the text. See also *The Prayer-Book Dictionary*, p. 312.

6. *The Geneva Bible* is the source of all subsequent biblical quotations.

7. *New Catholic Encyclopedia*, C. Smith, "Epiphany, Feast of," 5:481. See also Joseph B. Collins, *Christian Mysticism in the Elizabethan Age* (Baltimore: Johns Hopkins Press, 1940), p. 46.

8. Donne, *The Sermons,* 3:358; subsequent references to the sermons are cited in text.

9. Andrewes, *Ninety-Six Sermons,* 1:204; subsequent references are cited in the text. Nelson, *A Companion for the Festivals and Fasts,* p. 63, says of the Magi: "Lest they should expect a *Prince* accompanied with outward Pomp and Magnificence, the *Angel* describeth the Meanness and Obscurity of his Circumstances." And Donne in another Epiphany sermon adds, "He was God, *humbled in the flesh;* he was Man, *received into glory*" (3:206).

10. Davies, *Worship and Theology in England,* p. 67.

11. Northrop Frye, *Anatomy of Criticism* (Princeton: Princeton University Press, 1957), pp. 163-66, 287-88.

12. See also *New Catholic Encyclopedia,* s.v. "Epiphany."

13. Ibid., p. 481.

14. Meagher, *Method and Meaning,* p. 55; see pp. 19-20 for Jonson's comments.

15. Ibid., pp. 40-45; Lucier, "More Remov'd Mysteries," *DA* 24: 1162.

16. *Ben Jonson: The Complete Masques,* ll. 100-105; subsequent references are cited in the text.

17. *Hymenaei* was actually performed on the night of 5 January 1606 (Orgel, ed., *Ben Jonson: The Complete Masques,* p. 474).

18. *The Masque of Beauty* was performed on Epiphany Sunday 1608 (Orgel, ed., *Ben Jonson: The Complete Masques,* p. 474).

19. *The Prayer-Book,* p. 94; Meagher, *Method and Meaning,* pp. 134-36; *John Donne: The Anniversaries,* ed. Frank Manley (Baltimore: Johns Hopkins Press, 1963), pp. 20-40, notes.

20. John M. Rist, *Eros and Psyche* (Toronto: University of Toronto Press, 1964), pp. 207, 213-14 Meagher, *Method and Meaning,* p. 125; Walter N. King supports this contention in "Introduction," *Twentieth Century Interpretations of Twelfth Night* (Englewood Cliffs: Prentice Hall, 1968), p. 12: Christ in the Epiphany celebration becomes the "symbol and essence of all ordering principles."

21. Robert Ellrodt, *Neoplatonism in the Poetry of Spenser* (Folcroft, Pa.: Folcroft Press, 1969), pp. 175-80.

22. Barbara Lewalski, "Thematic Patterns in *Twelfth Night,*" p. 168; Hotson, *The First Night,* passim; and Barber, *Shakespeare's Festive Comedy,* pp. 3-35.

23. *Ben Jonson: The Complete Masques,* pp. 13-16.

24. See the discussion of Malvolio in the following chapter.

25. Orgel, *Jonsonian Masque,* p. 190. Mikhail Bakhtin, *Rabelais and*

His World, pp. 5–9 passim, and Welsford, *The Court Masque,* pp. 376–88, discuss other aesthetic implications of the feast of fools and misrule.

26. Middleton, *The Works,* 7: ll. 249, 261.

27. See Charles Seymour Robinson, *Annotations upon Popular Hymns* (New York: Hunt & Eaton, 1893), p. 147.

28. The next Epiphany masque is actually *Mercury Vindicated* (1616). Except for its motif of festive misrule, it is not apposite to Epiphany. Actually written for New Year's, and more appropriate to that occasion, the masque is included in the list of Epiphany masques to keep the final statistics accurate.

29. Both *The Fortunate Isles* and *Love's Triumph* were actually performed on the Sunday following Epiphany (Orgel, ed., *The Complete Masques,* pp. 506–7).

30. Andrewes, *Ninety-Six Sermons,* 5:54 ff. Welsford, *The Court Masque,* p. 217, mentions how popular this theme of false and true love was in the Caroline court, and how closely it was connected to a Neoplatonic craze among its ladies.

31. Manley, ed., *John Donne: The Anniversaries,* pp. 20–40, notes.

32. John Marbeck, *A Book of Notes and Commonplaces,* p. 634.

33. Meagher, *Method and Meaning,* p. 124.

34. Thomas Fuller, *The Holy State and the Profane State,* pp. 304–5.

35. Welsford, *The Court Masque,* pp. 355–56.

36. Ibid., p. 217.

CHAPTER 4

1. Hotson, *The First Night of Twelfth Night.* The critics are legion; see Peter G. Phialas, *Shakespeare's Romantic Comedies* (Chapel Hill: University of North Carolina Press, 1966), p. 258.

2. Hotson, *The First Night,* pp. 174–75, 190; Urlin, *Festivals, Holy Days, and Saints' Days,* p. 15.

3. Barber, *Shakespeare's Festive Comedy,* pp. 3–35; John Hollander, *"Musica Mundana* and *Twelfth Night,"* in *English Institute Essays,* ed. Northrop Frye (New York: Columbia University Press, 1957), pp. 55–82; Lewalski, "Thematic Patterns in *Twelfth Night,"* pp. 168–69.

4. The previous chapter, pp. 56–58, discusses edifying humiliations as a central motif of Epiphany. See notes 9–10. Alexander Nowell, *A Catechism,* p. 137, says: "We be by nature most inclined to the love of ourselves," exemplifying this commonplace. See also ibid., pp. 216–17, and Donne, *The Sermons,* 1:286, 314. Davies, *Worship and Theology in*

England, p. 36, suggests that edification is a primary Protestant concern during the sixteenth century.

5. Lewalski, "Thematic Patterns," pp. 169-77.

6. Meagher, *Method and Meaning in Jonson's Masques,* chaps. 3-5; Hollander, *"Musica Mundana,"* pp. 55-82; *The Annotated Book of Common Prayer,* p. 258; *New Catholic Encyclopedia,* s.v. "Epiphany, Feast of."

7. *Ben Jonson: The Complete Masques,* pp. 13-16, 35.

8. Shakespeare, *The Complete Works,* ed. Harbage; subsequent references to this edition are cited in the text.

9. Kaiser, *Praisers of Folly,* pp. 1-16; see also Battenhouse, "Falstaff as Parodist and Perhaps Holy Fool," pp. 32-52; John Colet, *An Exposition of . . . Corinthians,* p. 19. William Fulke, *A Comfortable Sermon of Faith,* sig. A2; and Donne, *The Sermons,* 10:125, 2:348, develop this often repeated expression of Donne the homilist. (Subsequent references to Donne's sermons are cited in the text.) Erasmus relates this paradoxical humiliation of the preacher to Christ's own humiliation at Epiphany. See *The Praise of Folie, Moriae Encomium,* trans. Sir Thomas Chaloner (London, 1549), sig. S1.

10. See *New Catholic Encyclopedia,* s.v. "Epiphany."

11. L. G. Salingar, "The Design of *Twelfth Night,*" *Shakespeare Quarterly* 9 (1958): 118, suggests that Feste is "mumming it as a priest and attempting a mock exorcism in the manner of the Feast of Fools."

12. Andrewes, *Ninety-Six Sermons,* 1:204; subsequent references are cited in the text.

13. *New Catholic Encyclopedia,* s.v. "Epiphany." One of Campion's wedding masques for Epiphany (1607) even contains a long debate about virginity. Diana, inevitably, loses. See Thomas Campion, *Songs and Masques,* pp. 156-58, and Appendix B.

14. Beaumont and Fletcher, *The Works,* 2:440; subsequent references are cited in the text.

15. Lyly, *The Complete Works of John Lyly,* vol. 2 (1.3. passim); subsequent references are cited in the text.

16. Warwick Bond, ed., Introduction, *The Complete Works of John Lyly,* 3:107.

17. Middleton, *The Works,* vol. 6 (1.1.10-12); subsequent references are cited in the text.

18. Bentley, *The Jacobean and Caroline Stage,* 7:85-86; Malone Society Collections, *Dramatic Records in the Declared Accounts . . . ,* 6:xxvii.

19. W. Mountague, *The Shepheard's Paradise,* p. 22; subsequent references are cited in the text.

20. Welsford, *The Court Masque,* p. 217, says one Epiphany masque, *Love's Triumph Through Callipolis,* "turned on the difference between false and true love. . . . This kind of subject was to prove popular at the Caroline Court, where spiritual or platonic love was a constant theme for discussion among the ladies."

CHAPTER 5

1. Lewalski, "Thematic Patterns in *Twelfth Night,*" pp. 168-81. Marion Bodwell Smith, *Dualities in Shakespeare.*

2. *The Prayer-Book of Queen Elizabeth 1559,* p. 25.

3. Donne, *The Sermons,* 7:325-26; 10:65; subsequent references are cited in the text.

4. Lewalski, "Thematic Patterns," pp. 169-77.

5. Shakespeare, *The Complete Works,* ed. Harbage; subsequent references are cited in the text.

6. Robert Nelson, *A Companion for the Festivals and Fasts,* pp. 148-49; subsequent references are cited in the text.

7. See also Kaiser, *Praisers of Folly*; cf. Nelson, *Companion,* p. 150.

8. *The Geneva Bible*; subsequent quotations will refer to this edition.

9. Donne repeatedly uses the phrases "the folly of preaching" and "fooles for Christ" to refer to his ministry (e.g., *Sermons of John Donne,* 10:125); see also Colet, *An Exposition of . . . Corinthians,* p. 19; and Fulke, *A Comfortable Sermon of Faith,* sig. A2.

10. Kenneth Muir, ed., *King Lear* (London: Methuen, 1972), p. xl.

11. *The Prayer-Book,* p. 25. See also *The Prayer-Book Dictionary,* pp. 341-42.

12. Theodore Spencer, *Shakespeare and the Nature of Man,* discusses this context of ideas in the opening chapters.

13. Peter Saccio, *The Court Comedies of John Lyly* (Princeton: Princeton University Press, 1969), pp. 175-76; subsequent citations of Saccio will be made in the text. Andrewes, *Ninety-Six Sermons,* 1:177, 179-80.

14. Lyly, *The Complete Works,* 3:23; subsequent references are cited in the text.

15. John Cook, *Greene's Tu Quoque,* 2:564.

16. Barnabe Barnes, *The Devil's Charter,* p. 12; subsequent references are cited in the text.

17. *Ben Jonson: The Complete Masques,* p. 181; subsequent references are cited in the text.

18. Ellrodt, *Neoplatonism in the Poetry of Spenser*, pp. 165-66.
19. Orgel, ed., *Complete Masques*, p. 122; subsequent references are cited in the text.
20. Middleton, *The Works*, ll. 157-60; subsequent references are cited in the text.
21. Shrove Tuesday always falls just before Ash Wednesday, which always falls forty-six days (forty non-Sundays) before Easter Sunday. But because Easter's placement in the church year depends upon the lunar rather than the solar calendar, that festival, and therefore these other feast and fast days determined by it, is a "movable feast." Evidently this year Shrove Tuesday comes too close in February for Candlemas's comfort. In fact, in the year of this masque, it comes quite early, just seven days after Candlemas (Bentley, *The Jacobean and Caroline Stage*, 7:30).
22. Mikhail Bakhtin, *Rabelais and His World*, pp. 16-29 passim, contains a provocative discussion of the place of these base epithets and "downward comparisons" in the satiric tradition.

CHAPTER 6

1. Joseph Whitaker, *An Almanack for . . . 1975* (London: William Clowes, 1975), p. 189; see also M. Louis Le Cte De Mas Latrie, *Trésor de Chronologie* (Paris: Librairie Victor. Palme, 1889).
2. *Extracts from the Accounts of the Revels*, pp. 204-5.
3. Frederick George Lee, *A Glossary of Liturgical and Ecclesiastical Terms* (London: Bernard Quaritch, 1877), p. 371.
4. Urlin, *Festivals, Holy Days, and Saints' Days*, pp. 41-42; Welsford, *The Court Masque*, p. 12.
5. Wright, *British Calendar Customs: England*, 1:1.
6. *The Prayer-Book Dictionary*, p. 749.
7. See marginal notes in *The Geneva Bible* and *The Interpreter's Bible*, 1:558-59, 582; *The Prayer-Book of Queen Elizabeth 1559*, p. 67.
8. *The Interpreter's Bible*, 1:551-52; see also C. H. George and Katherine George, *The Protestant Mind of the English Reformation*, pp. 95 ff., on the same dilemma. The Fathers of the English Church frequently discuss this precarious Shrovetide balance of presumption and despair. See particularly in the Parker Society series Latimer, *Works*, 2:182; and Hooper, *Early Writings of John Hooper*, 1:415-422. See also Andrewes, *Ninety-Six Sermons*, 5:513-15, 535.
9. Donne, *The Sermons*, 7:73, spoken to James at Whitehall, 24 February 1625/6. See also ibid., 2:165-67; 3:348-51.

10. These understandings are widely shared; they reflect particularly the work of Barbara K. Lewalski, "Biblical Allusion and Allegory in *The Merchant of Venice*," *Shakespeare Quarterly* 13 (1962): 327-43; and John Russell Brown, *Shakespeare and His Comedies* (London: Methuen, 1957).

11. See my articles "Antonio and the Ironic Festivity of *The Merchant of Venice*," *Shakespeare Studies* 6 (1970): 67-74; and "Shylock's Frustrated Communion," *Cithara* 13 (1974): 19-33. See also Thomas Fujimura, "Mode and Structure in *The Merchant of Venice*," *PMLA* 81 (1966): 499-511, for a sensitive discussion of the mixed modes.

12. In fact, Gobbo's cynical disrespect for his father reminds us not only of Jessica and Shylock, but also of Ham and Noah.

13. The paradoxical concept of surfeiting is mentioned twice in the play, both times preceptorially (1.25-6; 3.2.113-14). The Christians seem unable to profit from it.

14. Welsford, *The Court Masque*, pp. 12, 36.

15. R. H. Marijnissen, *Bruegel* (New York: Putnam, 1971), pp. 102-3.

16. Dekker, *The Dramatic Works*, vol. 1 (5.2.188-94); subsequent references are cited in the text.

17. George and George, *The Protestant Mind*, pp. 95 ff. Donne, *The Sermons*, 7:73; Andrewes, *Ninety-Six Sermons*, 5:535; subsequent references to Andrewes are cited in the text.

18. See R. H. Tawney, *Religion and the Rise of Capitalism* (Gloucester: Peter Smith, 1926), p. 210; and Mark Van Doren, *Shakespeare* (Garden City: Doubleday, 1953), pp. 138-39.

19. Lee, *Liturgical and Ecclesiastical Terms*, p. 371; Urlin, *Festivals, Holy Days, and Saints' Days*, pp. 252-54; *The Prayer-Book Dictionary*, p. 751.

20. *Vox Graculi*, p. 55.

21. Barber, *Shakespeare's Festive Comedy*, pp. 3-35; Mikhail Bakhtin, *Rabelais and His World*, pp. 5-9.

22. Batman, *The Golden Booke of the Leaden Goddes*, fol. 10^V-11.

23. Lyly, *The Complete Works*, vol. 2 (2.3; 3.2).

24. Beaumont and Fletcher, *The Works*, 8:336, 361, 370; subsequent references are cited in the text.

25. Chapman, *The Plays of George Chapman: The Comedies*, p. 557.

26. Beaumont and Fletcher, *The Dramatic Works*, ed. Bowers, 1:133.

27. James I requested a repeat performance of this masque during Shrovetide, as he did earlier for *The Merchant of Venice* (Orgel, ed., *Jonson: The Complete Masques*, p. 276).

28. *Ben Jonson: The Complete Masques,* pp. 284–88; subsequent references to the masques are cited in the text. Recall Othello's "goats and monkeys," describing Desdemona's presumed carnality.

29. Thomas Fuller, *The Holy State and the Profane State,* pp. 304–5.

30. Mercury, known as Messenger or "Embassadoure of the Gods" (Batman, *The Golden Booke,* fol. 4^V), is a frequent character in these Shrovetide masques. Because Christ is also traditionally called an Angel "for that he is the eternall fathers messenger, or Ambassador" (Arthur Golding, trans., *A Postill,* fol. 199), we might wonder if the Neoplatonically astute Caroline court would have connected this parallel in their roles, however whimsically.

31. Carew, *The Poems of Thomas Carew,* ed. Rhodes Dunlap, pp. 275–76, 279; subsequent references are cited in the text.

32. Giordano Bruno, *The Expulsion of the Triumphant Beast,* ed. Arthur D. Imerti (New Brunswick, N.J.: Rutgers University Press, 1964), pp. 47–65; subsequent citations will occur in the text. Bruno's *Lo Spaccio* would have been well known in the London court. Bruno himself resided in London during the decade before his trial for heresy in 1592, and was so close to Sir Philip Sidney and his circle of Protestant intellectuals that he warmly dedicated *Lo Spaccio* to him (p. 10).

33. George and George, *The Protestant Mind,* pp. 95 ff.

34. *The Tempest,* 4.1.154–56.

35. Davenant, *The Dramatic Works of Sir William Davenant,* p. 296.

36. Aurelian Townshend, *Poems and Masks,* p. 85; subsequent references are cited in the text.

37. Imerti, ed., *Triumphant Beast,* pp. 25–26.

38. The two titles excluded from the Shrovetide figures are *Luminalia* and *The Haddington Masque.* The first, a ballet rather than a masque, was written for the festival but never performed. The second was designed to celebrate a wedding. See Appendix B for five other wedding masques.

39. Only the last, *Salmacida Spolia* in 1649, is too politically topical in its defense of the tottering monarch to reflect the Shrovetide liturgical tradition. The informers barking at the heels of Charles are themselves the agents of this national shriving, but Davenant can hardly be expected to celebrate that event.

CHAPTER 7

1. *The Geneva Bible* is always cited for biblical references.

2. *The Prayer-Book of Queen Elizabeth 1559,* p. 72.

3. Nelson, *A Companion for the Festivals and Fasts,* pp. 187, 217-18.
4. Shakespeare, *The Complete Works,* ed. Harbage, 5.2.98-111, passim; subsequent references are cited in the text.
5. *The Prayer-Book,* p. 94.
6. *The Prayer-Book,* p. 103. The congregation acknowledges this perpetual state of sin when it repeats in the General Confession of the Communion Service these words: "we acknowledge and bewayle oure manifolde synnes and wyckednesse, which we from tyme to tyme moste grevously have committed, by thoughte woorde and deede, against thy divine Majestie, provokynge mooste justlye thy wrathe and indignation against us" (ibid., p. 100).
7. *The English Hymnal,* pp. 167-68, 179; John Donne, *The Divine Poems,* ed. Helen Gardner (Oxford: Clarendon Press, 1952), p. 11.
8. That "sacrifice," along with "satisfaction" or "expiation" and "oblation" are prominent liturgical terms concerning Christ's crucifixion, the Easter promise of eternal life, and the communion, is obvious from *The Prayer-Book.* It becomes even more obvious if one looks at *The General Index* of the Parker Society Publications, pp. 675-77.
9. Nelson, *Companion,* p. 217.
10. Ennis Rees, ed., *The Tragedies of George Chapman,* pp. 31, 38, 48.
11. George Chapman, *Bussy D'Ambois,* ed. Nicholas Brooke, pp. xlvii, l-liii.
12. Robert Ornstein, *The Moral Vision of Jacobean Tragedy,* p. 48.
13. Ibid., pp. 58-59.

CHAPTER 8

1. *The Prayer-Book of Queen Elizabeth 1559,* p. 90.
2. Prescribed in *The Prayer-Book,* pp. 26, 90.
3. *The Geneva Bible* is the source of all biblical quotations.
4. *The Prayer-Book Dictionary,* pp. 732-33.
5. John Milton, *A Maske: The Earlier Versions,* p. 42; subsequent references are cited in the text.
6. James G. Taaffe, "Michaelmas, The 'Lawless Hour,' and the Occasion of Milton's *Comus,*" *English Language Notes* 6 (1969): 262.
7. William B. Hunter, Jr., "The Liturgical Context of *Comus,*" *English Language Notes* 10 (1972): 11-15.
8. Davenant, *The Dramatic Works,* p. 26; subsequent references are cited in the text.

9. Bullinger, *The Decades*, 3:342.

10. Arthur Wilson, *The Inconstant Lady*, pp. 110-12; subsequent references are cited in the text.

11. Middleton, *The Works*, 1:218; subsequent references are cited in the text.

12. From *The Merchant of Venice*, 3.2.105; 2.7.9.

13. Dorothy Gladys Spicer, *Yearbook of English Festivals*, p. 136; A. R. Wright, *British Calendar Customs: England*, 3:80, 86.

14. *The Prayer-Book*, pp. 26, 91; see also *The Prayer-Book Dictionary*, p. 347.

15. Latimer, *Sermons by Hugh Latimer*, 1:487-88; subsequent references are cited in the text.

16. The story to which Latimer refers is told in Psalms 52. *The Geneva Bible* marginal notes show how commonly the passage, Doeg, and therefore evidently Hallowmas were associated with malicious, destructive slanderers: "Thy malice moveth thee by craftie flateries & lies to accuse and destroye the innocents." John Milton was sufficiently struck by the same associations to project "Doeg slandering" as a possible topic for a tragedy. See Milton, *The Works of John Milton*, ed. Frank Allen Patterson (New York: Columbia University Press, 1931-38), 18:236.

17. Wright, *British Calendar Customs*, 3:112. Urlin, *Festivals, Holy Days, and Saints' Days*, pp. 191, 199-200.

18. *The Prayer-Book*, pp. 25, 89.

19. *Speculum Sacerdotale*, ed. Edward H. Weatherly (London: Oxford University Press, 1936), p. 193, margin (lessons "addressed to parish priests of the festivals of the Christian year in English").

20. Urlin, *Festivals, Holy Days, and Saints' Days*, p. 176.

21. *Ben Jonson: Bartholomew Fair*, p. 182 (5.5.104-5).

22. J. A. Bryant, *The Compassionate Satirist*, pp. 135, 142, 155; and John Scott Colley, " 'Bartholomew Fair': Ben Jonson's 'A Midsummer Night's Dream,' " pp. 63-71, are both comfortable with the Christian context of this uncharacteristic vision. For other perspectives, see Robert Knoll, *Ben Jonson's Plays*, p. 148; Jonas Barish, *Ben Jonson and the Language of Prose Comedy* (Cambridge: Harvard University Press, 1960), pp. 185, 222-30; and Alan Dessen, *Jonson's Moral Comedy*, pp. 205-17.

CHAPTER 9

1. To reiterate, the three days of Shrovetide and the two days of Eastertide are counted one each because of their identical liturgical character.

2. J. Leeds Barroll, *The Revels History of English Drama*, 3:23–24; Glynn Wickham, *Early English Stages 1576–1660*, 2:25; subsequent references are cited in the text.

3. Muriel Bradbrook, *Elizabethan Stage Conditions* (Cambridge: At the University Press, 1932), p. 31.

4. Una Ellis-Fermor, *The Jacobean Drama*, 4th ed. (New York: Vintage Books, 1964), pp. 170–71, 153, 79, 191.

5. See F. S. Boas, *University Drama in the Tudor Age* (Oxford: Clarendon Press, 1914).

6. Mikhail Bakhtin, *Rabelais and His World*, would be an excellent starting place.

7. Robert G. Hunter, *Shakespeare and the Comedy of Forgiveness.*

Selective Bibliography

Adams, Joseph Quincy. *The Dramatic Records of Sir Henry Herbert.* New Haven: Yale University Press, 1917.

Andrewes, Lancelot. *Ninety-Six Sermons.* 5 vols. 1843. Reprint. New York: AMS Press, 1967.

The Annotated Book of Common Prayer. Edited by John Henry Blount. New York: E. P. Dutton, 1908.

Arviragus and Philicia. London: John Norton, 1639 (University Microfilms).

Bakhtin, Mikhail. *Rabelais and His World.* Translated by Helene Iswolsky. Cambridge: M.I.T. Press, 1968.

Barber, C. L. *Shakespeare's Festive Comedy.* Princeton: Princeton University Press, 1959.

Barnes, Barnabe. *The Devil's Charter.* 1607. Reprint. New York: AMS Press, 1970.

Barroll, J. Leeds. *The Revels History of English Drama.* Vol. 3, *1576-1613.* London: Methuen, 1975.

Batman, Stephen. *The Golden Booke of the Leaden Goddes.* London, 1577.

Battenhouse, Roy W. "Falstaff as Parodist and Perhaps Holy Fool." *PMLA* 90 (1975):32-52.

Beaumont, Francis and Fletcher, John. *The Dramatic Works of Beaumont and Fletcher.* Edited by Fredson Bowers. 2 vols. Cambridge: At the University Press, 1966.

____. *The Works of Francis Beaumont and John Fletcher.* Edited by A. R. Waller and Arnold Glover. 10 vols. Cambridge: At the University Press, 1905.

Becon, Thomas. *The Early Works of Thomas Becon.* Edited by John Ayre. Cambridge: The Parker Society, 1843.

Bentley, Gerald Eades. *The Jacobean and Caroline Stage.* 7 vols. Oxford: Clarendon Press, 1941-68.

The Book of Common Prayer, 1559. Edited by John E. Booty. Charlottesville: University of Virginia Press, 1976.

Bullinger, Henry. *The Decades of Henry Bullinger.* Edited by Thomas Harding. 3 vols. Cambridge: The Parker Society, 1850.

Campion, Thomas. *Songs and Masques.* Edited by A. H. Bullen. London: Bullen, 1903.

Carew, Thomas. *The Poems of Thomas Carew.* Edited by Rhodes Dunlap. Oxford: Clarendon Press, 1949.

Certaine Sermons or Homilies Appointed to be Read in Churches in the Time of Queen Elizabeth I. Edited by Mary Ellen Rickey and Thomas B. Stroup. Gainesville: University of Florida Press, 1968.

Chambers, E. K. *The Elizabethan Stage.* 4 vols. Oxford: Clarendon Press, 1923.

Chapman, George. *Bussy D'Ambois.* Edited by Nicholas Brooke. Cambridge: Harvard University Press, 1964.

———. *The Plays of George Chapman: The Comedies.* Edited by Alan Holaday. Urbana: University of Illinois Press, 1970.

Chytraeus. *A Postill, or orderly disposing of certayne Epistles.* Translated by Arthur Golding. London: Lucas Harryson, 1577.

Colet, John. *An Exposition of St. Paul's First Epistle to the Corinthians.* Edited by J. H. Lupton. London, 1874.

Colley, John Scott. "Bartholomew Fair: Ben Jonson's 'A Midsummer Night's Dream.'" *Comparative Drama* 2 (1977):63-71.

Cook, John. *Greene's Tu Quoque.* In *Ancient British Drama.* 3 vols. London: William Miller, 1810.

Davenant, William. *The Dramatic Works of Sir William Davenant.* Edited by James Maidment and W. H. Logan. 1872-74. Reprint. New York: Russell & Russell, 1964.

Davies, Horton. *Worship and Theology in England.* Princeton: Princeton University Press, 1970.

Dekker, Thomas. *The Dramatic Works of Thomas Dekker.* Edited by Fredson Bowers. 4 vols. Cambridge: At the University Press, 1953-61.

Dessen, Alan C. *Jonson's Moral Comedy.* Evanston: Northwestern University Press, 1971.

Documents Relating to the Office of the Revels in the Time of Queen Elizabeth. Edited by Albert Feuillerat. Louvain: A. Uystpruyst, 1908.

Donne, John. *The Sermons of John Donne.* Edited by George R. Potter and Evelyn M. Simpson. 10 vols. Berkeley and Los Angeles: The University of California Press, 1953.

The English Hymnal. London: Oxford University Press, 1906.

Extracts from the Accounts of the Revels at Court in the Reigns of Queen Elizabeth and King James I. Edited by Peter Cunningham. London: The Shakespeare Society, 1842.

Frye, R. M. *Shakespeare and Christian Doctrine.* Princeton: Princeton University Press, 1963.

_____. "Theological and Non-Theological Structures in Tragedy." *Shakespeare Studies* 4 (1968):132–48.

Fulke, William. *A Comfortable Sermon of Faith.* London, 1574.

Fuller, Thomas. *The Holy State and the Profane State.* Edited by M. G. Walton. 2 vols. New York: Columbia University Press, 1938.

The General Index. Edited by Henry Gough. Cambridge: The Parker Society, 1855.

The Geneva Bible, a facimile of the 1560 edition. Introduction by Lloyd E. Berry. Madison: University of Wisconsin Press, 1969.

George, C. H. and George, Katherine. *The Protestant Mind of the English Reformation (1570–1640).* Princeton: Princeton University Press, 1961.

Gesta Grayorum. Edited by W. W. Greg. Oxford: Oxford University Press, 1915.

Greg, W. W. *A Bibliography of the English Printed Drama to the Restoration.* 3 vols. London: Oxford University Press, 1932.

Grindal, Edmund. *The Remains of Edmund Grindal.* Edited by William Nicholson. Cambridge: The Parker Society, 1843.

Harbage, Alfred. *Annals of English Drama 975–1700.* Revised by Samuel Schoenbaum. Philadelphia: University of Pennsylvania Press, 1964.

Hardison, O. B., Jr. *Christian Rite and Christian Drama in the Middle Ages.* Baltimore: Johns Hopkins Press, 1965.

Higgs, Griffin. *The Christmas Prince.* The Malone Society Reprints. Oxford: Oxford University Press, 1922.

The Holy Bible (Douay Version). Baltimore: John Murphey, 1899.

Hooker, Richard. *Ecclesiastical Polity.* London: J. M. Dent, 1922.

Hooper, John. *Early Writings of John Hooper.* Edited by Samuel Carr. Cambridge: The Parker Society, 1843.

Hotson, Leslie. *The First Night of Twelfth Night.* London: Hart-Davies, 1954.

Hunter, Robert Grams. *Shakespeare and the Comedy of Forgiveness.* New York: Columbia University Press, 1965.

The Interpreter's Bible. Edited by George Arthur Buttrick, Walter Russell Bowie, Paul Scherer, John Knox, Samuel Terrien, and Nolan B. Harmon. New York and Nashville: Abingdon-Cokesbury Press, 1952.

Jonson, Ben. *Ben Jonson: Bartholomew Fair.* Edited by Eugene M. Waith. New Haven: Yale University Press, 1963.

___. *Ben Jonson: The Complete Masques.* Edited by Stephen Orgel. New Haven: Yale University Press, 1969.

___. *Every Man in His Humour.* Edited by G. B. Jackson. New Haven: Yale University Press, 1969.

___. *Volpone.* Edited by Alvin Kernan. New Haven: Yale University Press, 1962.

Jorgensen, Paul A. *Our Naked Frailties.* Berkeley and Los Angeles: University of California Press, 1971.

Knoll, Robert. *Ben Jonson's Plays.* Lincoln: University of Nebraska Press, 1964.

Kolve, V. A. *The Play Called Corpus Christi.* Stanford: Stanford University Press, 1966.

Latimer, Hugh. *Sermons by Hugh Latimer.* Edited by G. E. Corrie. Cambridge: The Parker Society, 1844.

___. *The Work of Hugh Latimer.* Edited by G. E. Corrie. 2 vols. Cambridge: The Parker Society, 1844-45.

Lewalski, Barbara K. "Thematic Patterns in Twelfth Night." *Shakespeare Studies* 1 (1965):168-81.

The Lost Lady. London: Jo. Oakes, 1639 (University Microfilms).

Lyly, John. *The Complete Works of John Lyly.* Edited by Warwick Bond. 3 vols. Oxford: Clarendon Press, 1902.

Malone Society Collections. *Dramatic Records in the Declared Accounts of the Treasurer of the Chamber, 1558-1642.* Vol. 6. Oxford: Oxford University Press, 1961.

Manley, Frank, ed. *All Fools.* Lincoln: University of Nebraska Press, 1968.

Marbeck, John. *A Book of Notes and Commonplaces.* London: Thomas East, 1581.

Martin, Gregory, ed. *The New Testament.* Rheims Version. Antwort: D. Vervliet, 1600.

Meagher, John C. *Method and Meaning in Jonson's Masques.* South Bend: University of Notre Dame Press, 1966.

Middleton, Thomas. *The Works of Thomas Middleton.* Edited by A. H. Bullen. 8 vols. Boston: Houghton, 1885-86.

Milton, John. *A Maske: The Earlier Versions.* Edited by E. E. Sprott. Toronto: University of Toronto Press, 1973.

Mountague, W. *The Shepheard's Paradise.* London: John Starkey, 1659.

Nelson, Robert. *A Companion for the Festivals and Fasts of the Church of England.* 19th ed. London, 1748.

New Catholic Encyclopedia. S.v. "Epiphany, Feast of."

Nowell, Alexander. *A Catechism.* Translated by Thomas Norton. Edited by G. E. Corrie. Cambridge: The Parker Society, 1853.

Orgel, Stephen. *The Jonsonian Masque.* Cambridge: Harvard University Press, 1965.

Ornstein, Robert. *The Moral Vision of Jacobean Tragedy.* Madison: University of Wisconsin Press, 1960.

The Prayer-Book Dictionary. Edited by George Harford, Morley Stevenson, and J. W. Tyrer. London: Sir Isaac Pitman & Sons, 1912.

The Prayer-Book of Queen Elizabeth 1559. London: Griffith Farran, 1890.

Rees, Ennis, ed. *The Tragedies of George Chapman.* Cambridge: Harvard University Press, 1954.

Ridley, Nicholas. *The Works of Nicholas Ridley.* Edited by Henry Christmas. Cambridge: The Parker Society, 1841.

Rossiter, A. P. *English Drama From Early Times to the Elizabethans.* New York: Hutchinson's House, 1950.

Shakespeare, William. *The Complete Works.* Edited by Alfred Harbage. Baltimore: Penguin Books, 1969.

Smith, Marion Bodwell. *Dualities in Shakespeare.* Toronto: University of Toronto Press, 1966.

Spencer, Theodore. *Shakespeare and the Nature of Man.* New York: Macmillan, 1942.

Spicer, Dorothy Gladys. *Yearbook of English Festivals.* New York: H. W. Wilson, 1954.

The Stage Acquitted. London: John Barnes, 1699.

Townshend, Aurelian. *Poems and Masks.* Edited by E. K. Chambers. Oxford: Clarendon Press, 1912.

Tyndale, William. *Doctrinal Treatises.* Edited by Henry Walter. Cambridge: The Parker Society, 1848.

Urlin, Ethel A. *Festivals, Holy Days, and Saints' Days.* 1915. Reprint. Ann Arbor: Gryphon Books, 1971.

Vox Graculi. London: Nathaniell Butter, 1622.

Webster, John. *The Complete Works of John Webster.* Edited by F. L. Lucas. 4 vols. New York: Oxford University Press, 1937.

Welsford, Enid. *The Court Masque.* 2nd ed. 1927. Reprint. New York: Russell and Russell, 1962.

West, Robert H. *Shakespeare and the Outer Mystery.* Lexington: University of Kentucky Press, 1968.

Whitgift, John. *The Works of John Whitgift.* Edited by John Ayre. 3 vols. Cambridge: The Parker Society, 1853.

Wickham, Glynn. *Early English Stages, 1576-1660.* 2 vols. New York: Columbia University Press, 1966-72.

Wilson, Arthur. *The Inconstant Lady.* Oxford: Samuel Collingwood, 1814.

Wright, A. R. *British Calendar Customs.* 3 vols. London: William Glaisher, 1936.

Index

211